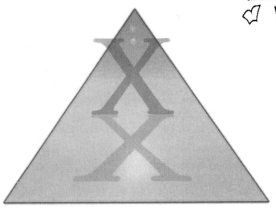

COMPbiblio:

Leaders and Influences
in Composition Theory and Practice

Allison D. Smith, Trixie G. Smith,
and Karen Wright, editors

Tanya McLaughlin,
production assistant

FOUNTAINHEAD
PRESS

Cover design by Pat Bracken
Page design by Susan Moore

Books may be purchased for educational purposes.

For information, please call or write:

1-800-586-0330

Fountainhead Press
100 W. Southlake Blvd. Suite 142, #350
Southlake, TX 76092

Web site: www.fountainheadpress.com
E-mail: customerservice@fountainheadpress.com

First Edition
ISBN 978-1-59871-070-0

Printed in the United States of America

Acknowledgements

A project of this size cannot be successfully completed without a fine production team that keeps collaborators on track and then helps to join disparate writing and organizational styles together. The production team for this project was led energetically by Tanya McLaughlin, who was assisted by Dianna Baldwin, Rebecca Bobbitt, and Kennie Rose. We are grateful to those who researched, revised, and edited until the manuscript was complete, and we also thank the team at Fountainhead Press—Felix Frazier, Susan Moore, and Scott Timian—for their assistance with this manuscript and their dedication to professional development. We thank all of the composition leaders who took time out of their busy schedules to help with this project. Our final thanks goes to the Graduate College at MTSU, which supported the development of the book proposal by funding a graduate faculty grant for Trixie and Allison in 2004-05. This project would not have been possible without the assistance and support of all those listed above. As with all research, final mistakes in this manuscript are our responsibility; however, please contact us with any necessary changes to information presented here or suggestions for additional composition leaders to include in future editions.

Table of Contents

Table of Contents

SECTION II: INFLUENCES FROM OTHER DISCIPLINES

Chapter:

SECTION III: INFLUENCES FROM WRITING PROGRAM ADMINISTRATION

Chapter:

 **Introduction**

The idea for this collection—a different type of annotated bibliography—came about in a composition pedagogy seminar Allison taught at Louisiana Tech for new TAs in the fall of 2000. Just like in many other courses that provide the same kind of introduction to new TAs, she asked each of her students to choose a leader in composition to research and report on, asking them to present the class with a handout that included biographical and bibliographic information. That semester, Stephanie Sims, one of her graduate students, decided to contact her composition leader—David Bartholomae—via email, not only asking him questions about his career and research, but also asking him for any advice he could give her as a beginning teacher. His response was both generous and supportive (see below), but it was the fact that he took the time to respond to Stephanie that made the standard composition leader project into something more important, something that allowed Stephanie to begin her journey as a composition teacher and invited her into the community of composition studies. Once Bartholomae shared his advice, other students in the class tried to connect with their composition leaders via email as well, thus developing the project into something more for all of them.

Date: Tue, 17 Oct 2000 15:00:59 -0400
From: David Bartholomae barth+@pitt.edu | **Block address**
Subject: **Re: FROM AN ADMIRER OF YOUR WORK**
To: Ssims@garts.latech.edu

Dear Stephanie Sims,

You shouldn't be nervous. I'm flattered that you wrote.

A piece of advice. Hmm. You didn't give much context: advice as teachers? as writers? as graduate students?

I will give you a little bit on all three. The hardest thing to learn to do as a teacher is to learn how to read student writing—to read it with care and attention, as you would read poems by Phillip Levine or a novel by

---

Margaret Atwood or an essay by James Baldwin or criticism by
Edward Said.

Student writing is hard to read because it is never quite any of the
above, but a teacher has to learn how and where to pay attention. And
students have to be enabled to aim high and to write beyond their
competence. And then the next hardest thing to do is to value student
writing, to know what to admire and when, what to worry about and
when. And so on.

As writers, I think the best advice is to find models, people who are
doing the kind of writing you admire (or are charged to produce), one
or two essays or chapters, and to work closely with them, reading as a
writer.

As graduate students. I don't know. I'm sure everyone tells you that
the market is a tough one. The best advice is to develop as broad a
teaching portfolio as your institution will allow. The job market values
generalists, people who can do several things. Everybody will have an
interesting dissertation and great letters of recommendation. Not
everyone teaches well and widely and speaks well about teaching.

Good luck on your project.

When Allison moved to Middle Tennessee State University to
take over as the director of the Writing Program and TA
Supervisor, she took this project into her fall Teaching College
Composition seminar, and once again, using Stephanie's model,
the graduate students began to contact their composition leaders
via email, and most of the leaders responded. As part of our
revision of the composition curriculum at MTSU, we developed
two new courses for TAs: English 6/7570—Practicum in
Composition Methodology offered in the spring, and English
6/7550—Writing Center Theory and Practice offered in the fall.
In the spring 2003 Practicum course, students were asked to
choose the topics that would be covered in class, and Allison
proposed that one of the units they might want to consider was
investigating how to get a book published in composition studies
and putting together a proposal for a collection on composition
leaders. The students did indeed choose this real-world activity,

helping to create a book proposal and writing chapters that would become the heart of this book. The next year, Trixie continued the project in her Writing Center Theory and Practice course, and Allison did the same again in her fall seminar. Stephanie, sadly, was taken from us as this project became a book; however, her spirit and initial spark will always be with us. Her longing to be part of the larger composition community and her passion for her work will always be remembered. Thus, we dedicate this book to Stephanie and all the other new TAs—past, present, or future—teaching writing for the first time.

COMPbiblio: Leaders and Influences in Composition Theory and Practice enables students and instructors to access biographical and scholarly information about leading figures in the field of composition and other fields directly related to the study and teaching of composition. The book's format is designed to serve equally well as a textbook for graduate seminars or as a reference manual for a wider audience. Bibliographic information is geared towards teachers early in their careers, and though its primary audience will be graduate students and new scholars interested in the theories, research, and practices of composition studies, the text is also accessible to students and teachers of literacy and writing at K-16 levels.

In the "Leaders" section, each chapter is devoted to a specific composition leader and contains a brief biographical narrative and an annotated bibliography of sources relating to the work of that individual; in the "Influences" sections, each chapter is focused on representative works in and around writing theory and practice to start your search. A collaborative project, this book includes the work of over 50 graduate student TAs who worked with the editors to share the lives and work of their favorite leaders in composition theory and pedagogy. Each living composition leader has been contacted, mostly through email, to share and confirm biographical information, provide some insight into a favorite publication or two, and recommend three sources that new teachers might want to read as they start on their journeys as writing teachers. We could not have completed this book without these composition leaders; their work in the field and their willingness to share with teachers new to the field is to be admired. In addition, the biographies—or stories—of the arcs of their careers are both informative and inspiring to the authors and to those graduate students or teachers considering composition as a teaching area.

The field of composition continues to evolve, and *COMPbiblio* traces this evolution by presenting how current leaders in composition came to their careers and continue to reinvent their research and teaching practices as new ideas arrive in composition studies.

Allison D. Smith, Trixie G. Smith, and Karen Wright

List of Acronyms

AAUP	American Association of University Professors
ADE	Association of Departments of English
ADFL	Association of Departments of Foreign Languages
AERA	American Educational Research Association
APA	American Psychological Association
CCC	*College Composition and Communication*
CCCC	Conference on College Composition and Communication
CE	*College English*
CEA	College English Association
CEE	Conference on English Education
CUNY	City University of New York
DAI	Dissertation Abstracts International
ELT	English Language Teaching
ERIC	Education Resource Information Center
ESL	English as a Second Language
ESOL	English for Speakers of Other Languages
FIPSE	Fund for the Improvement of Postsecondary Education
FYC	First-Year Composition
Gen-ed	General Education
IWCA	International Writing Center Association
JAC	*Journal of Composition Theory*
JLLAD	Journal of Language and Learning Across the Disciplines
L1	First Language
L2	Second Language
LSU	Louisiana State University
Miami-Ohio	Miami University, Ohio
MIT	Massachusetts Institute of Technology
MLA	Modern Language Association
MLN	*Modern Language Notes*
MTSU	Middle Tennessee State University

NCTE	National Council of Teachers of English
NEA	National Endowment for the Arts
NEH	National Endowment for the Humanities
NES	Native English Speaker(s)
NSF	National Science Foundation
NWCA	National Writing Center Association
RTE	*Research in the Teaching of English*
SIUP	Southern Illinois University Press
SUNY	State University of New York
TA	Teaching Assistant
TESL	Teaching English as a Second Language
TESOL	Teaching English to Speakers of Other Languages
TETYC	*Teaching English in the Two-Year College*
UC	University of California
UCLA	University of California, Los Angeles
UIUC	University of Illinois at Urbana-Champaign
UMass	University of Massachusetts
UNH	University of New Hampshire
WAC	Writing Across the Curriculum
WPA	Writing Program Administration/Administrator
WPA	*WPA: Writing Program Administration*
WPA Council	Council of Writing Program Administrators

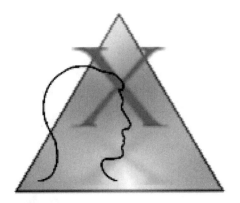

Section I:
Leaders in Composition

 **Chapter 1:
Chris Anson**

(b. 1954)

Chris Anson is an educator known primarily for his work with
WAC initiatives and theory as well as his work with
undergraduate education reform. Anson received his PhD
(1984) and a second MA (1982) with a specialization in
composition studies from Indiana University. He received his
first MA in English and Creative Writing (1980) and graduated
magna cum laude with a BA (1977) in English from Syracuse
University. Anson began his career in teaching at Syracuse
University as a TA and continued teaching at Indiana
University and then at the University of Minnesota. Anson
spent 15 years at the University of Minnesota, where he
directed the Program in Composition (1988-96) and was Morse-
Alumni Distinguished Teaching professor before moving to
North Carolina State University (1999) where he serves as the
director of the Campus Writing and Speaking Program and
teaches both graduate and undergraduate courses in language,
composition, and literacy.

A prolific writer, Anson has published 14 books and over 75
journal articles and book chapters and is on the editorial or
readers boards of ten journals, including *WPA, CCC, CE, RTE,*

JLLAD, Written Communication, Assessing Writing, and *The Journal of Writing Assessment.* His most recent book project, *The WAC Casebook: Scenes for Faculty Reflection and Program Development* (2002), is an edited collection of scenarios for faculty development in WAC. He is currently working on a book on the social construction of error.

Adding to his scholarship is Anson's extensive service. Anson served as President of the WPA (2003-05), on the CCCC Executive Committee (1993-96), the CCCC Resolutions Committee (2002, 2005), the *CCC* Editor Search Committee (2003-04), the CCCC Committee on Professional Standards (1990-03, co-chair 1993), the CCCC Committee on Issues in the Profession (2004-present), the CCCC Nominating Committee (1998, chair 1999), the CCCC Exemplar Award Committee (1996), the NCTE/CEE Nominating Committee (1987), the NCTE Committee on Language Across the Curriculum (1988-91), and the NCTE Board of Directors (1985-99). He chaired the NCTE Assembly for Research (1992-93) and was program chair of the NCTE Global Conference on Language and Literacy (2000) and the Sixth Conference of the National Testing Network in Writing (1987). He formed and chaired the Midwest MLA's Writing Across the Curriculum Section (1989-94).

Respected in his field for his work with literacy, undergraduate reform, and WAC, Anson has delivered over 325 conference papers, keynote addresses, and invited lectures and faculty workshops both nationally and internationally.

Gwendolyn Hale

 Sources for Biographical Narrative

▶ Anson, Chris M. "Professional Portfolio of Chris M. Anson." 29 June 2006 <http://www.home.earthlink.net/~theansons/mainp.html>.

▶ "Chris M. Anson." Dept.Graduate Faculty home page. North Carolina State University. 2006. 30 June 2006 <http://www.chass.ncsu.edu/english/maprog/grafa2.htm>

Chris Anson recommends these readings for novice composition instructors:

1. Hillocks, George. *Teaching Writing as Reflective Practice.* New York: Teachers College P, 1995.
2. Sternglass, Marilyn S. *Time to Know Them: A Longitudinal Study of Writing and Learning at the College Level.* Mahwah, NJ: Erlbaum, 1997.
3. Bloom, Lynn, Donald Daiker, and Edward M. White, eds. *Composition Studies in the New Millennium: Rereading the Past, Rewriting the Future.* Carbondale, IL: SIUP, 2003.

Annotated Bibliography

▶ Anson, Chris M. *The WAC Casebook: Scenes for Faculty Reflection and Program Development.* New York: Oxford UP, 2002.

This book is an invaluable resource for any instructor in any discipline who wishes to effectively incorporate writing into the classroom. Anson shares 45 different scenarios that cover the range of difficulties and situations instructors may encounter when engaging in WAC. Further, the cases are left intentionally open-ended in an effort to provoke questions and reflexive thought. The book covers important WAC topics such as writing to learn, designing effective assignments, roles of instructors and graduate students, and utilizing technology, and it also includes Web-based resources in its appendix to further assist instructors in their WAC endeavors.

▶ ---, ed. *Writing and Response: Theory, Practice, and Research.* Urbana, IL: NCTE, 1989.

This edited collection is divided into three parts with 22 distinguished composition theorists, practitioners, and researchers describing, illustrating, and analyzing responses to student writing. Part One of the collection, "Toward a Theory of

Response in the Classroom Community," includes four essays on the large picture: theories of literacy, the ways teachers mediate theory and practice, transactional theories of reading, and the whole language movement. Part Two, "New Perspectives for Responding to Writing," contains six essays on learning to praise, the use of Rogerian reflection, self-assessment strategies, responding to student journals, the writer's memo, and responding with computers. Part Three of the collection, "Studies of Response in the Instructional Context," concludes the volume with six descriptions of research on responses to student writing. This collection of essays with an introduction and conclusion by Anson, is often cited in critical works regarding composition.

▶ Anson, Chris M., et al, eds. *Dilemmas in Teaching: Cases for Collaborative Faculty Reflection*. Madison, WI: Atwood, 1988.

This collection, written by faculty members as part of a grant from The Collaboration for the Advancement of College Teaching and Learning, works to further undergraduate education reform. The cases will provoke discussion and exchanges among faculty and assist newer faculty and TAs in becoming acclimated to the ever-changing terrain of their chosen career. Further, these 29 cases are grouped into three sections focusing on the classroom, departments and institutions, and the changing culture of higher education. Finally, the collection features case abstracts, discussion questions, and useful material for faculty development.

▶ Anson, Chris M., et al. *Scenarios for Teaching Writing: Contexts for Discussion and Reflective Practice*. Urbana, IL: NCTE, 1993.

This collection offers college instructors—TAs, adjuncts, new and veteran faculty—meaningful and real world scenarios regarding the many aspects of teaching introductory college composition courses. The authors, all experienced WPAs, provide situations, syllabi, assignments, and journal entries from their own classrooms, while also presenting theoretical and practical topics for discussion among colleagues.

▶ Anson, Chris M., and Robert A. Schwegler. *The Longman Handbook for Writers and Readers.* 4th ed. New York: Longman, 2005.

This resource is an accessible reference book for writers who wish to improve their writing—academic, business, personal, and creative. The handbook also provides information on electronic research, documentation, citation, plagiarism, punctuation, and mechanics. Anson and Schwegler also provide instruction regarding special needs of ESL students and the writing process.

▶ Anson, Chris M., Robert A. Schwegler, and Marcia F. Muth. *The Longman Writer's Companion.* New York: Longman, 2002.

This unique textbook offers help for writing within the academic community and in other communities as well. Stressing writing as a tool essential for success in life as well as in the workplace, the text focuses on how community shapes all aspects of communication, including writing, critical reasoning, language, style, technology, evaluation, and documentation. The handbook also takes into account community when it addresses grammar and usage. Anson, Schwegler, and Muth utilize their "Read/Recognize/Revise" approach, which encourages students to see errors as their readers do. This easy-to-use resource is practical and helps writers connect successfully with their audience.

▶ Anson, Chris M., John E. Schwiebert, and Michael M. Williamson, eds. *Writing Across the Curriculum: An Annotated Bibliography.* Westport, CT: Greenwood Press, 1993.

This annotated bibliography is the first to trace the history of the WAC movement and to comment on its current state as well as its future. Covering 1,067 important resources taken from a variety of sources, this bibliography covers not only the history but the implementation and teaching of WAC. With author and subject indexes, this annotated bibliography provides easy access for those in any discipline.

▶ Anson, Chris M., and Lance E. Wilcox. *Field Guide to Writing*. Boston: Addison-Wesley, 1997.

This guide provides instruction in the forms and conventions of particular disciplines and how to better convey material and processes to students through their own writing. *The Field Guide* covers journal writing, writing-to-learn assignments, and research essays. Accessible to instructors and students alike, this guide offers scenarios, practices, and helpful advice.

▶ Campus Writing and Speaking Program, North Carolina State University. North Carolina State University, Raleigh. 2006. 29 June 2006. <http://www2.chass.ncsu.edu/CWSP/header/contact.html>.

Established in the 1990s to respond to growing interest by students, faculty, and area businesses, this Web site is home to a scholarly community of faculty and graduate TAs who work together to improve the undergraduate experience in writing and speaking. The numerous links and resources that can be accessed through the site map include sample publication and conference presentations, classroom strategies, national resources, student resources, and workshop archives. Further, the site provides information for faculty members and colleagues regarding upcoming and previous faculty seminars.

▶ Farris, Christine, and Chris M. Anson, eds. *Under Construction: Working at the Intersections of Composition Theory, Research, and Practice*. Logan: Utah State UP, 1998.

Chapters in this book examine the changes in the field of composition theory over the previous two decades. The chapters deal with the relationship between scholarship and teaching practices in the field of composition as well as the disparities between current theory and practice. This book calls into question the assumptions about composition by both students and instructors. Finally, later chapters examine the ways in which new teachers and scholars come into the field of composition.

Chapter 2:
David John Bartholomae

(b. 1947)

David Bartholomae received his BA (1969) from Ohio Wesleyan University, and earned his PhD (1973) in English Literature from Rutgers University. He has taught at the University of Pittsburgh as assistant professor (1975-81), associate professor (1981-87), professor (1987), and currently serves as Chair of the Department of English (1995-present). At one time he was the university's director of Composition (1980-89).

Bartholomae has served on the editorial boards of numerous journals, such as *CE* (1992-98) and *Pedagogy* (1999), and on the executive committees of numerous professional organizations, such as the MLA (1995-02) and CCCC (1982-89). For these services, Bartholomae has been awarded the University of Pittsburgh's Chancellor's Distinguished Teaching Award (1995), the Distinguished Achievement Award (1987) from the Educational Press Association of America for "Teaching Writing as a Learning Process," a Fulbright Fellowship (1982) to lecture on American Studies at the Universidad de Deusto in Bilbao, Spain, and the Richard B. Braddock Award (1980) for the best article in *CCC*.

Bartholomae has received numerous grants to study the composing process, including working with Erika Lindemann to manage an Institute for Teachers of Composition (NEH, 1977) and with Anthony R. Petrosky to develop test specifications (The National Assessment of Educational Progress, 1982). Bartholomae investigated the benefits of "Using Cognitive Research and Computer Technology to Improve Writing Skills in Low-Performing College Students" (Ford Foundation, 1983-86) and combined his interests in composition and computers to explore the "Varieties of Reasoning" (Mellon Foundation, 1989-93).

Bartholomae has contributed to our understanding of the composing process, especially as it is taught to students unfamiliar with academic discourse. His essays "Inventing the University" and "The Study of Error" have moved the focus of classroom instruction from grammar to rhetoric—from surface error to semantic and critical content—changing the typical skills-drills course into a theoretically centered seminar with demanding, integrated reading and writing assignments. In *Facts, Artifacts and Counterfacts* and *Ways of Reading*, Bartholomae and Petrosky demonstrate their methodology, first presented in Bartholomae's seminal article "Inventing the University," of initiating writers into the language, methods, and standards of academic discourse. By concentrating on the compositional stage before editing and error correction, they first engage their students in active research and intensive readings emphasizing the assumptions and context of their study. As the students explore the critical questions underpinning research topics like the sociological study of the transition from adolescence to adulthood or the role of the observer in analyzing cultural patterns in anthropology, they develop community standards of acceptable writing. Through extended discussions, contrasting critical readings and repeated revisions, they seek to produce writing that is not just acceptable, but excellent, worthy of publication and discussion by the academic community. In these courses, Bartholomae seeks to give basic writers the knowledge and skills necessary to move from the margins of the university to the center of the academic community where they can speak with authority and confidence to express their needs, criticisms and visions for the future.

Joe Ballantyne

Source for Biographical Narrative

▶ Bartholomae, David. E-mail to Joe Ballantyne. 29 Oct. 2004.

David Bartholomae recommends these readings for novice composition instructors:

1. Slevin, James F. *Introducing English: Essays in the Intellectual Work of Composition.* Pittsburgh: U of P, 2001.
2. Bartholomae, David. *Writing on the Margins: Essays on Composition and Teaching.* Boston: Bedford/St. Martin's, 2005.
3. Coles, William E., Jr. *The Plural I—and After.* Montclair, NJ: Boynton/Cook, 1988

Annotated Bibliography

▶ Bartholomae, David. "Composition: 1900-2000." *PMLA* 115 (2000): 1950-55.

As a brief, straightforward summary of the history of composition studies in the 20th century, this article is a useful introduction for beginning students. For more advanced students it alerts them to the institutional nature of the field and the political climate that gave birth to composition as an independent field in English studies with women's, gay and lesbian, Afro-American and film studies in the 1970s with a research agenda, professional alliances, strong debates and interest groups as well as a varied and distinguished literature. For students of education administration, the article challenges them to explain why the institutionalization of composition studies has largely been effected through the use of adjunct faculty and teaching assistants and identifies one of the most significant developments in 2000: writing across the curriculum, bringing many faculty members to the teaching of writing for the first time.

▶ ---. "Inventing the University." *When a Writer Can't Write: Studies in Writer's Block and Other Composing-Process Problems.* Ed. Mike Rose. NY: Guilford, 1985. 134-66.

In this seminal article, Bartholomae argues that basic writers or marginal students must invent the university for themselves when they attempt to satisfy academic standards with which they are not familiar. Although sometimes highly abstract, this article marks a landmark in the theory of composition studies, presenting a clear alternative for students of curriculum design, teachers, and administrators who can use this article to think about whether students must appropriate the privileged language of a specialized discourse, and appear comfortably fluent to successfully integrate into the academic community. Beginning student teachers might productively consider how they can provide sufficient exposure to this language to permit their students to locate themselves within this discourse.

▶ ---. "Response to Peter Elbow." *CCC* 46 (1995): 62-72.

Arguing that Elbow's work tries to "preserve and reproduce the figure of the author, an independent, self-creative, self-expressive subjectivity," Bartholomae asks whether the university should require students to "participate in a first person, narrative or expressive genre whose goal is to reproduce the ideology of sentimental realism . . . a narrative that celebrates a world of private life and whose hero is sincere" (69). His answer is tentatively affirmative but he questions the manner in which this approach reproduces the myth of American life, which obscures the social and political forces that form the identities of the writer and the reader. This spirited article can spark debate on the socio-political implications of composition studies for universities in introductory seminars, even though the dualistic nature of the debate simplifies the issue of authorial independence.

► ---. "The Study of Error." *CCC* 31 (1980): 253-69.

This classic article builds on Mina Shaughnessy's work on error analysis, emphasizing that errors in writing are complex with many sources, and suggests that composition teachers use oral readings as a diagnostic tool to help distinguish miscues from deeper errors that show evidence of some idiosyncratic language use. Using oral reconstructions, the composition teacher can diagnose the sources of error, instruct the student to read and edit more proficiently, and chart the student's progress when acquiring the second language of writing.

► ---. "The Tidy House: Basic Writing in the American University." *Journal of Basic Writing* 12 (1993): 4-21.

This reflective article argues that basic writing classes have become self-perpetuating, ensuring that the university will always have a steady supply of basic writers. Drawing on Mary Louise Pratt's concept of the contact zone, he warns instructors that the tendency to reproduce the procedures, protocols and formats of existing patterns of power and authority requires the marginal student to replicate dominant images of himself, and thereby reproduces the hierarchies of privilege which they sought to subvert. Instead of eliminating social differences, he challenges planners to use the classroom as the forum for discussion of these differences through a program of dense, difficult readings and writing projects that call for students to acquire a chosen field's professional academic discourse.

► ---. "What is Composition? And If You Know What That Is, Why Do We Teach It?" *Composition in the 21st Century*. Ed. Lynn Bloom, Donald Daiker, and Edward White. Carbondale: SIUP, 1996. 11-29.

Calling for a paradigm shift in composition studies, Bartholomae defines "composition" as a "record of institutional and professional responses to challenged standards, challenges to a standard of writing produced by writers who were said to be unprepared" (11). Making a clear argument that the failure of composition studies to ally with literary theory in order to confront the ideological program of the university to promote a romantic humanism supports the discursive and institutional formations that underpin existing systems of inequity and injustice. Bartholomae convincingly calls for a post-process movement in composition studies that takes the social roots of writing into account, posing a challenge for theorists, instructors, and administrators of composition studies alike.

▶ ---. "Writing on the Margins: The Concept of Literacy in Higher Education." *A Sourcebook for Basic Writing Teachers*. Ed. Theresa Enos. NY: Random House, 1987.

The problem confronting the composition teacher is to convey a command of the distinctive gestures of authority, key terms and figures and interpretive schemes of scholarship, to appropriate the specialized discourse of the academy. Building on Shaughnessy's work, Bartholomae asserts that error analysis reveals the student to be trying to speak the language of the center, not to be ignorant of the rules of grammar. This insight permits teachers to avoid needless instruction and to focus their work on key enabling structures of academic discourse.

▶ Bartholomae, David, and Anthony R. Petrosky. *Facts, Artifacts and Counterfacts: Reading and Writing in Theory and Practice*. Montclair, NJ: Boynton/Cook, 1986.

Focusing on problems of research and rhetoric, this book gives a detailed plan for an integrated reading and writing course that explores the transition from adolescence to adulthood. Although the book does not include the readings (most are full-length novels), it outlines the assignments, schedule and objectives. After interviewing their fellow students and examining literary and scientific models for describing and analyzing the transition, the students' writing is published as a text to be used for reference in subsequent classes, providing concrete validation of their work.

▶ ---. *Ways of Reading: An Anthology for Writers*. Boston: Bedford, 1987.

This innovative and groundbreaking book is designed for students entering the school unprepared for the distinctive difficulties of academic life. It is a course in Basic Writing that offers substantial material: long, difficult readings that required serious attention along with a method of reading and rereading designed to help students learn to read and think critically and respond in writing. Employing sequenced assignments that integrate a selection of readings and editorial features with advice on reading, writing, and critical thinking, the course provides a flexible structure that allows instructors to assign readings, or students to choose pieces that they themselves find important and engaging.

▶ ---. *Ways of Reading: Words and Images*. Boston: Bedford, 2003.

This new textbook brings visual culture into the composition classroom, including over 180 images that focus on the analysis of visual texts and help students engage with visual representation in an active way. The challenging readings on visual culture are drawn from important and influential books in cultural and academic debates. Because the assignments build on each other, they allow students to work with a selection, connect it to another, and bring the ideas of one writer to bear on another.

Chapter 3:
James A. Berlin

(1942-1994)

James Berlin is recognized nationally as a prominent figure in the field of rhetoric and composition, as well as a respected composition cultural studies theorist. Berlin believed that the English curriculum, and its undeniable influence on society, was the mode through which great social change and empowerment was possible for all people.

Born in Hamtramck, Michigan (1942), Berlin was the oldest of seven. He attended Central Michigan University on a sports scholarship, graduating *summa cum laude* with his BA (1964). He taught elementary school in Detroit and Flint, Michigan, before attending graduate school. He earned an MA and a PhD (1975) in Victorian literature at the University of Michigan. Shortly thereafter, he became assistant professor of composition at Wichita State University and served as the first director of the Kansas Writing Project, which is affiliated with the National Writing Project. He later became director of Freshman English at the University of Cincinnati (1981-85) and subsequently held visiting appointments at Penn State and the University of Texas before becoming a professor of English at Purdue (1987).

Berlin published numerous essays on rhetorical history, rhetoric, postmodernism, and cultural studies in journals such as *CE* and *Pre/Text*, and contributed to several major rhetoric and composition collections. His most notable books include *Writing Instruction in Nineteenth-Century American Colleges* (1984), *Rhetoric and Reality: Writing Instruction in American Colleges, 1900-1985* (1987), *Cultural Studies in the English Classroom* (edited with Michael J. Vivion, 1992), and *Rhetorics, Poetics, and Cultures: Refiguring College English Studies* (1996). He was also an active participant in CCCC and NCTE.

Berlin's posthumous work *Rhetorics, Poetics, and Cultures: Refiguring College English Studies* (1996) was awarded the CCCC Outstanding Book Award (1998) for its contribution to composition and communication scholarship. Since 1992 the CCCC James Berlin Memorial Outstanding Dissertation Award is awarded yearly to a graduate whose dissertation contributes to the field of composition studies or to its body of knowledge.

Berlin's work primarily focuses on social-epistemic rhetoric, which views reality as socially constructed and has a progressive or radical socialist agenda as its politics. He calls for a new English studies discipline that examines all forms of signifying practices, including the ideologies and the social institutions that support them, in order to prepare students for thoughtful, literate, and participatory citizenship in America's emerging multicultural democracy. Constantly petitioning for students' rights and those working in composition and rhetoric studies, Berlin is remembered as a voice of morality as well as a strong intellectual character in the academic community.

Adam McInturff

 Sources for Biographical Narrative

▶ CCCC Outstanding Book Award. 2 Aug. 2004
  <http://www.ncte.org/cccc/awards/123732.htm>.

►Lauer, Janice M. Afterword. *Rhetorics, Poetics, and Cultures:Refiguring College English Studies*. By James A. Berlin. Urbana, IL: NCTE, 1996.181-82.

►---. "Memories of Jim Berlin." *JAC* 14 (1994): 583-89.

Annotated Bibliography

►Berlin, James A. "Contemporary Composition: The Major Pedagogical Theories." *CE* 44 (1982): 765-77.

In an effort to establish how classic theory influences contemporary rhetoric and composition, Berlin examines the rhetoric of Neo-Aristotelians (Classicists), Positivists (Current-Traditionalists), Neo-Platonists (Expressionists), and New Rhetoricians (Social-Epistemics) in terms of their pedagogical techniques. He suggests that writing instructors re-evaluate their teaching strategies with respect to possibly contradictory methods and recommends assessing process-centered versus product-centered approaches. Though Berlin's review is perhaps biased with respect to his advocacy of New Rhetoric, composition teachers will find his suggestions insightful.

►---. "Poststructuralism, Cultural Studies, and the Composition Classroom." *Rhetoric Review* 11 (1992):16-33. Rpt. in *Professing the New Rhetorics: A Sourcebook*. Ed.Theresa Enos and Stuart C. Brown. Englewood Cliffs, NJ: Prentice Hall, 1994. 461-80.

Berlin uses postmodernism to understand complicated language and text, and he explores the ideological designations that are inherent in language and linked to social, political, and economic issues. Berlin proposes that students can better understand complicated language and text by researching their own language and culture in relation to the ideological designations of different mediums, such as articles, books, or films. Readers of this text need not be familiar with the details of postmodernism or poststructuralism to understand Berlin's article, as it is representative of his clear and understandable writing and provides an excellent theoretical base for conducting such a class.

▶ ---. "Revisionary History: The Dialectical Method."
   Pre/Text 8 (1987): 47-61.

Berlin proposes that society's material, social, political, and cultural conditions must be mediated through rhetoric and discourse. He claims this mediation should be the primary focus of education, especially through reading, writing, and speaking, and he convincingly argues that these learned dialectics validate those whom society deems worthy of being heard and grants those individuals social power. This article is a must-read as an introduction to Berlin's theory on the importance of dialectics in the classroom and its relation to society's power structure.

▶ ---. "Rhetoric and Ideology in the Writing Class." *CE* 50
   (1988): 477-94.

Berlin asserts that no rhetoric can be unbiased since they are all informed by socio-cultural and political ideologies. Berlin's critique of rhetorical approaches is broad, though he seems to promote certain rhetorics over others. For composition teachers, the article is a good source of material for debate, and the sections analyzing the classroom strategies of Ira Shor and Peter Elbow are insightful.

▶ ---. "Rhetoric and Poetics in the English Department:
   Our Nineteenth-Century Inheritance." *CE* 47 (1985):
   531-33.

Berlin chronicles the divergence of rhetorics and poetics, which originally shared a common epistemology but were relegated to different spheres. Berlin's analysis is based on 18th century rhetorical development and 19th century college curricular changes, which he recognizes as significant in the elevation of poetics and the corresponding diminution of rhetorics. This article is an excellent source for Berlin's historical perspective on how rhetoric and poetics developed in America, as well as how the disciplines may evolve in the future.

► ---. *Rhetoric and Reality: Writing Instruction in
        American Colleges, 1900 -1985.* Carbondale, IL:
        SIUP, 1987.

As an extension of another of his major works, *Writing
Instruction in Nineteenth-Century American Colleges,* Berlin
analyzes the development of rhetoric and composition during
the 20th century. He uses the terms objective, subjective, and
transactional, which closely resemble the communications
triangle, to create a discourse of an inclusive, epistemic rhetoric.
Through this text, the reader will surely discover tools to fulfill
Berlin's objective: "Study of the dynamics of change in writing
classes during the present century will serve as a guide in
charting the course of composition instruction in the future" (5).

► ---. *Rhetorics, Poetics, and Cultures: Refiguring
        College English Studies.* Urbana, IL: NCTE, 1996.

In this posthumously published text, Berlin discusses how
American English studies before the 1970s served to educate
the professional elite, but the emerging global economy and
growing disparity between society's economic and cultural
strata quickly shifted social power to the managerial class—to
those who could articulate, communicate, and collaborate with
others. Therefore, Berlin calls for a new English studies
discipline that examines all forms of signifying practices,
including the ideologies and the social institutions that support
them, in order to prepare students for thoughtful, literate, and
participatory citizenship in America's emerging multicultural
democracy. This is an important and often cited text that is
considered by many to be Berlin's seminal work.

► ---. *Writing Instruction in Nineteenth-Century
        American Colleges.* Carbondale, IL: SIUP, 1984.

This monograph traces the development of three rhetorical
forms—classical, 18th century epistemological, and 19th century
epistemological—that influenced 19th century writing
instruction. Berlin views rhetoric as a social construction and
examines its development in terms of dominant social
conditions such as rising nationalism. The text is rather brief
but provides a solid historical survey.

► Berlin, James A., and Michael Vivion, eds. *Cultural
    Studies in the English Classroom*. Portsmouth, NH:
    Boynton/Cook, Heinemann, 1992.

This text focuses on designing writing and literature courses
with a cultural studies focus, as it is divided into two sections,
"Cultural Studies Programs" and "Cultural Studies Courses."
The text further discusses university politics in regard to
undertaking department-wide revisions to curricula, as well as
using WAC to expose all disciplines as cultural inventions. The
text effectively encourages readers to develop their own
pedagogical approaches to the complexities of cultural studies.

Chapter 4:
Wendy Bishop

(1953-2003)

Known for her work combining creative writing, ethnography, and composition studies, Bishop received two BA degrees (1975) in Studio Art and English, both with honors, and two MA degrees in English Creative Writing (1976) and Teaching Writing (1979) from the University of California, Davis. She completed her PhD (1988) at Indiana University of Pennsylvania in English, Rhetoric and Linguistics.

Over the quarter-century she taught (1979-03), Bishop experienced a diverse career split between administrative and teaching duties, including receiving the Kellogg W. Hunt Distinguished Professor of English at Florida State University in 2001, where she taught English (1990-04) and acted as the director of the First Year Writing Program (1990-93). She served as visiting assistant professor of English and Writing Center Coordinator for the University of Alaska at Fairbanks (1985-89); Communications Chairperson for the Humanities and Fine Arts Division and director of Special Services for Disadvantaged Students at the Navajo Community College in Tsaile, Arizona. In 1980, Bishop spent a year lecturing at Bayero University in Kano, Nigeria.

Scholars associate Wendy Bishop with a number of subjects within the realm of composition studies. Coming to composition after an already successful career as a creative writer, Bishop brought her passion for creative writing with her. She published several books and essays about blending composition studies and creative writing, as her work emphasizes the strengths of both disciplines and causes scholars to question why a distinction between the two should even be assumed. The exemplary texts *Released into Language: Options for Teaching Creative Writing*, *Acts of Revision*, and *Colors of a Different Horse* are mandatory for the bookshelves of those interested in composition and creative writing pedagogies.

Her focus on validating ethnography as a viable means of research in composition studies also sets her apart in the field. Ethnography, Bishop suggests, gives writers a means of research that lends itself to a more creative and narrative voice in scholarly writing. Stemming from her dissertation on the topic, many of her articles and books utilize ethnography in enlightening and creative ways.

By reading any of her works, one can easily recognize that Bishop, above all, had the heart of a teacher—whether in the composition classroom or in the creative writing workshop. Her great loves were writing and pedagogy, whatever the genre. She insists that the expressivist approach to composition wrongly becomes demonized in composition studies as too "touchy-feely," as it still allows for valuable approaches in composition instruction by redirecting students to the act of writing and communicating matters that are important to them.

A continued commitment to writing program administration indicated her belief in the importance of a multi-faceted writing program at the collegiate level, stressing personal writing across curricular boundaries. By advocating creative nonfiction in the composition classroom, along with the use of personal narrative, Bishop encouraged her contemporaries to view all writing, no matter what its purpose, as creative.

Through her work, Bishop still touches countless scholars, students, and writers. Aside from winning grants and creative writing honors for her writings, Bishop even had the privilege of being appointed Chair of CCCC (2001). Her untimely death from leukemia in November 2003 left the composition and creative writing communities with a great sense of loss. The 2004 CCCC was dedicated in her honor.

Even now, her writing and research proves influential and inspiring to today's scholars. Husband Dean Newman is currently cooperating with publishers on collections of her work and a festschrift dedicated to her career.

Alan Coulter and Hillary Robson

Sources for Biographical Narrative

▶ Bishop, Wendy. *Curriculum Vitae*. Email to Hillary Robson. 23 June 2006.

▶ Newman, Dean. "Wendy Bishop." Email to Hillary Robson. 23 June 2006.

Annotated Bibliography

▶ Bishop, Wendy, ed. *Acts of Revision*. Portsmouth, NH: Boynton/Cook, 2003.

This comprehensive collection of 22 essays discusses the process and art of revision—and its importance to the writing classroom—through personal narrative. Practical advice and examples give writers from all walks of life tips for revising their work in a variety of genres, including nonfiction, research, essay, and creative and alternate styles. Text suggestions can help students and teachers create a community in the classroom based on their shared status as writers.

▶ ---. "Against the Odds in Composition and Rhetoric." *CCC* 53 (2001): 322-46.

This article originally served as a Bishop's conference chair address at the CCCC's (2001), incorporating the poetry of Gerard Manley Hopkins as a metaphoric bridge for introducing new professionals to the field. A must-read for professionals interested in or already working in the field of composition and rhetoric because Bishop details the institutional challenges for validation in a field constantly marginalized by the status-quo holders in a traditional English department, where literature outweighs composition studies. Bishop offers historical, social, and political views—along with the personal—to reflect composition's ever-evolving role at the university level.

► ---. "Co-authoring Changes the Writing Classroom: Students Authorizing the Self, Authoring Together." *Composition Studies/FEN* 23.1 (1995): 54-62.

Bishop focuses on the value of collaboration among students for writing projects, suggesting that student interaction and group feedback help illustrate the importance of the evaluation process—allowing for students to function in the role of audience, critical commentator, and educator. Bishop offers the perspectives of both the teacher and the student, and offers a variety of activities and assignments, complete with student examples of collaborative writing.

► ---, ed. *Elements of Alternate Style*. Portsmouth, NH: Boynton/Cook, 1997.

This collection of essays, including two penned by Bishop, introduces ways to invite students to try alternate writing styles, including fracture narratives, double-voiced discourse, and alternate research writing projects, highlighting the concept of creative play. Divided into parts, each essayist presents an alternate style concept and revisits that concept with pedagogical approaches in the classroom, complete with guidelines for crafting assignments, choosing curriculum, and grading, for both the first-year and advanced composition classrooms. This innovative and inspiring collection is also a practical guide for creating a positive writing environment in any classroom.

► ---. "I-Witnessing in Composition: Turning Ethnographic Data into Narratives." *Rhetoric Review* 11 (1992): 147-58.

Bishop elaborates on her own ethnographic research background from her doctoral dissertation and argues that ethnography lends itself especially well to composition studies.

She points to how ethnography allows for better, more well-written pieces of scholarly work and shuns any notion that ethnography is a lesser form of respectable research. This article provides great advice for writers but also offers ideas for writing teachers that could lead to successful writing assignments.

▶ ---. "Places to Stand: The Reflective Writer-Teacher-Writer in Composition." *CCC* 51 (1999): 9-31.

This article examines why debates between expressivists and "not-expressivists" exist and defends those who still practice expressivism in the classroom as writers who teach, not merely writing teachers. Referencing other composition leaders, Bishop also outlines the strong alliance between creative writing and literature studies, not creative writing and composition studies, and why this proves problematic. Bishop's conversational, entertaining, yet professional voice allows readers to easily access her ideas and apply them directly to their own pedagogical approaches.

▶ ---. "Suddenly Sexy: Creative Nonfiction Rear-Ends Composition." *CE* 65 (2002): 257-75.

The pedagogy of the student as author provides a framework for the continued promotion of creative non-fiction practices in the composition classroom. Bishop provides a detailed defense for a curriculum based on personal experience, with application examples, classroom themes, and ethnographic accounts. This civic-minded, historio-social approach to composition has the potential to reform teaching expectations and the scope and tone of writing in the first-year writing environment.

▶ ---. *Released Into Language: Options for Teaching Creative Writing*. Urbana, IL: NCTE, 1990.

At once both a historical account of practices employed in teaching creative writing and ways to change the creative writing learning environment to be more personable and productive, this text explores the traditional conceptualizations of the writing workshop, presents creative uses for crafting writing exercises, the benefits of collaboration, and tips for evaluation and response. Bishop culminates with a comprehensive and helpful annotated bibliography suited for any professional interested in expanding their teaching horizons to include, or augment, creative writing methodologies.

▶ ---. "Writing Is/And Therapy: Raising Questions about Writing Classrooms and Writing Program Administration." *JAC* 13 (1993): 503-16.

Here Bishop discusses writing as a therapeutic process and the writing professor acting in the role of counselor offering insight into the different spectrum of positive effects that personal writing can bring to both student and teacher. Bishop contends that the challenges to incorporating a more personal based writing curriculum stems from an uneasiness governing the concept of the self and writing and long-held romanticized truths about creative writing, and encourages a challenge to the pedagogy. Particularly useful for first-time writing instructors uncertain about their role in the classroom, with guidelines for approaching writing as studying both writers and the development of identity.

▶ Bishop, Wendy, and Hans Ostrom, eds. *Colors of a Different Horse: Rethinking Creative Writing Theory and Pedagogy*. Urbana, IL: NCTE, 1994.

This collection of essays, including one of Bishop's own, discusses the practices of creative writing instruction. Many topics within composition studies are addressed, such as writing center theory, the lines between creative writing and composition studies, collaboration, and pedagogy. The essays prove helpful to any writer-teacher, but they also provide one of the few sources that view such composition-oriented topics through a creative writing lens.

Chapter 5:
Patricia Bizzell

(b. 1948)

Patricia Bizzell graduated *summa cum laude* from Wellesley College (1970) and received a PhD (1975) in English Literature from Rutgers University. From 1975 to 1977, she served as director of the Remedial Writing Program at Rutgers. In 1978, she joined the College of the Holy Cross where she currently serves as Chair of the English Department. Bizzell is the current president of the Rhetoric Society of America (2004-06), serves on the Board of Directors for the Alliance of Rhetoric Societies (ARS), and belongs to many professional organizations, including the Coalition of Women Scholars in the History of Rhetoric, MLA, and CCCC. She also serves on the editorial boards of *Pedagogy* and the *Journal of Basic Writing*.

Bizzell's awards include the NCTE Outstanding Book Award (1992) for *The Rhetorical Tradition: Readings from Classical Times to the Present*, co-authored with husband Bruce Herzberg, and the WPA Best Book Award (2000) for *Coming of Age: The Advanced Writing Curriculum*, containing her essay "Writing as a Means of Social Change." Bizzell has also published a collection of her essays, *Academic Discourse and*

Critical Consciousness (1992). Her other work includes more than 40 published essays and numerous conference appearances.

Bizzell states that she sees herself as a teacher-scholar who writes as a way of thinking through problems that confront her in her teaching. Her goal as a teacher is, and has always been, to promote social justice by educating the unaware and disenfranchised. This quest has led her to significant work in the fields of composition studies and rhetoric where she stresses the need for multiple voices and ideologies in the academy. She has been an important figure in the adoption of rhetoric for composition and literary studies, with an emphasis on the non-traditional rhetoric of women and people of color. In addition to numerous published essays about feminist rhetorics, she recently served as guest editor for a special issue of *Rhetoric Review* that focused on feminist historiography.

She has been criticized for seeming to promote a return to traditional academic discourse in the classroom, a move that could rob students of their own voices, but these attacks ignore her arguments for students to appropriate academic style for their own use. Her recent work lies primarily in this path, in studying new discourses that have arisen from the introduction of diverse communities to the academy.

Throughout three decades of scholarship, Bizzell has sought consistently for methods of developing her students' critical consciousness, a critical self-awareness of their own intellectual processes. For Bizzell, rhetoric is key in this endeavor as it enables students to study the way a writer makes meaning within a community. But this self-awareness has the larger goal of introducing students to different perspectives and the struggles going on in the contact zones between communities.

Rebecca Bobbitt

 Sources for Biographical Narrative

▶ Bizzell, Patricia. *Academic Discourse and Critical Consciousness*. Pittsburgh: U of Pittsburgh P, 1992.

▶ ---. *Curriculum Vitae*. 23 Nov. 2004
   <http://www.holycross.edu/departments/english/
   pbizzell/cv.html>.

▶ ---. "Patricia Bizzell's Statement." Teaching Writing for
   Social Change: A CCCC98 Roundtable Discussion.
   CCCC Convention, Chicago, IL. 1998. 23 Nov. 2004
   <http://www.hu.mtu.edu/cccc/98/social/bizzell.htm>.

▶ Dobrin, Sidney I. "'Radical Pedagogy': An Interview with
   Patricia Bizzell." *Writing on the Edge* 5 (1994): 57-68.

▶ "Patricia Lynn Bizzell." *Literature Resource Center*. 17 Sept.
   2002. 23 Nov. 2004
   <http://galenet.galegroup.com.ezproxy.mtsu.edu>.

Patricia Bizzell recommends these readings for novice composition instructors:

1. Villanueva, Victor, ed. *Cross-Talk in Comp Theory: A Reader*. 2nd ed. Urbana, IL: NCTE, 2003. – "provides an excellent introduction to the development of composition theory, important controversies, etc."
2. Shaughnessy, Mina. *Error and Expectations: A Guide for the Teacher of Basic Writing*. New ed. New York: Oxford UP, 1979. – "a model of how to attend sensitively to student writing"
3. Bizzell, Patricia, Nedra Reynolds, and Bruce Herzberg, eds. *The Bedford Bibliography for Teachers of Writing*. 6th ed. Boston: Bedford/St. Martin's, 2003. – "a useful resource on many teaching topics for many people"

Annotated Bibliography

▶ Bizzell, Patricia. *Academic Discourse and Critical
   Consciousness*. Pittsburgh: U of Pittsburgh P, 1992.

This collection of essays surveys Bizzell's earlier work and
shows the formation of her ideas about teaching composition

and the development of composition studies. The introduction and afterword provide interesting background for the essays, explaining how each essay grew from her teaching and the influences of composition leaders. Together, these essays offer a useful exploration of the nature and value of academic discourse.

▶ ---. "Classroom Authority and Critical Pedagogy." *American Literary History* 3 (1991): 847-63.

Here Bizzell offers a survey of writing about classroom authority and the influences behind the debate. Her exploration of how Henry Giroux, bell hooks, and Mike Rose negotiate power in the classroom is instructive and emotionally charged. Geared toward literature teachers seeking to know more about the issue, this provides useful background and guides for further research.

▶ ---. "'Contact Zones' and English Studies." *CE* 56 (1994): 163-69.

This piece calls for a new approach to literary studies that would dissolve the traditional categories used for studying literature, such as time period or gender. Bizzell uses Mary Louise Pratt's term, contact zone, to describe this new method of approaching texts. Teachers interested in broadening the literary canon and promoting diversity will learn much from Bizzell's focus on multiculturalism and marginalized voices.

▶ ---. "Editing the Rhetorical Tradition." *Philosophy and Rhetoric* 36 (2003): 109-18.

This essay defends Bizzell and Herzberg's inclusion of alternate forms of rhetoric, specifically those of women and people of color, in *The Rhetorical Tradition*. She also addresses students' oppositions to the new forms, offering methods of approaching these figures in the classroom. This piece is accessible to those unfamiliar with the field and is useful to those interested in how the rhetorical tradition has evolved, especially in the last two decades.

▶ ---. "Feminist Methods of Research in the History of
      Rhetoric: What Difference Do They Make?" *Rhetoric*
      Society Quarterly 30.4 (2000): 5-17.

In this essay, Bizzell focuses on the inclusion of rhetoric from
women and racial minorities in *The Rhetorical Tradition*. Her
discussion of how feminine writing, non-normative discourse
containing passion and personal reflection, is maligned in the
academy, and her refutation of that attitude are important for
writing teachers and scholars. However, this piece targets
those familiar with on-going debates about research methods
within the field of rhetoric, and is therefore not highly
instructive.

▶ ---. "Foundationalism and Anti-Foundationalism in
      Composition Studies." *Pre/Text* 7 (1986): 37-58. Rpt. in
      Academic Discourse and Critical Consciousness.
      Pittsburgh: U of Pittsburgh P, 1992. 202-21.

This essay first describes Bizzell's realization that academic
discourse is not the best or only path to critical consciousness.
Using Stanley Fish's work as support, she examines the
practice of teaching academic discourse as a construct, but also
as a way to see through discourse to social truth. This essay
lays the foundation for Bizzell's work in rhetoric. Though
somewhat outdated, this work is instructive in regard to
discourse and social constructionism.

▶ ---. "The 4th of July and the 22nd of December: The Function
      of Cultural Archives in Persuasion as Shown by
      Frederick Douglass and William Apess." *CCC* 48 (1997):
      44-60.

Here Bizzell returns to the idea of contact zones, offering them
as sites of social/ historical/ political knowledge that can be
transformed into rhetorical strategies. She uses the rhetoric of
Frederick Douglass and William Apess to lead students to
examination of the struggles at contact zones while introducing
them to powerful rhetorical strategies. This essay is especially
useful as it both illustrates Bizzell's theories and shows how
they may be used within the classroom.

► ---. "The Intellectual Work of 'Mixed' Forms of Academic Discourse." *ALT DIS: Alternative Discourses and the Academy*. Ed. Christopher Schroeder, Helen Fox, and Patricia Bizzell. Portsmouth, NH: Heinemann Boynton/Cook, 2002. 1-10.

This call for new strategies in academic discourse offers a definition of standard academic discourse, that belonging to male, European Americans of the middle or upper classes. The mixed forms and non-traditional voices are important not only to democratize the academy, but also because these forms inspire new intellectual work. Most instructive to the reader is Bizzell's incorporation of other scholars' responses to non-traditional forms of discourse.

► ---. "On the Possibility of a Unified Theory of Composition and Literature." *Rhetoric Review* 4 (1986): 174-80.

The unified theory Bizzell proposes is that of rhetoric, in which literary scholars analyze all kinds of discourse, with culture becoming the studied text. This essay is useful in its examination of current debate, and it highlights how the study of rhetoric can benefit both literary criticism and student writers, but it is highly theoretical and relies too heavily on academic jargon.

► Bizzell, Patricia, and Bruce Herzberg. "'Inherent' Ideology, 'Universal' History, 'Empirical' Evidence, and 'Context-Free' Writing: Some Problems in E. D. Hirsch's *The Philosophy of Composition*." *MLN* 95 (1980): 1181-1202.

Bizzell describes this essay as the first articulation of her social-constructionist approach to the study of discourse. This essay, though largely confined to a refutation of E. D. Hirsch's *The Philosophy of Composition*, is an important step in the move from cognitive models to discourse communities. Bizzell and Herzberg's examination of Hirsch's terminology is instructive, but this essay focuses only on the problems inherent in teaching standard English to diverse communities rather than proposing solutions.

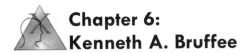

Chapter 6:
Kenneth A. Bruffee

(b. 1934)

A primary advocate of collaborative learning, Kenneth A. Bruffee graduated with a BA (1956) in English from Wesleyan University and earned a PhD (1966) in English from Northwestern University. During his career he taught at the University of New Mexico, Northwestern University, the University of Virginia, Columbia University, Cooper Union, and the University of Pennsylvania. Bruffee was a professor of English at Brooklyn College, City University of New York (CUNY, BC) and directed the Scholars Program and Honors Academy there for a major portion of his career. The college has honored Bruffee on several occasions, awarding him a Broeklundian Professorship (1991-94), an award granted to faculty demonstrating outstanding achievement in research and scholarship, and naming him a Wolfe Institute Faculty Fellow (1991-92), an honor awarded by the Ethyle E. Wolfe Institute for the Humanities to deserving full-time members of the CUNY, BC faculty.

Past accomplishments include being named first Chair of the MLA Teaching of Writing division (1976) and direction of The Institute in Peer Tutoring and Collaborative Learning (1979-82) at BC, a project supported by FIPSE. He also served as a member of the editorial advisory board for *Liberal Education* and was a founding editor of *WPA* (1979), a journal published by the WPA Council—a council which he co-founded (1977). He has been a highly sought-after speaker, including serving as the Keynote Speaker at the Brown University Conference on Peer Tutoring (1984, 1993). He also delivered the University of Memphis Marcus Orr Higher Education Lecture on "Changing Paradigms in College and University Teaching" (1996) and has led numerous colloquia on collaborative learning, authority in knowledge and liberal education.

Bruffee is generally considered the first compositionist to urge consideration of socially constructed knowledge, founding his theory on the works of Lev Vygotsky, Thomas Kuhn, and Richard Rorty. His writings encourage teachers to depart from traditional university teaching methods solely reliant on direct instruction. Rather, he suggests that knowledge is a set of concepts agreed upon by a knowledgeable community (normal discourse) and asserts that we create and validate this accepted body of knowledge through collaboration. Thus, instructors should use collaboration in the classroom, allowing students to participate in the "conversation of mankind" whether discussing literary works or evaluating each other's writing. As a result of the pedagogical rationale his work outlines, other scholars (e.g., Lunsford, Ede) have expanded the collaborative learning field in composition theory in a number of directions, particularly in relation to writing centers and new implications in this digital age.

Until his retirement in February of 2006, Bruffee continued to shape teaching practices at CUNY, BC, conducting collaborative learning workshops for the entire college and incorporating them into the workings of the Honors Academy. His work in the Honors Academy, which encompasses various disciplines and serves about 300 students, exposed the best and brightest students of CUNY, BC to the benefits of collaborative learning and rigorous academics.

Stephanie Harper

Sources for Biographical Narrative

► "Faculty." *BC Report (Self Study).* 7 July 2006
  <http://www.brooklyn.cuny.edu/bc/pubs/middle/
  body14.htm>.

► "The Flag of Excellence—The Honors Academy." 7 July 2006
  <http://www.brooklyn.cuny.edu/bc/texts/showcase/
  honorsacademy.htm>.

► Kennedy, Mary Lynch. "Kenneth Bruffee." *Theorizing
  Composition: A Critical Sourcebook of Theory and
  Scholarship in Contemporary Composition Studies.*
  Westport, CT: Greenwood, 1998.

► "Kenneth Bruffee: Brief Biography." English Dept. home
  page. CUNY, Brooklyn College. 2000. 1 July 2006
  <http://academic.brooklyn.cuny.edu/english/bruffee/
  bruffee_cv.html>.

Annotated Bibliography

► Bruffee, Kenneth, A. "The Brooklyn Plan: Attaining
  Intellectual Growth through Peer-Group Tutoring."
  Liberal Education 64 (1978): 447-68.

Bruffee cites Theodore Newcomb's 1962 study suggesting that
peer-group influence is the most powerful force in
undergraduate education, as well as other studies suggesting
the benefits of peer tutoring for students. As a result of these
studies, CUNY devised a writing program centered around peer
tutoring, and this article describes the program established at
CUNY, BC, The Brooklyn Tutoring Plan. While this article
might seem dated in its explanation of a collaborative model
developed over twenty years ago, it accomplishes two important
things—it describes an early writing center staffed by
undergraduates that addressed not only grammar but also
what Bruffee calls "intellectual paralysis," and it details
positive effects of peer tutoring on tutors as well as tutees.

▶ ---. "Staffing and Operating Peer-Tutoring Writing Centers."
*Basic Writing: Essays for Teachers, Researchers, and
Administrators.* Ed. Lawrence N. Kasden and Daniel R.
Hoeber. Urbana, IL: NCTE, 1980. 141-49.

This article makes a strong argument for the use of writing
centers staffed by peer tutors, noting not only the benefits for
tutees but also that tutors learn to "recognize, formulate, and
express ideas of their own and to integrate education into
everyday social, emotional, and practical life" (149). While
suggesting how a writing center can enhance writing education
for basic writers, Bruffee also addresses the fundamental
challenges of operating writing centers—staff, budget, training,
and location. This article addresses issues that have been
rehashed in many writings since then; however, it suggests still
useful and practical information about peer tutoring and
writing centers and how to support both tutors and center.

▶ ---. "Collaborative Learning and the 'Conversation of
Mankind'." *CE* 46 (1984): 635-52.

This work is a landmark essay in the arena of collaborative
learning and one of the first to outline a rationale for its
practice. It outlines the connections between conversation,
thinking, and writing and asserts the philosophy that
knowledge is constructed by agreement in knowledgeable
communities. Explanations of theoretical underpinnings are
clear; however, the article provides little practical application of
the practice in the classroom.

▶ ---. "Collaborative Learning: Some Practical Models." *CE* 34
(1973): 634-43.

This early effort seeks to do what "Collaborative Learning and
the 'Conversation of Mankind'" did not—it provides readers
with actual examples of real world and classroom collaboration.
Its practicality renders it both helpful and readable, as it
explains how to avoid pitfalls and how to succeed in
collaborative learning. Emphasis is on the need for the teacher
to become a facilitator while still providing necessary structure
to sometimes reluctant students.

► ---. *A Short Course in Writing.* 4th ed. Longman Classics
    Edition. New York: Longman, 2007.

Reissued in a series of classic textbooks and with a forward by
John Trimbur and Harvey Kail which discusses the historical
importance of the text, Bruffee's 1985 *Short Course* provides
teachers and writers an expository writing textbook intended
for use in a collaborative classroom. While writers are
instructed to mine their own experiences for ideas and to allow
those ideas to guide their topic choice, the acknowledged
drawback of the book is its restrictive nature in terms of form;
however, it does allow choice in subject and offers adaptive
models. Also, it includes activities conducive to collaboration,
ample modeling through sample essays, and concludes with a
useful appendix specifically for teachers desiring to establish a
collaborative classroom.

► ---. "Social Construction, Language, and the Authority of
    Knowledge: A Bibliographical Essay." *CE* 48 (1986):
    773-88.

Bruffee offers a foundation to social constructionist theory,
beginning with a detailed explanation of social constructionism
based on the work of Thomas Kuhn and Richard Rorty. He then
threads together general social constructionist works before
focusing on community-specific writings on the theory (i.e., in
literature or composition). The bibliographic article provides a
thorough and specific introduction, complete with suggested
order of reading in some cases.

► ---. "On Not Listening in Order to Hear: Collaborative
    Learning and the Rewards of   Classroom Research."
    Journal of Basic Writing 7 (1988): 3-12.

Originally a keynote address, this essay urges community
college humanities instructors to conduct research documenting
the diversity and cultural origins of their students. Through
collaborative learning, students feel confident enough to share
learning and writing processes with instructors who may then
discover how we negotiate among the diverse communities
around us. It is certainly true that benefits derived from

collaborative learning might especially enhance the learning experience of students in community colleges who need the reacculturation Bruffee discusses in other works; however, this address is primarily useful in the background it gives about the development of Bruffee's theory and its affirmation of community colleges as centers of important and valid learning.

▶ ---. "Sharing Our Toys: Cooperative Learning Versus
    Collaborative Learning." *Change* 27.1
    (January/February 1995): 12-18.

Bruffee asserts that while cooperative and collaborative learning are two versions of the same thing, there are essential differences between the two because of different assumptions about the nature of knowledge and the age of the students generally experiencing each practice. Cooperative learning is designed for primary education and to eliminate competition, while the teacher remains the primary authority; whereas, collaborative learning encourages disagreement within the group if it enhances learning, and the teacher does not intervene in or evaluate group activities at all. This article provides an interesting and readable overview of both practices, acknowledging the strengths and weaknesses of each.

▶ ---. *Collaborative Learning: Higher Education,
    Interdependence, and the Authority of Knowledge.* 2nd
    ed. Baltimore: John Hopkins, 1999.

Bruffee acknowledges that this book allowed him to piece through and evaluate his decades of thought on collaborative learning, ascertaining what really worked and constructing new thought from the original theory—careful considerations that add to the validity and usefulness of the work. Bruffee strongly suggests that college should be a place of reacculturation where students learn to be part of critically thoughtful communities rather than having knowledge poured into them in a foundationalist manner. Important additions to newer editions of the book are chapters on technology and the difference between cooperative and collaborative learning.

▶ ---. "Peer Tutoring and the 'Conversation of Mankind'." *The Allyn and Bacon Guide to Writing Center Theory and Practice*. Ed. Robert W. Barnett and Jacob S. Blumner. Boston: Allyn and Bacon, 2001. 206-18.

Bruffee applies the concepts outlined in his original "Conversation of Mankind" article specifically to the practice of peer tutoring. He explains the conceptual rationale for peer tutoring, discusses the view of knowledge that underlies the practice, and then returns to implications of social constructivism and peer tutoring for the humanities. This article is subdivided by headings useful to readers already conversant with Bruffee's general theory in that they can go immediately to pertinent portions of the article.

Chapter 7:
Peter Carino
(b. 1955)

Peter Carino began graduate work at Southern Illinois University at Edwardsville (1979), before receiving a PhD (1984) from UIUC, both in English. He has developed and taught undergraduate and graduate courses in writing, rhetorical theory, writing center theory and administration, and literature at Indiana State University as professor (1993-present); and was appointed visiting professor at the University of Pisa (1997). Accolades and esteemed distinctions consist of a position on the editorial board of *The Writing Center Journal* (1999), executive board membership in the East Central Writing Centers Association, with the elected titles of President (1991-92) and Treasurer (1993-96). He was honored with the Distinguished Service Award (1996) and the College of Arts and Sciences Educational Excellence Award (1993) both from Indiana State.

Carino has made great contributions to the field of composition and writing center theory as a published author of three books on first-year college writing; nine articles on writing centers, with topics such as politics, history, technology, and discourse analysis; and seven articles on the writing process in the introductory composition classroom. Carino's research methodologies are primarily grounded in a historio-social view, drawing from both his scholarship and near 22-year appointment as head of the Indiana State Writing Center.

Carino's dedication to university service includes continued involvement in the faculty senate, as Chair (1998-00), Vice-Chair, and Executive Committee Member; he is a member of both the University Club and Faculty Affairs, and has served on numerous Masters theses, papers, and examination committees in the fields of composition and American literature. He was university coordinator for the Conference on Baseball in Literature and American Culture (1995, 1996,

1999); co-coordinator of the English department Creative Writing Day (1994) and the Annual Conference on Teaching Composition (1986, 1987).

Carino has worked as supervisor of the Indiana State Writing Center since 1987, and many conference presentations and published articles stem from his work at the Center. His innovative ideas have fostered new developments in the Center's scope and overall accessibility; in the past two decades, he has conceptualized or sponsored successful plans to increase staff through recruitment initiatives, employed a tutor training program, created materials for staff skill development, and began several promotional campaigns for campus-wide awareness. A self-admitted technophobe, Carino encouraged an online writing center in 1998, an experience that prompted him to write about the challenges encountered in the process. As a result of his efforts for the center to reach the Indiana State community online and on campus, the center conducts approximately 2,000 tutorial sessions per semester; an average of 16 percent of the student population.

His articles, "Open Admissions and the Construction of a Writing enter History: A Tale of Three Models," and "Theorizing the Writing Center: An Uneasy Task." were winners of the NWCA Best Article of the Year Award in 1998 and 1995, respectively. Carino's continued support for excellence in teaching writing, for writing center development and writing across-the-discipline initiatives, and groundbreaking scholarship reflect his importance to composition and writing center theory.

Hillary Robson

Sources for Biographical Narrative

▶ Carino, Peter. *Curriculum Vitae.* English Dept. home page. Indiana State University. 2005. 25 June 2006 <http://web.indstate.edu/english/fac/carino.html>.

▶ Writing Center. Indiana State University. 2001. 15 June 2006 <http://isu.indstate.edu/writing/>.

Peter Carino recommends these readings for novice composition instructors:

1. Berlin, James A. *Rhetoric and Reality: Writing Instruction in American Colleges, 1900-1985.* Carbondale, IL: SIUP, 1987.
2. North, Steven. *The Making of Knowledge in Composition: Portrait of an Emerging Field.* Albany, New York: Boynton/Cook, 1987.
3. Barnett, Robert, and Jacob Blumner, eds. *Writing Center Theory and Practice.* Boston: Allyn and Bacon, 2001.

Annotated Bibliography

▶ Carino, Peter. "Early Writing Centers: Toward a History." *Writing Center Journal* 15 (1995): 16-27.

Carino's investigation into the history of writing centers at the university discusses the difficulties in locating reliable resources to reflect the start of writing centers prior to the 1970s. This seminal article provides insight to the early, and prevailing, issues at hand for the development of the writing center: that it often acts as an appendage of the English department, the challenges to staffing, administrative privileges and funding, and the misconstruction of the center as a place for remedial students to work on basic writing skills. This is a foundational article for all composition professionals.

▶ ---. "Open Admissions and the Construction of Writing Center History: A Tale of Three Models." *Writing Center Journal* 17.1 (1996): 30–48.

Carino contends that existing models of writing center history from 1968-1983 are inadequate, and that a cultural-model proves more appropriate. Furthermore, he claims the position of the writing center as a response to Open Admission policies, introducing the so-called remedial student, is inaccurate. This is an excellent article for understanding the history of the writing center from a more cultural perspective, with emphasis placed on the required quality of historical research.

▶ ---. "Posing Questions for Evaluating Tutorial Sessions on Audio Tape." *Writing Lab Newsletter* 14.1 (1989): 8-12.

Carino uses Muriel Harris's *Teaching One-to-One* and Meyer and Smith's *The Practical Tutor* as primary sources to determine tutor/tutee audio or video tape evaluation guidelines, where session objective, tutor/tutee talk and rapport, and bridging to classroom connections act as the frame for training writing center staff members. Carino suggests that trainees evaluate the tapes in small groups to develop methods for conducting their own tutoring sessions. Tips for writing center directors, including ethical editing practices and how to choose quality tapes for training complete this well-rounded presentation of a useful training and staff development tool.

▶ ---. "Theorizing the Writing Center: An Uneasy Task." *Dialogue: A Journal for Composition Specialists* 2.1 (1995): 23-37.

The political, administrative, and ideological forces at play that influence the theorizing process of the writing center opens the floor to discussion on the role of the tutor/writing assistant as socially conscious and transformative. Carino attributes this conflict to the praxis at play in the writing center, the duality between the writing center environment as one for honing and perfecting skills whereas the classroom is for learning and cultivating specific skills. His work documents the struggle in validating both composition studies and the writing center as entities along the same spectrum with similar, symbiotic goals.

▶ ---. "What We Talk about When We Talk about Our Metaphors: A Cultural Critique of Clinic, Lab, Center." *Writing Center Journal* 13.1 (1992): 31-41. Rpt. in *Landmark Essays on Writing Centers*, Ed. Christina Murphy and Joseph Law. Davis, CA: Hemagoras, 1995: 37-46.

This foundational article provides an historical, social, and cultural view of the development of terminology used within the writing center. Carino explores the use of the clinic metaphor as creating a diagnostic or curative type role, a designation of remedial development sought and achieved at the writing center, the evolution into lab, still medical/scientific in origin but somehow less diagnostic but still curative, and finally to center. This interesting look into the assignment of metaphorical value to this unique labeling process, and the significant impact a name has on the writing center environment, is valuable to all writing center directors and tutors.

▶ Carino, Peter, Lori Floyd, and Marcia Lightle. "Empowering a Writing Center: The Faculty Meets the Tutors." *Voices of Empowerment: Proceedings of the Eleventh Annual East Central Writing Centers Association Conference, 1989.* Ed. Lea Masiello. Indiana, PA: Halldin, 1990: 107-14. Rpt. in *Writing Lab Newsletter* 16.2 (1991): 1-5.

The three authors reflect on the struggle for authority, voice, and empowerment in the writing center and the university at large, and the struggle with self-identity and pride for tutors when there is a lack of communication between faculty and tutoring staff. Carino writes from an administrator's position, discussing the goal of communication among teachers and tutors started with session review forms, and followed with a meet and greet and informal question-and-answer session, with Floyd and Lightle sharing their experiences as tutors. Carino's attempt to empower and legitimize writing center work and the identity and professional respect among tutors and faculty proves groundbreaking for contemporary writing center practices in designating the writing center as a place for the improvement of writing from all writers—and not just in a remedial sense.

▶ Writing Center. Indiana State University. 2001. 15 June 2006 <http://isu.indstate.edu/writing/>.

Carino's center opened online in 1998, offering valuable resource tools and center information to visitors, including 250 worksheets available for download in topics ranging from grammar, to structuring a thesis, and editing techniques. With superlative online resources for any student studying all forms of writing, the site's mission statement clarifies Carino's concept of his writing center: a place where students from all disciplines can seek and find help with their writing projects, with tutors in a non-directive role of peer reader with a focus on improving the student's writing, not just the grade. An excellent source that reflects a contemporary environment that both employs and influences current theoretical perspectives in writing centers.

Chapter 8:
William Condon

(b. 1950)

A noted scholar in the field of composition, Bill Condon focuses on WAC, writing assessment, computer-enhanced pedagogy, and critical thinking, all of which reflect his exploratory approach to writing instruction. Condon earned his BA (1972) in English from the University of Georgia before attending graduate school at Miami University, Ohio, where he received his MA (1977). He later completed his PhD (1982) at Brown University, where he studied composition and literature. Though Condon began his career by teaching the 7th and 8th grade in 1974, he has spent the last few decades working as a WPA for various institutions, including the University of Oklahoma, Arkansas Tech University, the University of Michigan, and Washington State University.

Condon attributes his emphases on writing assessment, computer use, and WAC to his nine-year position on the University of Michigan's English Composition Board, an organization devoted to inventing, administering, and supporting WAC programs. Condon first used computers for pedagogical purposes in 1984 and has since advocated for their use, arguing that students' familiarity with such instruments

49

promises more active learning and encourages faculty to remain as electronically savvy as their students. Condon suggests that word processors encourage revision while providing students with access to the research processes of their selected area of study. Computers also provide an outlet for electronic portfolios, which invite an opportunity for assessing students' writing as well as cultivating the critical thinking and communicative skills necessary for the students' academic achievement.

Condon's interest in WAC and writing assessment evolved into a co-editorship with Liz Hamp-Lyons of the journal *Assessing Writing*, a refereed international journal that explores all issues of writing assessment. Condon was also a founding member of the Alliance for Computers and Writing, which is a free organization devoted to supporting teachers who use computer-based instruction. He currently works at Washington State as professor of English and director of the Campus Writing Program. Condon also teaches graduate seminars in writing assessment and composition theory as well as undergraduate courses that employ computer-enhanced pedagogies.

Jessica McKee

Sources for Biographical Narrative

▶ Condon, Bill. English Dept. home page. Washington State University. 2002. 2 Aug. 2006 <http://www.libarts.wsu.edu/english/faculty/condon.html>.

▶ Rutz, Carol. "The Tallest WAC Expert in North America: An Interview with Bill Condon." *The WAC Journal* 16 (2005): 70-75.

▶ "William Condon." *Directory of American Scholars*. 2002. 3 Aug. 2006 <http://galenet.galegroup.com>.

Annotated Bibliography

▶ *Assessing Writing*. Ed. L. Hamp-Lyons and W. Condon.
16 July 2006. Elsevier. 2 Aug. 2006
<http://www.elsevier.com>.

This Web site provides a history of *Assessing Writing* as well as
ordering and publication information. Edited by Condon and
Hamp-Lyons, *Assessing Writing* is a refereed international
journal devoted to scholarship on the practice of writing
assessment. The journal publishes essays on traditional and
experimental modes of assessment and welcomes work from all
fields of study.

▶ Butler, Wayne, and William Condon. *Writing the
Information Superhighway*. Boston: Allyn & Bacon,
1997.

This textbook responds to a culture shaped by the onset of
electronic media. Unlike traditional books on composition and
Internet use, *Writing the Information Superhighway* hopes to
bridge the gap between novice net users and writers by
creating a learning community of instructors and students
working together to develop traditional literacy skills while
cultivating their own technological literacy. With its directory
of URLs and comprehensive glossary, the book introduces the
Internet and its various forms of electronic communication. It
also provides model writing assignments and teaching
examples.

▶ Condon, William, and Susanmarie Harrington. "Don't Lower
the River, Raise the Bridge: Preserving Standards by
Improving Students' Performances." *The Dialogic
Classroom: Teachers Integrating Computer Technology,
Pedagogy, and Research*. Ed. Jeffrey Galinand and
Joan Latchaw. Urbana, IL: NCTE, 1998. 92-105.

Based on an experience with psychology students having
difficulties with writing and TAs having difficulties with
writing instruction, Condon and Harrington created software to
help students understand assignments and crucial writing

concepts while emphasizing to TAs the need for qualifying an assignment's requirements. This essay reports on the software and relays the concerns educators may address when creating interdisciplinary groups to support the needs of students writing across their curricula. This essay provides practical advice to all instructors who wish to improve their students' writing and their own instruction.

▶ *Critical Thinking Project.* 2 Aug. 2006
      <http://wsuctproject.wsu.edu/ph.htm>.

This Web site provides information on the *WSU Guide to Rating Critical Thinking*, a tool created by Condon and colleagues to measure critical thinking. Intended for instructors, the rating guide helps faculty from varying disciplines integrate and implement critical thinking into the course material and assignments by providing general criteria as evidence of mastery; it also helps determine the effectiveness of these critical thinking exercises.

▶ Hamp-Lyons, Liz, and William Condon. *Assessing the Portfolio: Principles for Theory, Practice, and Research.* Cresskill, NJ: Hampton, 2000.

This straightforward and informative book explores the multiple components of using portfolios for writing assessment. Divided into five chapters, the text provides a history of assessment   practices, including the principle characteristics of portfolio assessment as well as practical and theoretical implementation of portfolio assessment. Intended for English composition instructors and WPAs, this book provides useful information for anyone concerned with how to assess student writing.

▶ ---. "Questioning Assumptions about Portfolio Based Assessment." *CCC* 44 (1993): 176-90.

Hamp-Lyons and Condon report on their experience with portfolio-based writing assessment, revealing and debunking the assumptions made by faculty and by the authors. They also address the need for assessment criteria and the criteria's relationship to portfolio-based assessment. Straightforward and convincing, this essay challenges assumptions of portfolio use while espousing the value of such forms of assessment.

▶ Haswell, Richard H., ed. *Beyond Outcomes: Assessment and Instruction Within a University Writing Program.* Westport, CT: Ablex Publishing, 2001.

This book pulls together the work of numerous administrators and faculty involved in developing writing assessment and writing instruction at Washington State University. While written as a case study, their essays still offer advice for the construction or integration of similar programs at other universities. With an introduction by Condon as well as several collaboratively-written essays by him, this anthology reflects Condon's research in writing assessment.

▶ Monroe, Barbara J., Rebecca Rickley, William Condon, and Wayne Butler. "The Near and Distant Futures of OWL and the Writing Center." *Taking Flight with OWLs: Examining Electronic Writing Center Work.* Ed. James A. Inman and Donna N. Sewell. Mahwah, NJ: Erlbaum, 2000. 211-222.

This essay details the University of Michigan's creation of an OWL, an online writing and learning tutoring service that exceeds the traditional role of writing centers by providing services to communities outside the university, such as high schools and businesses. The authors persuasively argue that such programs help reclaim writing centers from their traditionally marginalized status because they encourage alliance building and corporate sponsorship, both of which work to increase the numbers of users as well as providing a positive public service role for universities.

▶ Kelly-Riley, Diane, Lisa Johnson-Shull, and William Condon. "Opportunities for Consilience: Toward a Networked-Based Model for Writing Program Administration." *The Writing Program Administrator as Theorist: Making Knowledge Work.* Ed. Shirley K. Rose and Irwin Weiser. Portsmouth, NH: Boynton/Cook Heinemann, 2002. 129-42.

In this book chapter, the authors assert that WPAs intuitively employ a networked model of administration that stems from their work with peer tutoring and their tendency towards collaboration. They argue that recognizing and identifying this as a form of networked administration allows for more connections between disciplines and administrators while legitimizing and solidifying the work of writing programs. Though intended for WPAs, this chapter reminds its audience of the academy's move from the hierarchical knowledge possessor/provider to a more egalitarian model where information flows back and forth rather than from top to bottom.

Chapter 9:
Robert Connors

(1951-2000)

Robert J. Connors' contributions to composition stand largely in the fields of classical and 19th century rhetoric and their connections to modern pedagogy and writing. He has authored, co-authored, or edited ten books and over 60 articles in the field of composition. Connors earned his BA (1973) from UMass-Amherst and his MA (1977) and PhD (1980) in composition and rhetoric from The Ohio State University. After earning his doctorate, Connors taught briefly at LSU before joining the faculty at the University of New Hampshire (UNH), where he helped establish the writing center that now bears his name. While at UNH, he was also instrumental in forming a WAC program as well as organizing the Beal Collection, a national collection of composition manuscripts.

His first scholarly publication came in 1979 for *CCC* with "The Differences between Speech and Writing: Ethos, Pathos, and Logos." Three years later, Connors produced his best-known and most influential work, "The Rise and Fall of the Modes of Discourse" (1982), which provides a brief history of rhetorical theories in American academia. This essay signaled his arrival on the academic scene and, in many ways, acted as a precursor to his work that melded history and rhetoric. His first book, *Essays on Classical Rhetoric and Modern Discourse* (1984), co-edited with Lisa Ede and Andrea Lunsford, covers a broad range of issues in rhetoric, its history, and its uses for today's academic writers. He also helped write and develop the *St. Martin's Handbook*, a textbook for composition classes. His final book, *Composition-Rhetoric: Backgrounds, Theory, and Pedagogy* (1997), highlights his specialization in composition. The work focuses on 19th century contributions to the field of rhetoric and how they connect with modern pedagogy. In many ways, this book represents the culmination of his research as a historian of rhetoric.

"The Rise and Fall of the Modes of Discourse" won the Richard Braddock Award (1982). Later Connors, along with Ede and Lunsford, was presented MLA's Mina P. Shaughnessey Prize (1985) for outstanding research in English pedagogy for their aforementioned *Essays on Classical Rhetoric and Modern Discourse*. His contributions were not limited to publications as he was an active and well-known presenter, serving as the featured speaker at the Penn State Conference on Rhetoric and Composition (1999).

Connors, through his research and writing, helped expand and clarify our understanding of rhetorical history while contributing to other aspects of the discipline. And due to his elegant research of obscure texts and teaching of young scholars, Connors has enriched rhetorical scholarship and furthered the field of composition.

Nicholas Bush

 Sources for Biographical Narrative

▶ Bloom, Lynn Z. "Canonical Bob." *JAC* 20 (2000): 483-504.

▶ Buckley, Louise. "New Reference Question." Email to Nicholas X. Bush. 12 July 2006.

▶ Ede, Lisa, and Andrea Lunsford, eds. *Selected Essays of Robert J. Connors*. New York: Bedford/St. Martin's, 2003.

▶ Kerr, Allan D. "UNH Loses 'Great Colleague'." *Union Leader* [Manchester]. 24 June 2000, all ed., sec. A: 6.

▶ Newkirk, Thomas. "In Memoriam: Robert J. Connors." *CCC* 52 (2000): 9-11.

▶ Sullivan, Patricia A. "In Memory of Robert J. Connors, 1951-2000." *JAC* 20 (2000): 483-504

Annotated Bibliography

▶ Connors, Robert J. *Composition-Rhetoric: Backgrounds, Theory, and Pedagogy*. Pittsburgh: U of Pittsburgh P, 1997.

This book defines the rhetoric of composition and classifies its many forms. It is an examination of how rhetorical pedagogy has been handed down to modern scholars from the 19th century. Connors also discusses what elements of rhetoric have survived into modern times and how they are implemented in modern classrooms. This work is more helpful for the preparation of the professor than any immediate instruction for students. A composition professor could use this to gain an understanding of the history of specific rhetorical techniques and perhaps use it as a reference guide for background in composition issues such as style theory, invention, and possible assignments.

▶ ---. "The Erasure of the Sentence." *CCC* 52 (2000): 96-128.

Connors chronicles the emergence and regression of sentence-centered writing instruction. He also classifies a type of sentence-based pedagogy by laying out the different ways in which sentence style and sentence structure are taught. Connors does point out the limits of sentence-based pedagogies but argues that using the sentence as a centerpiece in writing can, when used within the context of a given situation, be helpful.

This essay provides the different ways in which professors have taught sentence construction and the strengths and weaknesses of each.

▶ ---. "The Rise and Fall of the Modes of Discourse." *CCC* 32 (1981): 444-55.

This essay provides a brief history of the modes of discourse in American universities. The work recounts the why and how surrounding changes in discourse. Connors' essay is part examination of the subject and part criticism, providing an accurate presentation of the history of discourse. Novice composition instructors can use this as a means of strengthening their understanding of how written communication has been taught in the past, which would help the prospective professor gain a perspective on the context of his or her field.

▶ ---, ed. *Selected Essays of Edward P.J. Corbett.* Dallas: Southern Methodist UP, 1997.

This work anthologizes a selection of essays by Edward P.J. Corbett, who helped revive and modernize rhetoric in the 20th century. Connors has selected writings on the definition, history, and application of classical rhetoric; it also contains some writings that speculate on rhetoric's future. This book gives a glimpse into a professor who has influenced Connors' maturation as a scholar as well as providing the reader with ideas on classical rhetoric that are still relevant for today's classroom.

▶ ---. "Teachers' Rhetorical Comments on Student's Papers." *Selected Essays of Robert J. Connors.* Ed. Lisa Ede and Andrea Lunsford. Boston: Bedford/St. Martin's, 2003. 236-58.

This essay takes a unique look at the teaching of writing by focusing on what professors write on their students' papers. The work contains statistics and charts that help him in his attempt to connect what gets written and what gets learned. The essay gives an accurate look into how teachers interact with student's papers while grading. Inexperienced instructors finding their grading style can use this information to see how more seasoned professors approach student essays.

▶ ---. "Writing the History of Our Discipline." *Selected Essays of Robert J. Connors*. Ed. Lisa Ede and Andrea Lunsford. Boston: Bedford/St. Martin's, 2003. 202-20.

Connors looks at how the subfield of composition came from the larger discipline of rhetoric and how that history informs the way we teach composition today. He talks about how events, such as WWII, and rhetorical historians, such as Albert R. Kitzhaber, affected how colleges organized departments. The relevance for new instructors comes in the places where he draws the connection between past teachers and current ones by pointing out the similarities between the problems past professors faced in the classroom and the problems current ones face.

▶ Connors, Robert J., Lisa Ede, and Andrea Lunsford. "The Revival of Rhetoric in America." *Essays On Classical Rhetoric and Modern Discourse*. Ed. Robert J. Connors, Lisa Ede, and Andrea Lunsford. Carbondale, IL: SIUP, 1984. 1-15.

This essay recounts the rise and fall of classical rhetoric in American universities. The writers focus on why and how rhetoric devolved from a discipline that incorporated several genres to a discipline that focused on writing styles. They point out that, with the fusion of theory and practice, the late 20th century saw a revival in classical rhetoric. This article can help composition instructors see how their field has changed and can help them see what aspects of past rhetorical teaching they want to incorporate back into their respective curriculums.

▶ ---, eds. *Essays on Classical Rhetoric and Modern Discourse.*
   Carbondale, IL: SIUP, 1984.

This book is a compilation of essays that focuses on a wide
range of subjects concerning classical rhetoric and
contemporary pedagogy. The essays include broad subjects
from the history of rhetoric in US universities to how to teach
style. The book is a wellspring of information on the different
uses of classical rhetoric in the modern college classroom. And
provides a background on composition so that a professor can
gain an understanding of past and current trends and issues in
the field.

▶ Connors, Robert J., and Andrea Lunsford. *St. Martin's
   Handbook.* Boston: St. Martin's, 1989.

This handbook is a resource best used by students to provide
instruction in proofing and revising essays, yet it also contains
imitation exercises and professional writing samples. It can be
used strictly as a reference guide for grammar or style rules
such as understanding pronoun case or using strong verbs. It
can also be used as a preliminary source for learning
documentation, and it also containing chapters laying out the
basic steps of the writing process.

▶ Corbett, Edward P. J., and Robert J. Connors. *Classical
   Rhetoric for the Modern Student.* 4th ed. Oxford: Oxford
   UP, 1999.

This book focuses on the use and importance of classical
rhetoric in contemporary composition. The work is a textbook
that offers a brief definition and defense of classical rhetoric as
well in-depth examples of how and why it can work for the
modern student. The book has cogent, well-written ideas for
applying classical rhetoric in the contemporary classroom.

Chapter 10:
Edward P.J. Corbett

(1919-1998)

Edward P. J. Corbett is widely recognized as a key figure responsible for reintroducing classical rhetorical theory to composition studies. Corbett earned his undergraduate degree in English from Venard College (1942) and, after serving as a radar technician in the US Marine Air Corps (1943-46), returned to academe to earn an MA (1948) in English language and literature from the University of Chicago and a PhD (1956) from Loyola University, where he had decided to focus on rhetoric even though there were no courses offered in the subject at that time.

Corbett's first teaching job was as an instructor at Creighton University (1948-50, 1953-66) in Omaha, Nebraska, taking a three-year hiatus to complete his dissertation. Corbett continued his career at The Ohio State University (1966-90), during which time, in addition to teaching, he served as director of Freshman English, Vice-Chairman of the English department (1966-70) and associate editor of the *Quarterly Journal of Speech* (1972-74). Corbett held nearly every office in the CCCC, including the editorship of *CCC* (1974-79), which he viewed as a continuation of his education as it allowed him consideration of the full range of scholarship in the field.

Corbett received numerous honors and awards throughout his illustrious career, including the OSU Distinguished Scholar Award (1984) and the NCTE Distinguished Service Award (1986). Upon his retirement from OSU, he was named Professor Emeritus and received the CCCC Exemplar Award (1996).

Although Corbett's contributions to composition studies are numerous, it could be argued that his most important bequest to the field extends through his students who include Robert J. Connors, Lisa Ede, Andrea Lunsford, and Cheryl Glenn. Additionally, the importance of rhetoric in composition studies can be attributed, in part, to one of Corbett's most important contributions. It was while working at his first teaching job as an instructor at Creighton University that Corbett fortuitously stumbled across Hugh Blair's 18th-century text *Rhetoric and Belles Lettres*, ironically, while searching for help with explaining how to analyze prose works to his literature class. Blair's classical sentence-by-sentence analysis of prose style in Addison's *Spectator* led Corbett to further investigate classical rhetoricians such as Aristotle, Cicero, and Quintilian. This investigation resulted in Corbett's seminal textbook *Classical Rhetoric for the Modern Student* (1965). With this work, as well as through numerous editions of his *Little English Handbook* and *The Little Rhetoric Handbook*, Corbett made accessible to composition teachers the classical rhetorical theory that had been absent from modern composition classrooms.

Recognition of Corbett's commitment to and enthusiasm for rhetoric and composition scholarship is evidenced by several volumes of essays that have been collected in his honor, including *Composition and Its Teaching: Articles from College Composition and Communication During the Editorship of Edward P. J. Corbett* (1979), *Essays on Classical Rhetoric and Modern Discourse* (1984), and *Selected Essays of Edward P. J. Corbett* (1989). Additionally, awards established in his honor include the Edward P. J. Corbett Annual Award for the best article to appear in the Ohio Council of Teachers of English Language Arts *English Language Arts Bulletin* as well as the

Edward P. J. Corbett Fellowship and Edward P. J. Corbett Research Award, both awarded to outstanding OSU graduate students.

Patricia L. Baines

Sources for Biographical Narrative

▶ Connors, Robert J. "Introduction." *Selected Essays of Edward P. J. Corbett*. Dallas: Southern Methodist UP, 1989.

▶ Corbett, Edward P. J. Interview with Victor J. Vitanza. "Rhetoric's Past and Future: A Conversation with Edward P. J. Corbett." *Pre/Text* 8 (1987): 247-64.

▶ Ede, Lisa. "Remembering Edward P. J. Corbett." *JAC* 18 (1998): 401-04.

▶ Garnes, Sara, and Charles Zarobila. "A Bibliography of Works by Edward P. J. Corbett." *Essays on Classical Rhetoric and Modern Discourse*. Ed. Robert J. Connors, Lisa S. Ede, and Andrea A. Lunsford. Carbondale, IL: SIUP, 1984. 248-57.

▶ "OSU Board of Trustees: Board Meeting Minutes, 2 Oct. 1998." *Ohio State University*. 2 July 2006 < http://trustees.osu.edu/Minutes/1998October.html>.

Annotated Bibliography

▶ Connors, Robert J., ed. *Selected Essays of Edward P. J. Corbett*. Dallas: Southern Methodist UP, 1989.

A highly useful text offering selected essays written by Corbett from 1958 to 1986, the chronological order of the essays allows one to trace the progression of Corbett's thought during a time that rhetorical theory became increasingly important in composition studies. Additionally, each essay is contextualized through excerpts of a 1987 interview with Corbett conducted by Lisa Ede and Andrea Lunsford.

▶ Corbett, Edward P. J. *Classical Rhetoric for the Modern Student*. New York: Oxford UP, 1965.

This work is widely recognized as the seminal text that reintroduces classical rhetorical theory to composition studies. Organized so that the text's first section briefly explains classical rhetorical training in Western education, the main three sections examine invention, organization, and style; the work's final section gives a brief survey of rhetoric, including a bibliography. Although as a textbook this work may be more appropriate for advanced composition courses, it is a valuable resource for all composition teachers. 2nd edition, 1971; 3rd edition, 1990, and 4th edition co-authored with Robert J. Connors, 1999.

▶ ---. Interview with Victor J. Vitanza. "Rhetoric's Past and Future: A Conversation with Edward P. J. Corbett." *Pre/Text* 8 (1987): 247-64.

Corbett's discussion ranges from his first experiences teaching composition to some of the primary debates within the field, many of which remain topical. Most interesting is when the discussion shifts to the difficulties, as a teacher of rhetoric, in addressing the ethos of a speaker and the definition of "the good man speaking." Additionally, Corbett and Vitanza talk about making editorial choices, providing a helpful perspective to those seeking research topics.

▶ ---. "A Method of Analyzing Prose Style with a Demonstration Analysis of Swift's *A Modest Proposal*." *Reflections on High School English: NDEA Institute Lectures 1965*. Ed. Gary Tate. Tulsa: U of Tulsa, 1966. 106-24. Rpt. in *Selected Essays of Edward P. J. Corbett*. Ed. Robert J. Connors. Dallas: Southern Methodist UP, 1989: 23-47.

Among other key issues of style, Corbett addresses the common cry of frustrated students who know what they want to say but don't know how to say it, by extolling the benefits of having students comment on what they had learned from a series of stylistic studies. The initial section of the essay explains how Corbett arrived at this approach by giving a brief survey of prose style analysis. Subsequent sections on copying a writing selection as a means to know it and on the basics of critical assessment are especially helpful.

▶ ---. "Mutual Friends: What Teachers Can Learn from Students and What Students Can Learn from Teachers." *Balancing Acts: Essays on the Teaching of Writing In Honor of William F. Irmscher*. Ed. Virginia A. Chappell, Mary Louise Buley-Meissner, and Chris Anderson. Carbondale, IL: SIUP, 1991. 83-93.

This is an easy-to-read work, as teachers of writing will recognize their own thoughts and experiences in Corbett's. The essay offers an interesting view of perspective, beneficial to novice and experienced teachers alike. It is most useful as a theoretical approach to discussions of audience.

▶ ---. "The Rhetoric of the Open Hand and the Rhetoric of the Closed Fist." *CCC* 20 (1969): 288-96.

A highly recommended text for all rhetoric/composition teachers, this article situates a discussion of the history of and changes in rhetorical strategies through use of the title metaphor, contrasting the "old style rhetorical activity (open hand) with the new style (closed fist)," which Corbett sees as a more non-verbal kind of "body rhetoric." The first half of the article is devoted to the historical progress of rhetorical theory while the second half discusses a "new" (at the time of the article) shift to more non-verbal, often coercive, forms of rhetoric, making this an interesting discussion to consider for those teaching students conditioned by a text-message-truncated and emoticoned culture.

▶ ---, ed. *Rhetorical Analyses of Literary Works*. New York: Oxford UP, 1969.

This work is most useful for teachers wishing to incorporate literary analysis in composition courses. Essays examine familiar literary works through traditional rhetorical concentrations of argument, arrangement, audience, and style. The introduction provides a useful orientation to key figures and works in literary criticism, and headnotes situate each selection.

▶ ---. "Teaching Composition: Where We've Been and Where We're Going." *CCC* 38 (1987): 444-52.

This essay is a good resource for those entering the field and for anyone needing a general survey of the field. Corbett lists schools with strong graduate programs in rhet/comp (as of 1987), important books, journals and conferences in categories. The categorical listings make it especially easy to quickly find the information needed.

▶ ---. "Teaching Style." *The Territory of Language: Linguistics, Stylistics, and the Teaching of Composition.* Ed. Donald A. McQuade. Carbondale, IL: SIUP, 1986. 23-33.

This essay complements Corbett's earlier discussions of style ["A Method of Analyzing Prose Style ..." (1966) and the chapter on style in *Classical Rhetoric for the Modern Student* (1965)]. Corbett acknowledges the time constraints of modern curricula and the potential limits in students' understandings of style due to poor understandings of basic grammatical structures. Additionally, Corbett provides ideas for exercises to improve students' stylistic skills.

▶ Corbett, Edward P. J., and James L. Golden, eds. *The Rhetoric of Blair, Campbell, and Whately.* 2nd ed. New York: Holt, Rinehart and Winston, 1980.

This collection provides excerpts of Hugh Blair's *Lectures on Rhetoric and Belles Lettres* (1783), George Campbell's *The Philosophy of Rhetoric* (1776), and Richard Whately's *Elements of Rhetoric* (1828). The bibliographies listing primary and secondary sources are most helpful as is the Introduction, which provides a review of most of the works found in the rhetorical canon as a means of situating the works of the great triumvirate of British rhetoricians.

▶ Corbett, Edward P. J., Nancy Myers, and Gary Tate, eds. *The Writing Teacher's Sourcebook.* 4th ed. New York: Oxford UP, 2000.

With contributions from composition leaders, such as Peter Elbow, James Berlin, Donald Murray, David Bartholomae, and Mina Shaughnessy, this source book is intended to provide a starting point for new teachers to familiarize themselves with composition pedagogy. The included essays, which were written as early as 1970 and as late as 1998, combine theoretical discussions with concrete examples from the authors' personal experiences and some discussion of practical application within the classroom. Topics covered include student-teacher relationships, writing center theory, expressivism, formalism, rhetorical pedagogy, mimetic theories of writing, group work, collaborative learning, computers and composition, cultural diversity, using literature in the composition classroom, writing for an audience, critical pedagogy, and responding to and evaluating student writing.

Chapter 11:
Lisa S. Ede

(b. 1947)

Through her extensive teaching, administrative experience, and publishing, Lisa S. Ede has continuously proven herself as a leader in composition theory, research, and pedagogy. Ede has published six books and authored over 40 journal articles and book chapters. With a BS (1969) from The Ohio State University, Ede received her MA (1970) from The University of Wisconsin. She then returned to Ohio State, completed her PhD (1975), and immediately began her composition career.

Ede was hired at SUNY, Brockport in 1976 as assistant professor of English. In 1980, she took a position as an assistant professor at Oregon State University where she advanced to associate professor of English in 1985 and was promoted to her current position as professor of English in 1991. Ede has shown leadership in the composition field with her teaching and administrative experience. After serving as the director of Composition at SUNY, Brockport (1976-80), she became the Coordinator of Composition at Oregon (1980-1986). From 1980 until the present, Ede has served as the director of the Center for Writing and Learning at Oregon as well. She serves on the editorial boards of *Pre/Text: An Interdisciplinary*

Journal of Rhetoric, Textual Studies in Canada, Writing on the Edge, and *The Writing Center Journal*; she is also a member of the Board of Directors of the Coalition of Women Scholars in the History of Rhetoric and Composition.

Since 1977, when she was the recipient of the SUNY Summer Research Fellowship, Ede has received numerous grants and fellowships. She won the NEH Fellowship in Residence at Carnegie-Mellon University (1978-79), Oregon State's Faculty Development Award (1982), the Oregon Committee for the Humanities Summer Research Fellowship (1983), and Oregon State's Library Research Travel Grant (1995). Ede has also won several prestigious awards, such as the NWCA Award for outstanding scholarship on writing centers (1990), Oregon State's College of Liberal Arts Excellence Award (1993), Oregon State's General Research Fund Award (1995), Oregon State's Alumni Association Distinguished Professor Award (1996), and the CCCC Citation for Outstanding Classroom Practices (1998).

In 1982, Ede began a prolific co-authorship with Andrea A. Lunsford, with whom she won the Improvement of Post Secondary Education Shaughnessy Scholar grant (1984) and the Richard Braddock Award for outstanding article in *CCC* (1985). Ede and Lunsford won MLA's Mina P. Shaughnessy Prize (1985) with Robert J. Connors. Ede and Lunsford have co-authored and edited three books as well as 19 journal articles and book chapters.

Ede's major areas of interest and contributions to composition theory, research, and pedagogy include her work and influence in classical and contemporary rhetorical theory, collaborative writing, authorship, audience, writing centers, and intersections of feminism and rhetoric. Her work in collaborative writing, authorship, and audience has been extensively shared with Lunsford and has established Ede as a leader in the field of composition.

Andrew M. Coomes

Sources for Biographical Narrative

▶ "Administration." Oregon State University. 1 Feb. 2004
    <oregonstate.edu/admin/aa/
    2002/new/about/organizationalChart/ede.html>.

▶ "Conference Speakers." Northern California Writing Center
    Association. 1 Feb. 2004
    <http://ncwca.stanford.edu/speakers.htm>.

▶ Ede, Lisa. *Curriculum Vitae.* 29 Jan. 2004.

▶ "Lisa Ede." English Dept. home page. Oregon State
    University. 1 Feb. 2004
    <oregonstate.edu/dept/english/faculty/ede.htm>.

Lisa Ede recommends these readings for novice composition instructors:

1. Emig, Janet. *The Web of Meaning: Essays on Writing,
   Teaching, Learning, and Thinking.* Upper Montclair,
   NJ: Boynton/Cook, 1983. "an early collection of essays
   by a scholar who played a key role in the field in the
   1970s and 1980s"
2. Bullock, Richard, and John Trimbur, eds. *The Politics of
   Writing Instruction: Postsecondary.* Portsmouth,
   NH: Boynton/Cook Heinemann, 1991. "a collection of
   essays that marks composition's political turn in the
   late 1980s and early 1990s"
3. Bloom, Lynn Z., Donald A. Daiker, Edward M. White,
   eds. *Composition Studies in the New Millennium:
   Rereading the Past, Rewriting the Future.* Carbondale,
   IL: SIUP, 2003. "a relatively recent collection of essays
   that helps to situate current research in the field"

Annotated Bibliography

▶ Connors, Robert J., Lisa S. Ede, and Andrea A. Lunsford,
   eds. *Essays on Classical Rhetoric and Modern
   Discourse.* Carbondale, IL: SIUP, 1984.

This book examines a wide range of rhetoric theories, offering
an extensive survey of both the classical rhetoric and its
contemporary reactions. While the revolution of rhetoric had an
enormous impact on the teaching of composition, the
established connections between rhetoric and writing by
Edward P.J. Corbett inspired the majority of these changes.
The essay by Ede and Lunsford closely examines the
distinctions between classical and modern rhetoric and
epitomized the purpose of this book, linking reading, writing,
and speaking in the writing classroom. Though some of the
essays are a little dense, the usability of this source is
extremely beneficial to those surveying classical rhetoric.

▶ Ede, Lisa. "Audience: An Introduction to Research." *CCC* 35
   (1984): 140-54.

Relying on the fact that composition is an interdisciplinary
enterprise, Ede argues that, like any other subject, the nature
of audience must be clearly understood and researched by the
teacher before the students can be expected to fully grasp the
concept. This article effectively surveys previous research of
audience and examines the different approaches to analysis,
cognitive-based research, and theory of audience. Ultimately,
there is still much work left to be done in audience research,
but the analysis of audience in written discourse is imperative
to the success of writers, whether teachers or students. Ede's
introduction is beneficial to those of us interested or getting
started in the research of audience.

▶ ---. *Work in Progress: A Guide to Writing and Revising.* 6th
   ed. Boston: St. Martin's, 2004.

Serving as an easily readable and useful guide to teachers and
students alike, Ede's Work in Progress journeys through the
writing process with practical ideas, examples, and activities.
While she emphasizes the importance of appropriate choices for

various writing situations, Ede also provides strategies for writers as individuals and collaborators. This book is designed to accompany college students through their composition classes, demonstrating some effective techniques that can be utilized throughout the writing and revision process. Additionally, several chapters highlight the necessity of reading and research skills in order to produce informed and evaluative writing.

▶ ---. "Writing as a Social Process: A Theoretical Foundation for Writing Centers?" *Writing Center Journal* 9.2 (1989): 3-14.

In this useful article, Ede provides a convincing argument that writing centers are in need of a theoretical foundation that will link them more efficiently with other professionals in their field and discipline. As a writing center director herself, Ede identifies with the challenges of establishing this theory, but previous theories of collaboration and writing as a social process serve as templates for a new writing center theory. While writing centers are currently at the heart of many composition theories, this easily readable article demonstrates the earlier challenges that were faced in the late 1980s and early 1990s. Writing center directors and assistants have a unique opportunity to view small-group collaboration and participate/publish in the theoretical conversations of composition and writing as a social process.

▶ ---, ed. *On Writing Research: The Braddock Essays, 1975-1998*. Boston: Bedford/St. Martin's, 1999.

This book compiles the essays honored by the CCCC's Braddock Award from 1975 until 1998. Focusing on topics from the writing process and revision to Ede's own essay on audience, the included essays are significant contributions to composition research and pedagogy. Additionally, Ede included an afterword by the original author with each essay; each afterword outlines the author's current viewpoints on the topic(s) discussed in the essay. Ede's collection is extremely beneficial to writing teachers, allowing us to view the evolution of 23 years of composition research, as well as the author's own retrospective thoughts on the award-winning essays.

► Ede, Lisa, and Andrea Lunsford. "Audience
      Addressed/Audience Invoked: The Role of Audience in
      Composition Theory and Pedagogy." *CCC* 35 (1984):
      155-71.

This seminal work and award-winning essay emphasizes the importance of fully understanding, knowing, and identifying the audience for both writers and readers. The authors both praise and criticize composition theorists, such as Walter Ong, Herbert Simons, and James Moffett, who have previously studied audience, noting that the distinctions between audience and reader and oral and written communication have not been fully investigated. Ede and Lunsford concentrate on presenting the stresses on writers as they try to both create and write for an audience, as well as the stresses on readers as they try to both understand and relate to the intended audience. This article is essential to those researching the importance of audience in both theory and pedagogy.

► ---. "Collaboration and Concepts of Authorship." *PMLA* 116
      (2001): 354-69.

Ede and Lunsford tackle the questions that surround being an author in this essay, and they conclude that the contradictions between theory and practice in the academy are partially due to the credibility of authorship and the current viewpoints of individualistic ideologies. While the authors do not propose eliminating single authorship, collaboration seems to be a step toward linking contemporary theory with practice. This article is not as readable as the others by Ede and Lunsford, but their ideas are still beneficial to those in the academy, whether attempting to publish or not. Collaborative research allows different perspectives to unite, but traditional authorship (solitary scholarship) is the current choice for most academic institutions.

► ---. *Singular Texts/Plural Authors: Perspectives on
      Collaborative Writing.* Carbondale, IL: SIUP, 1990.

Discussing in-depth topics from primary and secondary authorship to students' collaboration in their writing, Ede and Lunsford work to change the academy's viewpoint of collaboration through their own example. While the entire book is easily readable and extremely beneficial to composition teachers, the most useful chapter is "The Pedagogy of Collaboration," outlining specifically the challenges of collaborative writing and the incorporation of collaboration in the classroom. Additionally, the authors include helpful tables and graphs that delineate the results of their research surveys.

▶ Lunsford, Andrea A., and Lisa Ede. "Collaborative Authorship and the Teaching of Writing." *Cardozo Arts & Entertainment Law Journal* 10 (1992): 681-702.

The authors examine both the historic and contemporary views of collaborative authorship, challenging the criticisms and equating the prestige of collaboration with single-author scholarship. Though never dominant, collaborative authorship has existed throughout history in such works as the Bible and the Oxford English Dictionary, but collaboration has never been on par with solitary authorship. Lunsford and Ede argue that collaborative writing is a logical extension of collaborative learning, which has been proven effective and essential at times. This article serves as a useful guide to those teachers wishing to either incorporate collaborative writing in their classrooms or participate in collaborative writing in their own field.

▶ ---. "Representing Audience: 'Successful' Discourse and Disciplinary Critique." *CCC* 47 (1996): 167-79.

Lunsford and Ede revisit their essay "Audience Addressed / Audience Invoked" (AA/AI) and offer a critique of their own work, noting what was present and what was missing from their previous essay. The main point that AA/AI lacked was its failure to explore "the ways in which audiences cannot only enable but also silence writers and readers" (170). The authors argue that their own audience in AA/AI allowed their essay to be successful, but it was unsuccessful in terms of meeting the more general audience that should have been intended. In short, AA/AI failed to fully examine the common-sense understandings of the purposes and impacts of education.

Chapter 12:
Peter Elbow

(b. 1935)

Peter Elbow is a true leader in composition and has remained
true to his ideologies throughout his life as a student, a writing
center director, and an educator. First earning BA degrees in
English from Williams College (1957) as well as Oxford (1959),
Elbow later earned an Oxford English MA (1963). He then
studied at Harvard (1959-60) and transferred to receive a PhD
(1969) in English from Brandeis. Challenged at Oxford and
Harvard, Elbow vowed to master writing. Elbow became
interested in writing simply because he had been told by
numerous professors that he could not write well. With little
help from professors, Elbow began his own personal odyssey to
write.

Boldly expressive, Elbow had an unparalleled career as
professor and writer, teaching at MIT (1960-63,1968-72),
Franconia College (1963-65), Evergreen State College (1972-
81), and SUNY, Stony Brook (1982-87), where he directed the
Writing Program. Furthermore, while at the University of
Massachusetts (1987-96), Elbow directed the Writing Program
(1996-2000) and published numerous works including *A
Community of Writers* with Pat Belanoff. Currently, Emeritus

Professor of English at UMass, Elbow has remained active in the field.

Elbow holds many honors including the James Squire award (2001), the Honorary Woodrow Wilson fellowship (1957), the Danforth fellowship (1957), the English Institute essay prize, the Kent postdoctoral fellowship, the Wesleyan University Center for Writing award, the CCCC's Braddock Award (1986), the James A. Berlin Prize for best essay of the year in *Rhetoric Review* (1993), and the CEE's James N. Britton award (2002). Moreover, Elbow has served on the Executive Council of the MLA and the Executive Committee of the CCCC (1994-97) as well as NCTE's Executive Committee. Currently, many colleges and universities fervently seek Elbow to speak and conduct workshops.

A pioneer of freewriting, peer response, and the process method, Elbow supports multiple drafts. In addition, Elbow backs classroom writing, contract grading, high and low stakes grading, portfolios, teachers as writers, and saving grammar for editing. For Elbow, confusion among professional writers requires specific methodologies to counteract the writing anxiety phenomenon. This focus on the individual learner promotes Elbow's theories of expressivism.

Elbow views hierarchical teaching as perverse, granting predatory teachers control of student thought. He even questions his own early desire to be the perfect student. However, when forming radical pedagogy, Elbow, surprisingly, turns classic, referring to educator John Dewey as one of the cornerstones of the democratic classroom.

Doubtless, Elbow's theories have generated waves of support as well as ripples of opposition in the community of composition and rhetoric. Somewhat in agreement with Elbow, well-known theorist Edward White supports both process and product; others like David Bartholomae and Andrea Lunsford stand more opposed. Thus, whether theorists agree or disagree with Elbow, his ideas always stimulate thought, contributing to the ever-growing community of composition scholars.

Gwendolyn Hale and Carlotta Jones

Sources for Biographical Narrative

► Briggs, John Channing. "Edifying Violence: Peter Elbow and the Pedagogical Paradox." *JAC* 15 (1995): 1-27. 9 Feb. 2004 <http://jac.gsu..edu/jac.15.1/Articles/5.htm>.

► Elbow, Peter. *Curriculum Vitae*. English Dept. home page. UMass. 14 Aug 2006 <http://scholarworks.umass.edu/peter_elbow/cv.pdf>

► ---."Illiteracy at Oxford and Harvard: Reflections on the Inability to Write." *Everyone Can Write—Essays toward a Hopeful Theory of Writing and Teaching Writing*. New York: Oxford UP, 2000. 91-114.

► Hirsch, David. "Penelope's Web." *Sewanee Review* XC 1 (1982): 119-31.

► "Houses Divided: Processing Composition in a Post-Process Time." *College Literature* 29 (2002): 171-79.

► "Peter Elbow." English Faculty home page. UMass. 18 Feb. 2004 <http://www.umass.edu/english/eng/facProfiles/Elbow.html>.

► "Peter Henry Elbow." *Contemporary Authors Online*. Literature Resource Center. Middle Tennessee State University, James E. Walker Library, Murfreesboro, TN. 4 Apr. 2001. 1 Jan. 2004 <http://galenet.galegroup.com>.

► *TESOL*. 9 Feb. 2004 <http://www.tesol.org/conv/t2003/pp/online/elbow.html>

► White, Edward M. "Post-Structural Literary Criticism and the Response to Student Writing." *CCC* 35 (1984): 186-95.

Peter Elbow recommends these readings for novice composition instructors:

1. Elbow, Peter. "Embracing Contraries in the Teaching Process." *CE* 45 (1983): 327-39.
2. ---. "A Map of Writing in Terms of Audience and Response." *Everyone Can Write: Essays Toward a Hopeful Theory of Writing and Teaching Writing.* New York: Oxford UP, 2000.
3. ---. "Reflections on Academic Discourse: How It Relates to Freshmen and Colleagues." *CE* 53 (1991): 135-55.

 Annotated Bibliography

▶ Elbow, Peter. "Closing My Eyes As I Speak: An Argument for Ignoring Audience." *CE* 49 (1987): 50-69.

In this article, Elbow explores the benefits of ignoring audience, at least initially. Elbow begins with the explanation that students often do not understand audience as they have only ever written for an instructor. Moreover, writing is usually a solitary activity, and most would agree that we need more practice in taking into account other viewpoints. Elbow agrees with Linda Flower in that writer-based prose is often weaker than reader-based prose. However, Elbow entertains the notion that writer-based prose has a place in composition classrooms in that it helps students, particularly ones who struggle to get started and wrestle with ideas, to become comfortable with their own abilities and language before moving on to reader-based writing. Keeping an audience in mind, especially for beginning or self-conscious students, often further exacerbates feelings of inadequacy and insecurity.

▶ ---. *Embracing Contraries.* New York: Oxford UP, 1986.

This collection of 12 essays focuses on the nature of learning and teaching to suggest a comprehensive philosophy of education. Elbow argues that natural learning and teaching are not tidy; rather they are full of contradictions. Elbow further argues that we need to re-examine our notion of how teaching and learning occur. This collection includes four sections on the processes of learning, teaching and evaluation, and on the nature of inquiry.

▶ ---. *Everyone Can Write: Essays Toward a Hopeful Theory of Writing.* New York: Oxford UP, 2000.

This collection of essays is the next collection of Elbow's essays published after *Embracing Contraries.* Including sections on voice, the experience of writing, teaching, and evaluation, this collection focuses on the need to humanize the profession through non-adversarial arguments and a decentered classroom. Moreover, Elbow stresses the necessity of binary thinking. *Everyone Can Write* is essential to all teachers of writing and is an asset to any composition course at any level.

▶ ---. Homepage. Nov. 2001. 12 Oct. 2003
       <http://writingprogram.hfa.umass.edu/alumni/
       elbow.asp>.

Centering on Elbow's career moves as well as his theoretical beliefs, this page concisely lists basic biographical information. While it emphasizes Elbow's argument that all students can write, it also raises issues of writing communities. Elbow also offers a brief sketch of himself in which he discusses how he was derailed from the academy for several years before discovering his love of teaching. The site also offers other biographical information as well as contact information.

▶ ---. "Writing Assessment at SUNY Stony Brook." *What is English?* Ed. Peter Elbow. New York: MLA, 1990. 176-78.

After arguing that English is a profession in which the professionals cannot define themselves, Elbow tells the story of Stony Brook when 40 percent of the freshmen were exempt from English 101. He uses this scenario to promote portfolios. Elbow calls for teacher accountability, saying that they must be bold enough to fail the students who do not perform at certain standards, stop blaming the legislators, and regain public trust.

► ---. *Writing with Power*. New York: Oxford UP, 1981. 59-77.

This handbook emphasizes that the essential activities needed for good writing are not difficult at all. While writing is often shrouded in mystery or cloaked in the notion that one is born with the talent to write well, Elbow provides the reader with numerous methods for getting words down on paper, getting feedback, and recognizing the power of written communication. This work shows writers, both novice and experienced, that they must embrace two opposite mentalities: creative and logical. The text is also designed either to be read straight through or by skipping around.

► ---. *Writing without Teachers*. 2nd ed. New York: Oxford UP, 1998.

Elbow outlines a practical program for learning how to write. This book and its approach are particularly helpful to those who suffer from writer's block. Nevertheless, the approach extends beyond academic writing to creative and business writing. Elbow encourages writing without initial editing as the editing obstructs the natural flow of writing. Finally, Elbow's approach encourages self-confidence and seeks to assist writers in finding inspiration.

► Elbow, Peter, and Pat Belanoff. *A Community of Writers: A Workshop Course in Writing*. 3rd ed. New York: McGraw-Hill, 2000.

This guide, known for its practical workshop approach, addresses students as writers and features numerous writing activities and assignments that are challenging. Writers are encouraged to explore the writing processes and to share their writing with others. Another feature of this guide is its in-depth treatment of research and argumentation as well as its coverage of Internet usage and web page design. Understanding that writing is no longer confined to the classroom and paper, the authors explore computer-based writing and visual literacy along with traditional writing.

▶ Elbow, Peter, Pat Belanoff, and Sheryl I. Fontaine. *Nothing Begins with N: New Investigations of Freewriting.* Carbondale, IL: SIUP, 1991.

Providing a theoretical grounding for the strategy of freewriting, this book consists of 16 essays from different authors, instructors, and theorists, varying in focus, methodology, and point of view. From organization to focus and from creative writing to technical and scientific writing, this book addresses the numerous facets and benefits of free writing in present-day composition. This text is useful for any instructor in any discipline who finds her students struggling with topics and focus.

▶ Scorcinelli, Mary Dean, and Peter Elbow, eds. *Writing to Learn: Strategies for Assigning and Responding to Writing Across the Disciplines.* San Francisco: Jossey-Bass, 1997.

This text provides instructors with numerous strategies and philosophies for teaching writing. Addressing the reality that many instructors in other disciplines have not had a great deal of experience in responding to student writing, the authors focus on the best ways to provide feedback regarding written work. Understanding that each instructor has a personal teaching style, the authors provide numerous feedback alternatives that are firmly grounded in research and theory.

Chapter 13:
Janet Emig

(b. 1928)

Janet Emig is an educator known primarily for her studies of the composing process. Born in Cincinnati, Ohio, her education initially prepared her for a career in the medical profession. She graduated cum laude from Mount Holyoke College with her BA (1950), and from there she attended the University of Michigan for her MA (1951). While at Michigan, Emig was influenced by an instructor who emphasized the revision process in composition. Also while at Michigan, Emig encountered what some, including Gerald Nelms and Emig herself, have reported to be sexism, and she was not admitted into the doctoral program there.

After not being admitted into a doctoral program, she began to teach high school, and it was during this time that she began experimenting with student conferencing as a means to assist in teaching the composing process. She attended the CCC convention where she was influenced by Priscilla Tyler, with whom she later studied. After some years of teaching high school, Emig then enrolled at Harvard where she eventually took over the writing program. She graduated with her EdD (1969) from Harvard. After encountering documented sexism at both University of Chicago and Lethbridge University of Canada, she was denied tenure, and went on to teach at Rutgers where she is now Professor Emeritus. She became the president of the NCTE (1989).

Emig's remarkable career has been filled with scholarly activities and awards, a Danforth Fellowship being only one of many (1962-63). Her poetry is anthologized in *Anthology of Sports Poems* (1971), and she is the contributor of about 25 articles to language journals. Other memberships have included that of the editorial board of *Harvard Educational Review* (1962-64) and that of the *Alumnae Quarterly* committee at Mount Holyoke College (1968-72). She was the recipient of the CCCC Exemplar Award (1992).

Some themes in Janet Emig's works include an interest in pedagogy, writing as a process, the complexities of composing, the developmental aspects of composing, physiological aspects of composition, the didactic functions of writing, a constructivist philosophy of writing, and the academic profession. Emig values education and has written many essays about her passion for educating. Still, her name became associated forever with composition pedagogy when she wrote *The Composing Process of Twelfth Graders* (1971). The case study used methods such as protocol analysis, tape-recorded interviews, and discourse analysis. By using such techniques, Emig was able to map out the process by which students effectively compose their writing. Emig discovered that twelfth grade writers engage in two modes of composing, reflexive and extensive. These differences can be ascertained and characterized through having the writers compose aloud during their composition process. Her studies may very well be the most influential in demonstrating how students compose and how instructors effectively help them.

Each year, the Janet Emig Award is given to the author of an article published in *English Education. The Composing Process of Twelfth Graders* not only put Emig on the map as a composition leader, but it also paved the way for the process approach in writing.

Gwendolyn Hale

Sources for Biographical Narrative

▶ Emig, Janet, *The Composing Process of Twelfth Graders.*
    Urbana, IL: NCTE, 1971.

▶ "Janet Emig Award Criteria and Nomination Process."
    NCTE. 2004. 23 Jan. 2004
    <http://www.ncte.org/groups/cee/awards/emig/
    108850.htm>.

▶ Nelms, Gerald. "A Brief Case History of Janet Emig:
    Introduction to 'The Contributions of Janet Emig.'"
    CCCC Convention, Cincinnati, OH. Mar. 19-21, 1992.
    23 Sept. 2003
    <http://search.epnet.com.ezproxy.mtsu.edu>.

▶ "Writing @ CSU: Writing Guides." Welcome to Writing @
    CSU. 2006. 4 Sept. 2006.
    <http://writing.colostate.edu/teaching_guides.cfm>.

Annotated Bibliography

▶ Bannister, Linda. "The Feminine Rhetorics of Janet Emig
    and Andrea Lunsford." CCCC Convention, Boston, MA.
    Mar. 21-23, 1991. 18 Sept. 2003.
    <http://search.epnet.com.ezproxy.mtsu.edu>.

Emig calls for a community of writers where teachers write
along with their students. This article also deals with another
important contributor to the new rhetoric, Andrea Lunsford,
who has presented a dialogic model of communication based on
collaboration. While this article is informative, it proves
difficult to read at times in that it is laden with jargon which
those not specializing in composition will have a difficult time
comprehending. However, if one can get past the density of the
language, the article has a vast amount of information and
insight.

► Emig, Janet. "Literacy and Freedom." *The Web of Meaning: Essays on Writing, Learning and Thinking.* Ed. Dixie Goswami and Maureen Butler. Upper Montclair, NJ: Boynton/Cook, 1983. 171-78.

Emig points out that in years past, literacy was the ability to sign one's own name and nothing more. In the present, Emig holds that literacy has little more meaning than it did in previous years. Her startling claim is that this is going on in universities as well. This is an important work in the study of not only comprehension but also the philosophy and reasoning behind the process movement. It is eloquently written and easily comprehended.

► ---. *The Composing Process of Twelfth Graders.* Urbana, IL: NCTE, 1971.

This book describes the entire research that Jane Emig conducted during her experiments with the composing process and read aloud protocols. This book/study is essential to anyone who wishes to gain a firm grounding in the paradigm shift of composition in the sixties and seventies as well as for anyone who wishes to know about the origins of the composing process. This book is highly accessible, and its information is easily digested.

► Emig, Janet, James Fleming, and Helen Popp, eds. *Language and Learning.* New York: Harcourt, Brace and World, 1966.

This book is comprised of articles by many who tend to believe that there must be a reform or a re-examination of formal verbal learning from kindergarten through college. This book is a criticism of the once current teaching of a first language at all academic levels. This book provides great insight into not only language acquisition and use, but also the educational climate of the 1960s when the process movement was first gaining notice. Some articles are more accessible than others.

► Nelms, Gerald. "A Brief Case History of Janet Emig:
    Introduction to 'The Contributions of Janet Emig.'"
    CCCC Convention, Cincinnati, OH. 19-21 Mar. 1992.
    EBSCO. 23 Sept. 2003
    <http://search.epnet.com.ezproxy.mtsu.edu>.

This paper presentation discusses the accomplishments of
Janet Emig from her experience with sexism at the University
of Michigan to her research and teaching at Rutgers
University. Nelms clearly explains the frustrations of Emig
throughout her academic career, but he also describes how
these frustrations and setbacks profoundly influenced and
motivated Emig. This article is profoundly interesting in its
biographical sketch and is easily accessible.

► ---. "An Oral History of Janet Emig's Case Study Subject
    'Lynn.'" CCCC Convention, Cincinnati, OH. 19-21 Mar.
    1992. EBSCO. 23 Sept. 2003. <http://web6.epnet.com/>.

This article discusses the true identity of Janet Emig's "Lynn,"
the primary subject of Emig's "The Composing Process of
Twelfth Graders." According to Nelms, two major criticisms of
Emig's book by Stephen North and Ralph Voss are not accurate
because the interview methodology used by Emig was
acceptable research. This article is very insightful in that is
reiterates what Emig was saying in her monograph. Nelms's
article is pertinent in that it lends credibility to Emig's work
thirty years later.

► ---. "Reassessing Janet Emig's The Composing Process of
    Twelfth Graders: An Historical Perspective." *Rhetoric
    Review* 13.1 (1994): 108-30.

Nelms discusses Janet Emig's experiences with sexism in the
academic community in the 1950s and 1960s, as well as her
composing process theory in the 1960s. Nelms addresses
pedagogical implications of Emig's composing theory, cognitive
development as a factor in composition pedagogy, and the
publication of the monograph. This is, by far, the best article I

have found on Janet Emig and her work. It is thorough and touches on the positives as well as the negatives of her work and research.

▶ Schreiner, Steven. "A Portrait of the Student as a Young Writer: Re-evaluating Emig and the Process Movement." *CCC* 48 (1997): 86-103.

In 1964, Janet Emig entered the field of process composition with an article arguing for the artistic nature of the writing student. Schreiner states that while this was and still is a noble pursuit, it oftentimes is not enough for the majority of today's students who are not as well-read as Emig's Lynn. This article is profoundly useful in not only the study of Janet Emig but also the process movement in that it offers historical background while also delineating the pros and cons of Emig's study.

Chapter 14:
Lester Faigley

(b. 1947)

A major contributor to research and practice in computers and composition, visual rhetoric, and writing center theory, Lester Faigley received his BA (1969) in English from North Carolina State University and his MA (1972) from Miami University, Ohio. He earned his PhD (1976) at The University of Washington, Seattle, where he completed a dissertation examining the poetic style of Old English. After a few years of teaching middle school English and History, Faigley joined the English Department faculty at The University of Texas, Austin (1979) and began focusing on composition.

Faigley has remained a steadfast member of the UT-Austin faculty since he started. Over the last 27 years, he has made major contributions to the strength of the writing programs in his department, founding and directing the Division of Rhetoric and Writing (1993-01) and a concentration in Science, Technology, and Society (1998-00). He currently directs the Undergraduate Writing Center and holds the Robert Adger Law and Thos. H. Law Professorship in Humanities, teaching courses in visual rhetoric and digital technology. In addition to his work at UT-Austin, Faigley has undertaken appointments as a senior fellow at the National University of Singapore (1986-87), visiting professor at Pennsylvania State University (1990), and visiting professor at Oxford University, Brasenose College (1992). In deference to his profession, he spent four years serving in various chairing positions for CCCC: Assistant Chair (1994), associate Chair (1995), Chair (1996), and Immediate Past Chair (1997).

Initially, Faigley's publications dealt primarily with scientific studies of the problems of teaching syntax, sentence complexity, and revision, but his work progressed to more global writing concerns, eventually encompassing process theory, writing in the disciplines, and the writing needs of employers. In his 1996 speech at CCCC, he shared with his audience a deep concern for the outside economic and technological forces affecting the entire discipline of composition. In his most recent publications, Faigley explores effective Internet use in classroom instruction and the use of visual rhetoric in the classroom to prepare students for jobs in a world that is no longer exclusively text-based and linear. His 1992 book, *Fragments of Rationality,* earned him the MLA Mina P. Shaughnessy Prize for an exceptional scholarly publication with application in teaching English (1992) and the CCCC's Outstanding Book Award (1994).

Having entered college with plans to become an architect, Faigley's passion for design still colors his work through the study of visual rhetoric. In *Fragments of Rationality,* he uses metaphors of art and architecture to explain writing, connecting the three as the book progresses. In the 2003 textbook *Picturing Texts,* co-authored with Diana George, Anna Palchik, and Cynthia Selfe, Faigley and his colleagues use the combination of traditional rhetoric and visual rhetoric to teach students how to examine and create texts that are both visually and textually meaningful, considering both the visual and textual needs of a modern audience. His current works radiate a belief that the Internet and other modern, visual media necessitate an educational system that prepares students to work confidently with multiple genres of both visual and traditional texts.

Claire Bates

Sources for Biographical Narrative

▶ "About Lester Faigley." English Dept. home page. University
   of Texas, Austin. 10 July 2006. 4 Sept. 2006
   <http://www.cwrl.utexas.edu/~faigley/ >.

▶ "Annual Symposium." English Composition Program home
   page. University of Miami. 7 July 2006
   <http://composition.miami.edu/symposium>.

▶ "Lester Faigley." *Biography Resource Center*. Thomson Gale,
   2006. MTSU, James E. Walker Lib., Murfreesboro, TN.
   7 July 2006.
   <http://galenet.galegroup.com/servlet/BioRC>.

Annotated Bibliography

▶ Faigley, Lester, et al. *Assessing Writers' Knowledge and
   Processes of Composing*. Norwood, NJ: Ablex, 1985.

Faigley's earlier work concerning the processes of composing at
the sentence and syntactical level weaves a thread throughout
this book; many of the ideas from earlier articles are compacted
here and shared with ideas of his co-authors. The text discusses
three generations of studying the processes of composing; it
breaks the research down by stages such as planning,
producing texts, revision, and writers' knowledge and lays out
the methodologies for attempting to assess writers' processes.
Anyone interested in how writers compose and how we can and
should assess those compositions will find this text helpful.

▶ Faigley, Lester. "Competing Theories of Process: A Critique
   and a Proposal." *CE* 48 (1986): 527-42.

Faigley gives an overview of three kinds of process theory:
expressive, cognitive, and social, listing the famous proponents
of each and arguing for a theoretical approach to composition
as a discipline. He asserts that process theory assigns more
value to student writing than the current-traditional model.

For teachers who plan to use process methods, especially when incorporating technology, this article provides a theoretical backdrop.

▶ ---. *Fragments of Rationality: Postmodernity and the Subject of Composition*. Pittsburgh: U of Pittsburgh P, 1992.

Receiving awards from MLA and CCCC for his exploration of postmodernity in composition studies, Faigley draws on his knowledge of architecture to illustrate how outdated modernist principles are still applied to writing instruction. His chapters cover the politics of composition, issues of the self, problems with writing textbooks, and the non-linear postmodern structure of hypertext documents and their impact in the writing classroom. This entertaining and thought-provoking book sees writing instruction in a way that situates it squarely within contemporary culture.

▶ ---. "Judging Writing, Judging Selves." *CCC* 40 (1989): 395-412.

Faigley takes on the often arbitrary guidelines set by English departments defining good or A papers, charging that teachers are often more concerned with constructing certain selves they see appropriate in student writers than in examining how they write. He questions how often judgments of writing are principally matters of taste and whether simply wanting students to write in an authentic voice constitutes good writing. New and experienced teachers could benefit from exploring the questions asked but not always resolved and keeping them in mind when evaluating student writing.

▶ ---. "Literacy After the Revolution." *CCC* 48 (1997): 30-43.

In this 1996 Chair's address to CCCC, Faigley laments the second-class status writing teachers usually hold in English departments; he illustrates how the larger, global forces have sparked two revolutions, digital and a revolution of the rich, responsible for the current conditions in the field. He examines the impact of an unregulated market on higher education and asks educators to think critically about the transformative effect of the Internet without dismissing that effect as negative.

Forces that are still in effect today, its prophetic look at issues of socio-economic policy and technology make this article useful for administrators and teachers of English

▶ ---. "Names in Search of a Concept: Maturity, Fluency, Complexity, and Growth in Written Syntax." *CCC* 31 (1980): 291-300.

In this article, Faigley questions and rejects some of the terms used to describe the constructions of writing because the terms have connotations that don't really apply to their intended usefulness. He discredits former studies that connect syntactic maturity to increases in holistically judged writing quality and claims that increased clause length cannot measure an increase in writing maturity; however, he does advocate teaching sentence-combining as a way to better student writing. He does not, in this article, discuss practical ways for teachers to do this and laments that grammar cannot adequately describe the complexity of texts.

▶ Faigley, Lester, Diana George, Anna Palchik, and Cynthia Selfe. *Picturing Texts*. New York: Norton, 2004.

Designed to help composition students interpret visual compositions and design their own, *Picturing Texts* does not see text and image as separate entities, but rather investigates how the two can, should, and are used together. The textbook differs from most in its striking design and its use of images not for illustration but as actual content for discussion and interpretation. Composition courses with an emphasis in visual rhetoric would benefit from using this text.

▶ Faigley, Lester, and Thomas P. Miller. "What We Learn From Writing on the Job." *CE* 44 (1982): 557-69.

Because of the proliferation of electronic written communication, mostly due to e-mail, since this article was written, some of the extensive statistics presented here are outdated; however, Faigley and Miller argue in 1982 that college educated professionals write often at work, with their employers typically requiring a variety of compositions.

Therefore, the basic findings of this study, that college graduates will need to write effectively in their professions, remains true. It bolsters the argument for both required writing classes for non-English majors, professional writing classes, and for WAC and writing in the disciplines.

▶ Faigley, Lester, and Stephen Witte. "Analyzing Revision." *CCC* 32 (1981): 400-14.

This article attempts to investigate both the types of revisions made by writers and the different methods writers of basic, intermediate, and expert skill levels use in revising. It debunks the common assumption that the more basic and intermediate writers revise, the better their work becomes by illustrating that these writers sometimes make unconstructive changes with revision whereas expert writers revise less and more constructively. It calls for teachers to think about the global issues surrounding revision and not just ask students to revise more.

▶ Witte, Stephen P., and Lester Faigley. *Evaluating College Writing Programs*. Carbondale, IL: SIUP, 1983.

Faigley and Witte, colleagues at UT-Austin, co-wrote this evaluation of four major universities' writing programs, asking questions about the existence of the programs, the stability, the goals, and the effectiveness in improving student writing. They develop a framework for evaluating even the most complex of writing programs, which includes five components necessary for evaluation and an analysis of the interactions between these components. It provides potential evaluators with background theory, a framework on which to build an evaluation, and a list of useful questions.

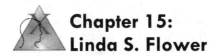

Chapter 15:
Linda S. Flower

(b. 1944)

Linda S. Flower received her BA (1965) from Simpson College in English and French and her PhD (1972) in English from Rutgers University and has been a professor of English and Rhetoric at Carnegie Mellon University since 1980. In addition to her role as professor at Carnegie Mellon, she has been the Co-director of the Center for University Outreach since 1996 and is currently the director of the Center for Study of Writing and Literacy.

Her early interest in the cognitive processes that students use to write led to her groundbreaking article, "A Cognitive Process Theory of Writing," co-authored with John R. Hayes (1981). Their research helped connect cognitive theory to composition studies; established the need for strategic, problem-solving approaches to writing instruction; and introduced the think-aloud protocol research tool to composition. As such, one of Flower's main contributions to composition theory, research, and pedagogy lies in the general area of cognition.

After this early work, Flower continued to be on the cutting edge in composition studies and rhetorical research and has helped us all explore the new areas of cognitive rhetoric theory, intercultural rhetoric and education, and community literacies. More recently, she has focused on creating an integrated approach to describing and teaching writing that includes both social and cognitive aspects of writing. How writers construct negotiated meaning while being influenced by internal and social voices is at the heart of this current research, and she is now looking at how negotiated meaning is arrived at in literacy classes and inner city communities. Although Flower has done a considerable amount of important work in cognition, she feels that her most important contribution to composition is this recent research in community literacy. Her article "Community Literacy," co-authored with Wayne Campbell Peck and Lorraine Higgins, is truly a groundbreaking and influential work in this area.

Attesting to the influence her research has had in composition studies, Flower received the Richard Braddock Award for Best Article in *CCC* twice, once in 1987 for "Detection, Diagnosis, and the Strategies of Revision," co-authored with John R. Hayes, Linda Carey, Karen Schriver, and James Stratman, and once in 1989 for "Rhetorical Reading Strategies and the Construction of Meaning," co-authored with Christina Haas. Flower is currently a member of NCTE, CCCC, and AERA. In addition, she serves as a member of the Advisory Committee for Pittsburgh Public Schools' project PROPEL and as a member of the CCCC Service-Learning and Community Literacy Committee. She is also an active member of the Pittsburgh community in general, taking part in many community literacy and service learning projects each year.

Allison D. Smith

Sources for Biographical Narrative

▶ "Faculty." English Dept. home page. Carnegie Mellon University. 5 Aug 2006. <http://english.cmu.edu/people/faculty/faculty.html>.

▶ Flower, Linda S. *Curriculum Vitae.* 29 January 2004.

► "Linda S. Flower." *Biography Resource Center.* Thomson
    Gale, 2006. MTSU, James E. Walker Lib.,
    Murfreesboro, TN. 29 January 2004.
    <http://galenet.galegroup.com/servlet/BioRC>.

 Annotated Bibliography

► Flower, Linda S. *The Construction of Negotiated Meaning: A
    Social Cognitive Theory of Writing.* Carbondale, IL:
    SIUP, 1994.

In this important introduction to the socio-cognitive approach,
Flower suggests that a focus on both social and cognitive
aspects of literacy skills provides a good model for viewing and
teaching literacy skills. The beginning teacher often gets
distracted by the mechanics of writing and the sometimes
opaque theoretical foundations inherent in freshman
composition texts; Flower addresses this problem head-on and
provides a strong socio-cognitive foundation that new teachers
can use to examine the context of literate actions.

► ---. "The Construction of Purpose in Writing and Reading."
    CE 50 (1988): 528-50.

Although rather dated in its solitary cognitive view of writing,
this article introduces some usable ideas for the novice teacher.
Flower focuses on the use of reading webs, where students can
draw out an author's purpose, goal, and support. These webs
can become quite complex as student readers take on more
complicated texts, and the detailed web or frame created can
assist with understanding. This essay could be useful for those
teachers who are looking for some effective reading strategies
to introduce into the writing classroom.

► ---. "Intercultural Inquiry and the Transformation of
    Service." *CE* 65 (2002):181-201.

This essay is an excellent introduction to both intercultural
inquiry and service learning. By providing an overview of
different types of service learning and its underlying principles

and motivations, Flower presents both the possible positives and negatives in making service learning the focus of a composition course. In addition, her examples drawn from community projects in the Pittsburgh area show the nitty-gritty of doing community literacy research and setting up service learning projects.

▶ ---. *Problem Solving Strategies for Writing.* Fort Worth: Harcourt Brace, 1998.

This textbook is a good example of how research and pedagogy can connect. Flower uses her research in cognition and the rhetoric of community literacy to ground a textbook that allows students to problem solve as the impetus to writing. While there are many other textbooks available for the new teacher to use in a freshman composition course, this one was revolutionary when first published and illustrates a research-based rhetorical approach to writing and the teaching of writing.

▶ ---. "Talking Across Difference: Intercultural Rhetoric and the Search for Situated Knowledge." *CCC* 55 (2003): 38-68.

In the context of describing the intercultural inquiry that takes place in the community based projects in the Pittsburgh community, Flower asks how any teacher can encourage meaningful talk about culturally significant issues across often very wide differences in race, gender, ethnicity, belief systems, and experience. She describes how the rhetoric of intercultural inquiry draws its participants into a discourse that requires negotiation, an invitation to every member to move from a position of argument and into a rhetoric of problem solving. This essay provides a strong rationale for bringing the concepts of intercultural rhetoric into the writing classroom, especially since talking about difference can show students how to actively listen, question, and be ready to investigate.

► Flower, Linda S., and John R. Hayes. "A Cognitive Process
Theory of Writing." *CCC* 32 (1981): 365-87.

In this landmark essay that describes writing as a hierarchical
and recursive process, Flower and Hayes create a vivid picture
of the flow of the composing process. Their model is based on
their analysis of think-aloud protocols captured as writers both
wrote and talked or thought aloud about their writing tasks
and strategies. For those new to teaching or composition
studies, this is a must-read essay, even though the solitary
focus on cognition is now outdated.

► Flower, Linda S, John R. Hayes, Linda Carey, Karen
Schriver, and James Stratman. "Detection, Diagnosis,
and the Strategies of Revision." *CCC* 37 (1986): 16-55.

The winners of a Braddock Award in 1987, the authors focus on
some differences between beginning and skilled writers,
especially in the area of revision. They suggest that beginning
writers have limited detection skills when reading their own
writing, and this often stymies their diagnoses of particular
problems in their writing, thus also preventing them from
using effective revision strategies. The focus on strategies that
will help student writers find a clearer purpose and audience
are very useful for those teaching composition, especially those
new to the writing classroom.

► Flower, Linda S., Elenore Long, and Lorraine Higgins.
*Learning to Rival: A Literate Practice for Intercultural
Inquiry*. Mahwah, NJ: Erlbaum, 2000.

Following the approach of John Dewey's experimental way of
knowing, the authors describe how literacy practices can move
across communities through the acts of members seeking rival
hypotheses and negotiating alternative perspectives. Flower
and her colleagues share observations and insights about how
the natural intercultural inquiry that takes place in teenage
and college communities can be an effective model for the
writing classroom, WAC studies, service learning, and

community based projects. This is a wonderfully engaging study of how what already takes place in student communities can be harnessed effectively in the classroom.

▶ Flower, Linda S, David L. Wallace, Linda Norris, and
    Rebecca E. Burnett, eds. *Making Thinking Visible:
    Writing, Collaborative Planning, and Classroom
    Inquiry.* Urbana, IL: NCTE, 1993.

The editors provide theory-supported essays, including a few by Flower herself, which encourage teachers, new and experienced, to think critically about how student writers think about their own writing. In addition, there are also first-hand reports of the discoveries made by some of the 33 teachers taking part in the four-year Thinking Visible Project sponsored by the Center for the Study of Writing at Carnegie Mellon. This is an excellent source for new teachers, as Flower and others show how to accomplish observation-based theory building, a strong foundation for teacher research.

▶ Haas, Christina, and Linda S. Flower. "Rhetorical Reading
    Strategies and the Construction of Meaning." *CCC* 39
    (1988): 167-83.

In this 1989 Braddock Award winning essay, Flower and Haas synthesize previous work published on reading as a constructive, rather than receptive process, and extend this rhetorical view of reading by asking and trying to answer two questions: How does the constructive process actually work in the thinking process of reading? And are all readings really aware or in control of their discourse acts? Their well-supported and appealing suggestion to teachers is to move beyond the view of reading and writing as a simple exchange and reconsider literacy within a more complex rhetorical model.

▶ Peck, Wayne Campbell, Linda S.Flower, and Lorraine
    Higgins. "Community Literacy." *CCC* 46 (1995):
    199-222.

Once again, Flower, along with her co-authors, is on the cutting edge of new rhetorical boundaries, this time focusing on how intercultural communities affect literacy practices. This essay is a description of how the Community Learning Center in Pittsburgh promotes literacy and provides opportunities for the writing of public texts relevant to the members of the Pittsburgh community. Community literacy, therefore, happens as people come together, cross boundaries, and work to take action. A wealth of community literacy projects and research was influenced by this essay, one that shows the importance of everyday literacy, not just academic writing.

Chapter 16:
Toby Fulwiler

(b. 1942)

Toby Fulwiler is best known for his revolutionary work with
WAC, but he has skillfully interwoven his other significant
contributions—the promotion of journals as a major form of
college writing and the emphasis of writing as a process—to
advance the field of contemporary pedagogy. Born on
December 6, 1942, in Milwaukee, Wisconsin, Fulwiler attended
the University of Wisconsin at Madison where he earned his
BA (1965), MA (1967), and PhD (1973) in English with a focus
on American Literature. Fulwiler has taught at the University
of Wisconsin, Stevens Point (1967-69), UWM (1973-76),
Michigan Technological University (1976-83), and the
University of Vermont (1983-present). He was awarded the
Kroepsch-Maurice Award for Teaching Excellence (1993) at
Vermont and is currently Professor Emeritus there.

The turning point in Fulwiler's teaching career occurred in
1977 when he attended a seminar held by the NEH. There he
was introduced to the work of James Britton, Peter Elbow,
James Moffett, and Janet Emig, among others, who have
argued that unless students practice writing everyday in all of
their academic classes, they will never improve. Such

provocative ideas sparked within Fulwiler an interest in the teaching of writing, and he returned to Michigan Tech to teach literature, serve as director of the freshman writing program, and develop a WAC program with Art Young. Through interdisciplinary writing workshops, Young and Fulwiler encouraged faculty across the disciplines to incorporate more writing more often in their courses to enhance and develop students' composition skills.

In an effort to extend the influence of WAC beyond Michigan Tech, Fulwiler has conducted interdisciplinary writing workshops in 44 states, Washington, D.C., Puerto Rico, England, and Canada (1977-01) where he utilizes a process-oriented approach to teaching, introducing instructors to expressive writing through journals, collaboration, and freewriting. Instructors learn techniques and strategies for integrating this writer-based, introspective form of composition into the classroom as a tool for generating class discussion and knowledge.

Fulwiler emphasized writing to learn in his own literature classrooms by replacing formal assignments and examinations with dialogue journals, which provided his students an ideal space for thinking and writing freely, without the fear of being penalized. A stimulus for both personal reflection and class discussion, journal writing promotes student knowledge in an uncritical environment where the focus is not on grammar but comprehension. Fulwiler similarly has used journal writing in his interdisciplinary writing workshops to reinforce what has been learned and to facilitate small group activities as well as to help student writers brainstorm, analyze, and reflect.

Fulwiler further advocates his process-oriented approach to composition in conventional handbooks such as *The Blair Handbook*, *The College Writer's Reference*, and *Pocket Reference for Writers*. In these handbooks, he incorporates contemporary trends in pedagogy, such as collaboration, journal writing, and computers and composition, with standard conventions of written English within the context of the writing assignment.

Currently, Fulwiler manages his 90-acre forest for both timber harvest and sugar bush and revises *The Blair Handbook* and companion volumes.

Keri L. Mayes

 Source for Biographical Narrative

▶ Fulwiler, Toby. "FWD: Answers to Questions." Email to Keri Mayes. 3 Nov. 2004.

▶ ---. "RE: Comp Leader Project." Email to Keri Mayes. 11 Nov. 2004.

▶ ---. "Responding to Student Journals." *Writing and Response: Theory, Practice, and Research*. Ed. Chris M. Anson. Urbana, IL: NCTE, 1989. 149-73.

▶ ---. "Showing, Not Telling, at a Writing Workshop?" *CE* 43 (1981): 55-63.

▶ ---. *Teaching With Writing: An Interdisciplinary Workshop Approach*. Portsmouth, NH: Boynton/Cook, 1987.

▶ ---. "Writing Research." Email to Keri Mayes. 14 July 2006.

▶ Young, Art, and Toby Fulwiler, eds. *Writing across the Disciplines: Research into Practice*. Portsmouth, NH: Boynton/Cook-Heinemann, 1986.

Toby Fulwiler recommends these readings for novice composition instructors:

"I don't have a list of three books to introduce 'comp theory' to new comp teachers, but I'd recommend some of the now classic authors who said, plainly and clearly, the most useful things about 'learning to write' and 'writing to learn' some time ago: Don Murray, Ken Macrorie, James Britton, James Moffett, Janet Emig, Shirley Brice Heath, and Peter Elbow. None of these authors privilege theory above practice and that counts for a lot if becoming a good writing teacher is the goal."

Annotated Bibliography

▶ Fulwiler, Toby. *College Writing: A Personal Approach to Academic Writing.* 3rd ed. Portsmouth, NH: Boynton/Cook, 2002.

In this uniquely conversational textbook, Fulwiler provides essential information about how to be a successful writer in college through a process rather than product-oriented approach to writing. Organized in a clear, logical format, the book begins with a general discussion about why writing is so important and how writing facilitates critical thinking which leads to knowledge and then proceeds to answer how-to questions in the composing process. While useful for college students and instructors who understand the value of writing as a means of integration into the academic community, this book encourages exploration of the student's voice and elicits suggestions, not stringent rules.

▶ ---. "How Well Does Writing Across the Curriculum Work?" *CE* 46 (1984):113-25. Rpt. in *Writing Across the Disciplines: Research Into Practice.* Portsmouth, NH: Boynton/Cook-Heinemann, 1986.

This article is Fulwiler's effort to assess the overall effectiveness of Michigan Tech's WAC program. He reflects on their plan to improve student writing by influencing change first within the faculty and then within the students followed by a clear explanation of the specific problems they encountered as well as benefits to the university. Pertinent to academic faculty interested in developing WAC programs within their own institutions, Fulwiler clearly delineates potential pitfalls and strategies to employ by drawing on the research he and his colleagues have conducted.

▶ ---, ed. *The Journal Book.* Portsmouth, NH: Boynton/Cook, 1987.

This book is a collection of 42 articles written by teachers in a variety of disciplines and grade levels about the importance of journal writing in the classroom. Fulwiler asserts the benefits of utilizing journal writing as a learning tool by pointing out how journals encourage active learning by giving the student a free space to think about, speculate on, and explore ideas without fear of penalty and contribute to the student's overall improved writing and critical thinking skills. Easy-to-read, practical, and persuasive, this book provides teachers with necessary guidelines to follow for use of journals in their classrooms.

▶ ---. "Showing, Not Telling, at a Writing Workshop?" *CE* 43 (1981): 55-63.

This article presents Fulwiler's early exploration into the writing workshop as a place where teachers across the discipline can come together, collaborate, and learn different writing techniques that they may use in the classroom at their own discretion. Through the illustration of five successful workshops in which he utilizes group work and expressive writing, particularly in the form of journals, Fulwiler encourages teachers in non-English fields who may feel insecure about writing. Clear, logical, and easy-to-read, Fulwiler's article promotes a nondirective approach to integrating writing into the curriculum.

▶ ---. *Teaching With Writing: An Interdisciplinary Workshop Approach*. Portsmouth, NH: Boynton/Cook, 1987.

In this book addressed to teachers at both the high school and college levels in all subject areas, Fulwiler argues that writing within any discipline creates knowledge and improves critical thinking. Organized in an attempt to emulate one of his interdisciplinary writing workshops with interactive questions and collaborative activities, Fulwiler provides teachers with practical suggestions and innovative techniques for introducing writing into pedagogy. The book is insightful, easy-to-read, and effective for teachers at any level who want to improve their students' thinking and writing skills.

▶ Fulwiler, Toby, and Alan R. Hayakawa. *The Blair Handbook*. 5th ed. Upper Saddle River, NJ: Prentice Hall, 2005.

This handbook for college writers incorporates both contemporary trends in pedagogy and standard conventions of written English within the context of the writing assignment. Organized according to the five stages of the writing process—planning, drafting, researching, revising, and editing—with additional sections on methods for presenting the text, WAC, and integrating computers into writing, this handbook is committed to writing as a process. It is easily accessible and provides fundamental information for college students at any writing level with the inclusion of student writing samples and strategies and tips for more effective writing habits.

▶ ---, eds. *The College Writer's Reference*. 4th ed. Upper Saddle River, NJ: Prentice Hall, 2005.

This compact writing handbook for college students and instructors, first published in 1996 and now in its fourth edition, is colorful and easily navigable with its spiral binding. Fulwiler's influence is pervasive throughout this process-oriented approach to composition with a chapter on journal writing and an underlying philosophy that writing is complex but should not be taught as an arbitrary set of rules. Editing, the last step of the writing process, is afforded four of the book's six parts thus emphasizing the importance of clear, effective communication.

▶ Fulwiler, Toby, and Art Young, eds. *Language Connections: Writing and Reading across the Curriculum*. Urbana, IL: NCTE, 1982.

This collection of 12 essays written by Michigan Tech faculty calls for teachers in all disciplines to examine and recognize the function of language in learning. Based on the theory that language promotes learning in all disciplines, this book addresses the need to improve student's basic language skills in order to enhance knowledge. With practical, effective suggestions and strategies for integrating a variety of writing forms into the classroom, contributors to this book acknowledge that not all approaches will work for every teacher but that the ideas presented will certainly encourage mental stimulation.

▶ ---, eds. *Programs That Work: Models and Methods for Writing across the Curriculum*. Portsmouth, NH: Boynton/Cook, 1990.

Through the collaboration of 14 colleges and universities' WAC programs, this book details the benefits of this interdisciplinary program, which encourages student learning through writing not only in English courses but in all disciplines. Each chapter is written by a different college or university's WAC program and includes its history and development, characteristics and descriptions, funding methods, problems encountered and how handled, successful practices, future plans, and implications. A fundamental source for WAC program developers, this book effectively proves that there is no formula for creating a successful WAC program but offers a variety of approaches for its organization and maintenance.

▶ Young, Art, and Toby Fulwiler, eds. *Writing Across the Disciplines: Research into Practice*. Portsmouth, NH: Boynton/Cook-Heinemann, 1986.

Based on the research collected from 14 interdisciplinary writing workshops at Michigan Tech from 1977 to 1984, Young and Fulwiler seek to assess the efficacy of these workshops specifically to determine if and how faculty and students' attitudes toward writing have changed. The book is comprised of 18 essays written by faculty and program participants from a variety of disciplines and evaluates the impact WAC has had on both the university overall and the classroom and addresses successes and failures. Written and organized like a scientific report, this book would be useful for administrators and faculty interested in starting a WAC program as it provides an in-depth look at one institution's approach to the introduction of writing through the disciplines.

Chapter 17:
Anne Ruggles Gere

(b. 1944)

A distinguished advocator of writing groups, Anne Ruggles Gere has published or edited numerous books and articles on the history and theory of writing groups. Gere received her BA (1966) in English from Colby College, her MA (1967) in English from Colgate University, and her PhD (1974) in English and Education from The University of Michigan.

After teaching English at Princeton High School in New Jersey for three years, Gere began teaching courses at Michigan (1971). In 1975 she relocated to the Pacific Northwest to teach at the University of Washington. She returned to Michigan in 1987, and she has chaired their joint PhD Program in English and Education since 1989. In addition to teaching, during 1998-2002 she alternately served as Vice President and President Elect of the NCTE. She was also the founding director of the Puget Sound Writing Project, a site of the National Writing Project, based at the University of Washington's Seattle Campus, from 1978-87. She has been a reviewer for *CCC* since 1986 and for *Research in the Teaching of English* since 1983.

Gere has won numerous awards, particularly for her research into the roles of women in writing. In 2001 she was granted a Research Award from the Institute for Research on Women and Gender. Her *Intimate Practices: Literacy and Cultural Work in U.S. Women's Clubs 1880-1920* won her the National Women's Studies Association Manuscript Prize (1995). Michigan recognized her prominence and value as a professor with its Career Development Award (1999). She also received the NEH Award for the "Making American Literatures" Project (1997). Gere is consistently asked to deliver keynote addresses at a variety of universities and institutions. Past addresses have reflected her expertise in such areas as collaborative writing, cognitive development and composition, and the politics behind writing instruction.

Gere has devoted much of her career to promoting practical guides and methods for writing, particularly tailored for use in the classroom. According to Gere, writing groups and peer evaluations are especially useful in advancing student writing and should be incorporated into the curriculum well before high school. Gere believes that the best work comes from an understanding that writing is a social and collaborative discipline; students and other writers should work together to enhance their voices. In addition, Gere has made numerous efforts to ensure that writing move beyond the provenance of English departments. She has advanced WAC theory with contributions to such textbooks as *Into the Field: Sites of Composition Studies* and *Roots in the Sawdust: Writing to Learn Across the Disciplines*.

Ben Strickland

 Source for Biographical Narrative

▶ "Anne Ruggles Gere." Department of English, Language, and Literature. University of   Michigan. 2006. 16 June 2006
<http://www-personal.umich.edu/~argere/ ita.html>.

Annotated Bibliography

▶ Gere, Anne R.,ed. *Into the Field: Sites of Composition Studies*. New York: MLA, 1993.

These essays look at the relationship between composition and other disciplines by first dispensing with the traditional bridge-building metaphor in favor of restructuring their relationship. Gere argues that to restructure is to rework or deconstruct those disciplines in light of how they intersect with composition. New teachers will find a useful introduction to philosophical and postmodern theory with practical advice on how to approach composition in the classroom.

▶ ---. "Kitchen Tables and Rented Rooms: The Extracurriculum of Composition." *CCC* 45 (1994): 75-92.

Drawing on her studies of women's writing groups at the turn of the 20ᵗʰ century, Gere extrapolates that culturally imposed silences are forms of communication. Writing is primarily a method of self-exploration, which relies heavily on performance and the need for constructive feedback. Gere is persuasive in arguing that since classrooms are finite and ultimately limiting artificial arenas, teachers should expand their curriculums to include the environment because students and teachers can learn much by listening to voices other than one's own.

▶ ---. "Revealing Silence: Rethinking Personal Writing." *CCC* 52 (2001): 203-23.

Gere advocates expanding the concept of personal writing beyond the typical autobiographical narratives, which tend to focus on some traumatic event in the student's past, through an emphasis on collaboration and peer response. Teachers too often praise self-disclosure as bold, brave, and honest, while neglecting the larger social contexts, e.g., race or sexual orientation, which may make a student uncomfortable about revealing personal information. Students can learn to express themselves without revealing too much, and teachers should respect their silence by recognizing that the writing is the commodity, not the writer.

▶ ---, ed. *Roots in the Sawdust: Writing to Learn Across the Disciplines*. Urbana, IL: NCTE, 1985.

Born from her work with other writing teachers in the Puget Sound Writing Program, Gere makes it plain that this is not another WAC guidebook. Composition skills demand a place across the curriculum; however, increasing skill in writing does not necessarily mean that the students are learning to write well, only that they are becoming more polished, and Gere aims at improving writing by improving thinking. The essays in this book investigate how to tailor practical strategies for substantive writing in every subject.

▶ ---. *Writing Groups: History, Theory, and Implications*. Carbondale, IL: SIUP, 1987.

Gere examines the history of writing groups with a keen focus on writing as a social phenomenon. By counteracting the (still) traditional view that writers work in solitude, Gere points to the many artistic and communal benefits of collaboration. Novice writing teachers will find a new perspective on the discipline but will have to sift through much history and theory before arriving at the more immediately useful "Practical Directions" chapter that speaks to ways of constructing a classroom and increasing student self-confidence.

▶ ---. "Written Composition: Toward a Theory of Evaluation." *CE* 42 (1980): 44-48, 53-58.

Teachers should be aware of and respect their tremendous power and influence over students' assignments by recognizing their unique position as evaluators of writing. Gere juxtaposes New Criticism's formal semantics (the idea that meaning is embedded in the text) with her own preference of communication intention (in which the writer's and reader's intentions and expectations are taken into account). Beyond the theory, Gere pushes teachers to consider all of the factors that contribute to their assignments, e.g., time allotted, context within other lessons, length, point of view, and punctuation, and use these tools to their greatest effect.

▶ Gere, Anne R., and Robert D. Abbott. "Talking about Writing: The Language of Writing Groups." *Research in the Teaching of English* 19 (1985): 362-81.

Gere and Abbott look at how middle and high school students participate in peer reviews of their writing with a particular emphasis on *what* the students say and *how* they express themselves to one another. The students tend to center their critiques on subject rather than style. By examining and explaining what may make students needlessly uncomfortable, this essay is a useful reminder of the value behind seeing an assignment from the student's point of view.

▶ Gere, Anne R., Leila Christenbury, and Kelly Sassi. *Writing on Demand: Best Practices and Strategies for Success.* Portsmouth, NH: Heinemann, 2005.

Gere et al develop strategies for helping students prepare for the essay section of such standardized tests as the SAT, ACT, and AP. Sample essays are provided along with an insightful behind-the-scenes explanation of how they are scored. Abundant practical advice includes how to make students organize their thoughts efficiently and effectively, and though the book is designed around standardized tests, these lessons are useful for any pressured on-demand writing assignments.

▶ Gere, Anne R., Colleen Fairbanks, Alan Howes, Laura Roop, and David Schaafsma. *Language and Reflection: An Integrated Approach to Teaching English.* New York: Prentice-Hall, 1991.

The authors challenge teachers to reflect on their own training and acquired assumptions about writing and language. Philosophical theories behind language are broken down and examined in terms of art, archeology, anthropology, and psychology. The history of teaching is interesting, but the overall emphasis on how teachers must recognize their own personal, historical, and social issues as potentially impacting their classrooms is particularly effective.

▶ Schutz, Aaron, and Anne R. Gere. "Service Learning and English Studies: Rethinking 'Public' Service." *CE* 60 (1998): 129-49.

Gere and Schutz argue that academies should not try to exist independently of their communities, and that since English classrooms are naturally inclined towards promoting and enhancing discourse, service learning and English studies make fitting counterparts. Students who tutor in traditional literacy programs find that when they are asked to keep a journal of their activities, they acquire a keener ability to see situations from another's point of view. While this point about writing is well taken, the article makes many assumptions about the nature of public service and how it affects volunteers (such as the savior complex) and it is sometimes difficult to keep the authors' unique connotations of private and public in mind.

Chapter 18:
Keith Gilyard

(b. 1952)

A noted contributor to rhetoric, composition, and poetry studies, Keith Gilyard has written, lectured, and taught extensively, focusing primarily on critical race studies, language and literacy, sociolinguistics, and composition pedagogy. Gilyard earned his BS from CUNY, an MFA from Columbia University, and an EdD from New York University.

In 1981, Gilyard became a faculty member at CUNY, Medgar Evers College. He continued at CUNY as a teacher and WPA until 1994, followed by a period as professor of writing and English and director of the Writing Program at Syracuse University. Since 1999, he has been a professor of English at The Pennsylvania State University. Gilyard is actively involved in the NCTE, serving as a member of the editorial board and the executive committee. He is also affiliated with the CCCC where he served in several positions including Chair (2000).

One of Gilyard's most notable achievements is an American Book Award (1992) for his monograph *Voices of the Self: A Study of Language Competence*. Gilyard's efforts as an educator have earned him several distinctions at Penn State including

Distinguished professor status (2005), the Penn State Class of 1933 Medal of Distinction in the humanities (2005), and an Arts and Humanities Medal (2006). In 2005, Gilyard was inducted into the International Literary Hall of Fame for Writers of African Descent for his achievements as a literary critic.

Although a prolific writer of scholarly essays on rhetoric, language, and pedagogy, Gilyard's interests are not restricted to composition studies. Gilyard is also a poet, a political activist, a noted lecturer, and a literary critic. He has edited an array of scholarly works from composition texts (*Rhetorical Choices: A Reader for Writers* with Deborah Holdstein and Charles I. Schuster) to literature anthologies (*African American Literature*, with Anissa Wardi).

Interested in the complex interplay between race, ethnicity, language, composition, and politics, Gilyard exposes the differences between authentic student voice and the dominant discourse of the academy. His primary interest lies in identifying intersections of African American English and composition practices, which he explores in his monographs *Voices of the Self* and *Let's Flip the Script*. Advocating African American English as a legitimate discourse, Gilyard is a prominent voice in a movement to challenge Standard English and recognize other ethnic and cultural discourses as equally valid, a topic covered in *Race, Rhetoric, and Composition* as well as *Race and Ethnicity*.

Gilyard continues to lecture and produce critical essays. He is currently writing a *Literary Biography of John Oliver Killens* as a follow-up to *Liberation Memories: The Rhetoric and Poetics of John Oliver Killens*.

Adam McInturff

 Sources for Biographical Narrative

▶ Black Writers Hall of Fame. 26 May 2002. 17 June 2006 < http://www.csu.edu/GwendolynBrooks/ WritersConference/halloffame.htm>.

▶ "Faculty Teaching Awards." *LA Times.* May 2006. 15 June
　　2006 <http://www.la.psu.edu/CLA-News/
　　Latimes/may06/issue.shtml>.

▶ Gilyard, Keith. "Basic Writing: Cost Effectiveness and
　　Ideology." *Journal of Basic Writing* 19.1 (2000): 36-42.

▶ "Keith Gilyard." *Biography Resource Center.* Thomson Gale,
　　2006. MTSU, James E. Walker Lib., Murfreesboro, TN.
　　15 June 2006
　　<http://galenet.galegroup.com/servlet/BioRC>.

▶ "Keith Gilyard." The Department of English – Faculty
　　Directory. The Pennsylvania State University. 15 June
　　2006 <http://English.la.psu.edu/facultystaff/
　　Bio_Gilyard.htm>.

▶ Lewis, Rudolph. "Interview with Keith Gilyard on *Liberation
　　Memories.*" 15 June 2006 <http:www.nathanielturner.com/
　　interviewwithkeithgilyard.htm>.

Annotated Bibliography

▶ Gilyard, Keith. "African American Contributions to
　　Composition Studies." *CCC* 50 (1999): 626-44.

Gilyard chronicles the contributions of African Americans to
composition studies, from the efforts of rhetors to educational
theorists to modern scholars. Gilyard acknowledges how
diverse many groups are in their scope, from back-to-basics
proponents to supporters of Ebonics, yet he particularly
highlights the important developments that arose from those
struggles. This article provides a good overview for those
wanting to understand how modern discourse theory developed.

▶ ---. "Basic Writing, Cost Effectiveness, and Ideology."
　　Journal of Basic Writing 19.1 (2000): 36-42.

Gilyard responds to the debate over the eradication of basic
writing courses, examining each argument in terms of a

question: Will eliminating remedial courses in the name of cost effectiveness prove costly to student success? Justifying or negating the usefulness of basic writing courses is no easy task, and no conclusive solution is reached as Gilyard examines issues such as the efficacy of obtaining empirical evidence. Composition instructors, especially those teaching remedial courses, may find new insights within this fair treatment of the basic writing debate.

▶ ---. "Cross Talk: Toward Transcultural Writing Classrooms." *Writing in Multicultural Settings.* Ed. Carol Severino, Juan C. Guerra, and E. Johnnella. New York: MLA, 1997. 325-31.

Advocating a concept he terms "transculturalism," Gilyard refuses to accept simple solutions found within multicultural dialogue, encouraging an environment where students contribute to the knowledge base and accept new cultural constructions. Though his overall argument mirrors his other texts, Gilyard's role as a reactionary sparks new dialogue. Gilyard does not propose any definitive solution himself, though readers may use his review as a guide to understanding the issues posed in the chapter.

▶ ---. "Holdin It Down: Students' Right and the Struggle over Language Diversity." *Rhetoric and Composition as Intellectual Work.* Ed. Gary A. Olson. Carbondale, IL: SIUP, 2003. 115-27.

Examining the debate over authentic student discourse versus Standard English, Gilyard advocates an acknowledgement of student identity and attempts to refute the notion that it is necessary for students to acquire standard academic discourse to properly express their ideas. The argument focuses primarily on the Ebonics controversy and the accusations of those wanting to undermine the validity of non-standard discourses. The article encourages mutual inclusiveness within composition courses and suggests composition instructors affect a teaching style that encourages individual voice.

▶ ---. "Kinship and Theory." *American Literary History* 11.1
    (1999): 187-95.

Gilyard analyzes the problem of African American identity
present within modern culture, particularly token inclusiveness
and its potential to dissolve identity and produce false
harmony. Though he recognizes heterogeneity within the
African American community, Gilyard advocates the existence
of a clear community in order to understand social barriers and
work toward a collective racial progress. Implications within
progressive composition classrooms involve teachers
recognizing broad cultural differences without striving toward
a uniform racial unity that does not take into account real
social constructions.

▶ ---. *Let's Flip the Script: An African American Discourse on
    Language, Literature, and Learning.* Detroit: Wayne
    State UP, 1996.

Gilyard blends scholarly essay with personal narrative in this
examination of language, citing numerous examples of how
words illuminate or obfuscate. He recognizes the power of
language in different contexts and the importance of promoting
students' interest and participation in writing, debate, and
society in general. Readers may find the text's wide scope
valuable in assessing various pedagogical approaches to
composition instruction.

▶ ---. "Literacy, Identity, Imagination, Flight." *CCC* 52 (2000):
    260-72.

Through various metaphors and examples, Gilyard
acknowledges the difficulties in navigating constructed
meanings in racial identity, assuming a postmodernist stance
by which composition teachers recognize frameworks such as
black or white and attempt to modify these constructions.
Gilyard presents a moderate view that seeks to overcome
barriers through imagination and playfulness while
acknowledging the inherent problem of true communication.
New composition teachers attempting to construct a
progressive classroom may struggle with the essay's overall
readability but may benefit from the basic ideas found in study.

▶ ---, ed. *Race, Rhetoric, and Composition*. Portsmouth, NH: Boynton/Cook, 1999.

Essayists in this collection discuss the complex issue of race in relation to composition and rhetoric, including concepts of race as a social construction, the history and development of racial rhetoric, and the impact of racial—and racist—discourse in composition classrooms. The text's most salient aspect is its attempt to provide critical rather than emotive analyses of racial rhetoric. Composition instructors would benefit from using the text to promote dialogue about race in their classrooms.

▶ ---. *Voices of the Self: A Study of Language Competence*. Detroit: Wayne State UP, 1991.

In his examination of language, Gilyard alternates autobiographical narrative with critical analysis, offering a view of his experiences as a student navigating between Black English and Standard English. The odd-numbered chapters provide an examination of language acquisition and cite various sources. For composition teachers, the work gives an overview of Gilayrd's overall arguments and may serve as an introduction to more objective studies concerning language acquisition.

▶ Gilyard, Keith, and Vorris Nunley, eds. *Rhetoric and Ethnicity*. Portsmouth, NH: Boynton/Cook, 2004.

Gilyard and Nunley arrange a series of essays in which authors attempt to clarify ethnic concepts and how they influences writers' voices, personal awareness, and reception by an intellectual community and its dominant, often exclusivist discourse. Contributors analyze historical and political movements as well as pedagogical developments in terms of critical ethnicity, which Gilyard promotes as a potential starting point for examining how ethnicity is socially constructed. Potentially, composition teachers could use these essays to open discourse concerning differences and similarities in voice to create a greater sense of community.

 # Chapter 19:
Cheryl Glenn

Due to her extensive teaching, administrative, and research experience, Cheryl Glenn has become a recognized specialist in rhetorical theory, the history of rhetoric, and composition pedagogy. She earned a BS, MA (1981), and PhD (1989) from The Ohio State University, where her studies ranged from composition theory to Medieval and Renaissance literature.

Since 1997, Glenn has functioned in both teaching and administrative roles at The Pennsylvania State University (Penn State), where she is currently professor of English and Women's Studies. From 1989 until 1997, she held positions as assistant and associate professor at Oregon State University. In addition to her academic appointments, she has served as Chair of the CCCC (2007), president of the Coalition of Women Scholars in the History of Rhetoric and Composition, and a member of the editorial board for numerous scholarly publications, including *Rhetoric Society Quarterly*, *Rhetoric Review*, *Quarterly Journal of Speech,* and *CCC*. She has also been an active voice in the Rhetoric Society of America, which bestowed her with the Outstanding Service Award (2000).

Glenn has received countless other awards and fellowships, including the NEH Summer Stipend (1993, 2001), the NEH Fellowship for College Teachers (1995), and the Penn State Liberal Arts Research and Graduate Studies Faculty Award (1999). Her academic publications have received numerous accolades, such as The Society for the Study of Early Modern Women Best Book Award (1998) and the CCCC Braddock Award for outstanding article (1995). In addition, she has been recognized for her superb teaching, acquiring Penn State's College of Liberal Arts Outstanding Teaching Award (2006) and Oregon States's Elizabeth P. Ritchie Distinguished Professor Award (1996). Recently, she was granted an Administrative Fellowship in Penn State's Executive Vice President and Provost's Office (2004), and she was a Fellow for the Committee on Institutional Cooperation's Academic Leadership Program (2004).

Mostly, Glenn's research has focused on the patriarchal bias of the rhetorical tradition. Her book *Rhetoric Retold: Regendering the Tradition from Antiquity Through the Renaissance* discusses the contribution of female rhetoricians, including Aspasia, Margery Kempe, Anne Askew, and Elizabeth I. Since 2000, she has also edited and co-edited the "Studies in Rhetorics and Feminisms" series from SIUP. In addition, her work often explores the intersection of composition pedagogy and rhetorical study; *Making Sense* and *Hodges' Harbrace Handbook* discuss the usage of rhetorical methods of development. Her collection of essays, *Rhetorical Education in America*, discusses the history of courses in writing and speaking, the exclusion of various groups from rhetorical education, and the impact of cyber-literacy and the Internet on the curriculum.

Over the last few years, Glenn's research has explored the rhetorical use of silence. In her recent book *Unspoken: A Rhetoric of Silence* (2004), she examines silence in human communication, using examples ranging from Bill Clinton's scandals to Native American cultural practices. Currently, she is editing an essay collection, *Silence and Listening as Rhetorical Arts*, and she is finishing *The Harbrace Guide for College Writers: The Rhetorical Situation*.

Kennie Rose

Source for Biographical Narrative

▶ Glenn, Cheryl. "Re: Research Project." Email to Kennie Rose.
16 Jun. 2006.

Cheryl Glenn recommends these readings for novice composition instructors:

1. Lindemann, Erika. *A Rhetoric for Writing Teachers.* New York: Oxford UP, 1982.
2. Quintilian's *Institutio Oratoria*
3. Anything by Peter Elbow!

Annotated Bibliography

▶ Glenn, Cheryl. *Making Sense: A New Rhetorical Reader.* 2nd
ed. New York: Bedford/ St. Martin's, 2005.

Making Sense is a freshman textbook patterned on the
rhetorical methods of development: description, narration,
exemplification, classification, comparison and contrast,
process analysis, cause-and-consequence, and definition. It also
focuses on the development of visual literacy, and the pages are
littered with images and Web sites. For instructors looking for
a rhetorical reader, *Making Sense* provides a fantastic
collection of models, a concise explanation of each rhetorical
strategy, and a variety of classroom activities.

▶ ---. "Remapping Rhetorical Territory." *Rhetoric Review* 13
(Spring 1995): 287-303.

Glenn argues that rhetoricians must interrogate the male-
dominated tradition of their discipline. If scholars want a more
inclusive discourse, they must construct a historical map that
recognizes women—to demonstrate her point, she briefly
discusses the work of Aspasia, a female rhetorician from
ancient Greece. For those interested in the history of rhetoric,

this article is a must-read; however, it requires a strong knowledge of feminist theory.

▶ ---. *Rhetoric Retold: Regendering the Tradition from Antiquity through the Renaissance.* Carbondale, IL: SIUP, 1997.

Rhetoric Retold examines the contribution of women to the rhetorical tradition; her book stretches from ancient Greece to the Renaissance, discussing figures such as Aspasia, Margery Kempe, Anne Askew, and Elizabeth I. According to Glenn, if rhetorical scholars want to produce a more inclusive discourse, they must interrogate their discipline's paternal narrative. *Rhetoric Retold* is Glenn's most influential text; however, because it assumes an understanding of feminist theory, it might be difficult for some readers.

▶ ---. "Silence: A Rhetoric Art for Resisting Discipline(s)." *JAC* 22 (2002): 261-92.

Glenn discusses the potential of silence as a rhetorical tool—through an examination of the Anita Hill and Lani Guinier controversies, she demonstrates that silence can often be more powerful than the spoken word. In this article, Glenn does not address the function of silence in the classroom, but her argument has numerous pedagogical implications for both composition and writing center theory. For newcomers to her work on silence, this article supplies a wonderful introduction.

▶ ---. *Unspoken: A Rhetoric of Silence.* Carbondale, IL: SIUP, 2004.

In this groundbreaking work, Glenn depicts silence as a rhetorical tool, one with the same potential as spoken language. According to Glenn, silence can demonstrate submission, torture a loved one, exercise power, communicate frustration, or invite more speech—it all depends on the situation. All composition instructors should read the first two chapters, which discuss the function of silence in both administrative meetings and high school classrooms.

► ---. "When Grammar Was a Language Art." *The Place of Grammar in Writing Instruction*. Ed. Susan Hunter and Ray Wallace. Portsmouth, NH: Boynton/Cook, 1995. 9-29.

Looking back at the history of grammar instruction, Glenn argues that unlike contemporary teachers, who often administer isolated drills and worksheets, classical rhetoricians imagined grammar as an organic part of the writing process. According to Glenn, grammar encourages students to aim for more sophisticated prose; she cites the teaching strategies of Edward P. J. Corbett, who required students to record their average sentence length, transcribe passages from respected authors, and incorporate more sentence variety. Her historical study offers much to the field of composition; however, because Glenn focuses on the work of classical rhetoricians, other voices are left out of the equation, which leaves one curious about the impact of her ideas on students.

► Glenn, Cheryl, Melissa Goldthwaite, and Robert Connors. *The New St. Martin's Guide to Teaching* Writing. 5th ed. Boston: Bedford/St. Martin's, 2003.

A basic guide for young composition teachers, this book is divided between practical advice, theoretical issues, and scholarly articles. It contains detailed sections on in-class activities, student evaluation, the first week, and creating assignments. In addition, *The St. Martin's Guide* features basic descriptions of the major theoretical models, and the scholarly anthology includes respected figures such as David Bartholomae, Peter Elbow, Janet Emig, Linda Flower, and Mike Rose.

► Glenn, Cheryl, and Loretta Gray. *Hodges' Harbrace Handbook*. 16th ed. Boston: Thomson Wadsworth, 2007.

The latest edition of the classic handbook features detailed information about spelling, grammar, and punctuation. In addition, it contains a section on writing for literature and business, MLA and APA documentation guides, and hints for effectively using rhetoric. The handbook is concise and detailed, and many instructors consider it a fantastic resource; however, some would criticize its emphasis on grammar, which often comes at the expense of advice on the writing process.

▶ Glenn, Cheryl, Margaret Lyday, and Wendy Sharer, eds. *Rhetorical Education in America.* Tuscaloosa: U of Alabama P, 2004.

A collection of invited essays on rhetorical education, this volume's selections address an impressive range of topics. For example, in the second article, Thomas P. Miller traces the historical rise of literary studies, and in the final essay, Laura Gurak argues that the notion of literacy must expand to include technological advances. The contributors often explore unusual subjects; therefore, the essays tend to be extremely provocative, and they offer a wealth of useful information for composition scholars.

▶ Lunsford, Andrea, and Cheryl Glenn. "Rhetorical Theory and the Teaching of Writing." *On Literacy and Its Teaching: Issues in English Education.* Ed. Gail E. Hawisher and Anna Soter. Albany: SUNY P, 1990. 174-89.

Lunsford and Glenn provide an overview of rhetoric's seminal theories, such as the communication triangle, Aristotle's rhetorical elements, and Kenneth Burke's terministic screen. According to the authors, when a classroom is informed by these concepts, students will take an active role in their own learning; in addition, teachers will have the tools to craft effective writing assignments. For composition instructors unfamiliar with rhetoric, this article provides an accessible introduction to the field.

Chapter 20:
Muriel "Mickey" Harris

(b. 1937)

Born and raised in Chicago, Illinois, Muriel Harris began her work in the education field at UIUC where she received her BA (1959) in English Education and her MA (1960) in English Literature. She ventured off to Germany for a year with her husband Sam Harris and then returned to Columbia University where she eventually completed her education with a PhD (1972) in English, specializing in the English Renaissance.

When Harris's husband accepted a faculty position at Purdue University in 1969, the couple moved to Indiana. After her children started school, Harris taught as a part-time lecturer in the composition program and then volunteered to start a tutoring center when she realized that she would be more effective when meeting her students in one-to-one settings. After supporting a provisional writing center for a year, Purdue's English Department agreed to its establishment and then offered Harris a job as the director of the Writing Lab (1976). Writing centers, synonymous with the term writing labs, were still new, and no one really knew what they really were or what to do with them. Harris began the long process of trying what worked, discarding what did not, and eventually became an important name in the scholarship of writing center theory and practice. Most of her research focuses on writing center theory, administration, and pedagogy, and she is particularly interested in individualized instruction. Mentoring the tutors in her Writing Lab has resulted in over 30 of them moving on to accept directorships of writing centers in other institutions, a result she is particularly proud of.

Still heavily active in writing center scholarship, Harris changes with the times. While she began to spread, and continues to spread, awareness of writing centers and their rightful purposes, she aided in meeting the growing demand for organizing and uniting writing centers, to create ways for writing centers to collaborate as well as to validate their work in composition studies. Shortly, after the CCCC conference in 1977, Harris and a few of her colleagues discussed how a newsletter could inform, educate, and offer a forum for concerns and dialogue within the writing center community. By April 1977, Harris launched *The Writing Lab Newsletter,* using a typewriter and Scotch tape. Now the newsletter has matured to a more sophisticated journal, many editions of which are available and searchable online through Purdue's Online Writing Lab (OWL).

The very existence of Purdue's OWL shows another groundbreaking accomplishment by this composition pioneer. As technology advanced, Harris saw an opportunity to make instructional materials accessible on request and answer writing questions by e-mail. Looking for an easily remembered login for the earliest incarnation of the online e-mail service, Harris and a grad student decided on OWL, a term that has passed into the vocabulary of writing centers. As technology advanced and Web browsers were developed, Harris teamed up with Dave Taylor, a graduate student in educational technology. Moving from an e-mail service that attracted thousands of users from all over the world, to a Web-based one, the OWL took off in 1993, when millions of users downloaded materials and sent in questions to the online tutors. Visitors from all over the globe log onto Purdue's OWL to download grammar handouts, PowerPoint presentations, and tutorials; to submit questions; or to borrow ideas for other OWLs that are continuously hatching.

Though her professional accomplishments are respected and honored by an ever-growing writing center community, Harris has established a more than personable reputation among her colleagues. Her contributions and accolades decorate a 25-page curriculum vitae. Not counting multiple editions, Harris has authored five books, 29 chapters for other books, 55 journal articles, and has been a keynote speaker or invited workshop leader over 40 times. Of course, these numbers continue to grow and do not take into account her numerous conference paper presentations, time spent responding to questions on the WCenter listserv, and personal e-mail correspondences around the world with people who seek her advice with varying types of scholarship and the formation of new writing centers. This advice-giving character has led people to lovingly refer to her as "Mickey" because of her outgoing personality and roles as forerunner, expert, mentor, mother, and friend.

Harris is now Professor Emerita of English at Purdue University and Director Emerita of the Purdue University Writing Lab where she still serves as editor of *The Writing Lab Newsletter.*

Alan Coulter

 Sources for Biographical Narrative

▶ Harris, Muriel. Email to Alan Coulter. 22 Oct. 2004.

▶ ---. "Meet Muriel Harris." *Purdue's Online Writing Lab.* 24 Nov. 2004 <http://owl.english.purdue.edu/lab/staff/ HomePages/mickey.html>.

▶ Pemberton, Michael, and Joyce Kinkead. "Introduction: Benchmarks in Writing Center Scholarship." *The Center Will Hold.* Logan, UT: Utah State UP: 2003. 1-20.

▶Smith, Trixie. Personal communication. Nov. 2004.

Muriel Harris recommends these readings for novice composition instructors:

1. Murray, Donald M. *Write to Learn*. 6th ed. New York: Harcourt Brace College, 1998.
2. ---. *A Writer Teaches Writing (Revised)*. 2nd ed. Belmont, CA: Heinle, 2003.
3. Tate, Gary, and Erika Lindemann. *Introduction to Composition Studies*. New York: Oxford UP, 1991.

 Annotated Bibliography

▶ Harris, Muriel. "Collaboration Is Not Collaboration Is Not Collaboration: Writing Center Tutorials vs. Peer-Response Groups." *CCC* 43 (1992): 369-83.

In this article, Harris defines the role of the tutor by contrasting it with peer-response groups in the classroom. Harris offers a brief background for both groups, but she also shows how their histories forked, leaving them with two different purposes and goals. This article would be extremely useful for the composition teacher who innocently mistakes writing centers as a substitute for the in-class peer evaluation. Harris's conversational, yet professional style makes the article easy to read and comprehend.

▶ ---. "Individualized Diagnosis: Searching for Causes, Not Symptoms of Writing Deficiencies." *CE* 40 (1978): 318-23.

Harris affirms her belief in teaching the process on a one-to-one basis, not the rules of writing. She argues that dysfunctional or disabling writing habits can be changed if teachers go back to the source of ideas behind their students' writing by offering a list of questions she finds important for students to answer. She states that instructors will know how to better approach their students after evaluating their answers. This article is designed specifically for the composition instructor, but directors of writing centers or writing programs may find it useful in learning how to motivate their tutors and teachers.

▶ ---. "Making the Writing Lab an Instructor's Resource Room." *CCC* 28 (1977): 376-78.

Harris promotes the image of the center to composition professors, describing how her writing center at Purdue University became a place to offer knowledge and help to professors, rather than some ominous structure that nobody really understood. Written toward the beginning of her career, this article, almost a sidebar, shows how academic politics forced Harris to bridge a gap between centers and departments. Directors can still relate to this article and find inspiration in Harris's dedication to the writing center community.

▶ ---. "Mending the Fragmented Free Modifier." *CCC* 32 (1981): 175-82.

In her attempt to understand how and why students write fragments, Harris researched hundreds of fragments in student writing and found that the vast majority are created because of dependent clauses being separated from their related independent clauses. This suggests that students need help with understanding how to combine these related parts into whole sentences rather than instruction on the basics of parts of speech. Harris also advises instructors not to warn their students completely against using fragments in their writing because some fragments strengthen writing when used wisely and effectively. Harris shows her skill as a writer and teacher by her knowledge of the craft and the wisdom she brings to students' perceptions of writing. This article is extremely helpful for teachers who face the difficult task of balancing grades, mechanics, and the improvement of their students' abilities.

▶ ---. *Prentice Hall Reference Guide to Grammar and Usage.* Upper Saddle River, NJ: Prentice Hall, 1991. (Subsequent editions in 1994, 1997, 2000, 2003, 2005)

This handbook, which acknowledges the variety of writing processes and ways of learning, explains rules and the ins and outs of English grammar, with hints and strategies learned from Harris's many years of tutoring and listening to students' questions. The book addresses the entire spectrum of writing, from the process to details like word choice and ESL troubleshooting to larger issues of research and evaluating sources. While the book may not be a page-turner, it proves to be helpful and successful, with its seventh edition to be released in 2008.

▶ ---. "Talking in the Middle: Why Writers Need Writing Tutors." *CE* 57 (1995): 27-42.

Exploring the affective benefits of one-to-one interaction with tutors Harris explores student comments regarding how and why the tutoring benefited them. She also lends insight into what students are thinking or expecting when they walk into a university's writing center. She debunks the notions of centers as fix-it shops, and she also reflects on the importance of student confidence in their writing skills and suggests how students wish to write things they can be proud of. While some may see this as a Utopian depiction of writing centers, it seeks to explain why writing centers are effective and how difficult it is to prove their usefulness.

▶ ---. *Teaching One-to-One: The Writing Conference.* Urbana, IL: NCTE, 1986.

One of Harris's most popular works, *Teaching One-to-One* discusses the theory and practice of writing conferences in one book. Harris justifies the writing conference, explaining why it is effective, but she also gives readers ideas for how to conduct successful sessions. The appendices offer great exercises that benefit writers and tutors alike. Sections of this book may seem dated, but the ideas and concepts still apply to contemporary writing centers.

▶ Pemberton, Michael, and Joyce Kinkead. *The Center Will Hold: Critical Perspectives in Writing Center Scholarship.* Logan, UT: Utah State UP, 2003.

Winner of the IWCA and WPA 2004 Best Book Award, *The Center Will Hold* is a festschrift serving as Kinkead and

Pemberton's tribute to the scholarship and dedication of Muriel Harris. The book's ten articles from respected leaders of writing center theory, such as Nancy Grimm and James Inman, cover topics from patriarchal structures to WAC to online writing centers. Anyone unfamiliar with the wide range of topics under the writing center umbrella should read this book to see how diverse Harris's contributions have been to the field.

▶ *Purdue University's Online Writing Lab - The Owl Family of Sites.* 10 June 2006 <http://owl. english.purdue.edu>.

An offshoot of the brick-and-mortar Purdue Writing Lab, this OWL became a Web site in 1993 through the efforts of Harris and Dave Taylor and continues to serve as the model for many online writing centers. Most OWLs link to this site, which offers its own handouts, search engines, and tutorials on various writing issues. Purdue's OWL answers e-mailed questions from all over the world because of its user-friendly format. The older version of the OWL, with the original extensive collection of handouts, tutorials, and PowerPoints, is still available at <http://owl.english.purdue.edu/oldindex.html>.

▶ *Writing Lab Newsletter.* Ed. Muriel Harris. West Lafayette, IN: Purdue U.

In April 1977, Harris started this newsletter with a typewriter and scotch tape in response to the great interest shown at a CCCC session for a way to communicate with others in writing centers. The newsletter has matured into a more sophisticated forum for tutors and directors to offer theory; describe pedagogy; discuss administrative concerns such as publicizing a center and training tutors, as well as to voice concerns, review books, announce jobs and conferences, and share ideas within the writing center community. As of 2006, Harris continues to edit the journal (harrism@purdue.edu) with the help of a Managing Editor (wln@purdue.edu) who handles subscriptions and receives manuscripts. Digital versions of the print source are archived and searchable at Purdue's OWL. Although the most recent volumes are not available online, visit <http://owl.english.purdue.edu/wln> for accessible digital copies of back issues.

Chapter 21:
Gail E. Hawisher

(b. 1943)

A prominent researcher in writing technologies, Gail E.
Hawisher has published numerous books and articles detailing
her work in computers and composition, literacy, and feminism
and composition. Hawisher earned her BA (1970) in English
from Augusta College. She completed graduate work in
Linguistics, German, and English (1972) at the University of
Georgia; in German and Linguistics (1975) at the University of
South Carolina; and in Rhetoric, Literature, and Linguistics
(1982) at The Ohio State University. Hawisher received her
PhD (1986) in Composition Studies from UIUC, with an
emphasis in computers and composition.

A former high school English teacher and department head,
Hawisher began her collegiate teaching career at Parkland
College (1982), a community college in Urbana. Since 1985, she
has held various teaching assignments at UIUC, leading up to
her current positions as English professor and founding
director of the Center for Writing Studies. Beyond teaching,
Hawisher has served professionally on CCCC's Committee on
Computers (1987-94), NCTE's Executive Committee (1995-98),
MLA's Advisory Committee on the MLA International

Bibliography (1999-02), and MLA's Committee on Computers and Emerging Technologies (1996-99).

Hawisher's innovative teaching methods have secured her a consistent spot on UIUC's List of Excellent Teachers since 1992. Furthermore, she can claim several awards, such as the Robert Schneider Award for Outstanding Teaching and Service, Department of English, UIUC (2000), the Lynn M. Martin Distinguished Award for Women Faculty, College of Liberal Arts and Sciences, UIUC (2004), and CCCC's Outstanding Technology Innovator Award (2000).

Hawisher has won numerous grants for her research in technology and literacy. She shared an NCTE Research Foundation Grant (2000) with her collaborator Cynthia Selfe for their project "Technological Literacy in America: Tracing the Paths of the Technology-Linkage." Likewise, Hawisher's joint proposal with Patricia Sullivan, "How Do Computers Make a Difference? The Activities of Writing and Teaching Writing in an Electronic Classroom," led to a FIPSE Grant (1989).

Early in her career, Hawisher recognized the potential of computers to revolutionize composition and the way it is taught. She has written extensively about her research in computer-assisted instruction, asynchronous learning networks (ALN), and electronic communication between instructors and students. Along with Selfe, Hawisher has edited several books about computers and composition, including *Passions, Pedagogies, and 21st Century Technologies*, which won a Distinguished Book Award at Computers and Writing (2000). Additionally, Hawisher and Selfe presently co-edit the *Computers and Composition* international academic journal.

In 1990, Hawisher became a pioneer in WAC when she founded the Center for Writing Studies at UIUC. Home to a scholarly community of faculty and graduate students from three affiliated departments (English, Education, and Speech Communication), the Center promotes research and professional development in composition and related areas. Through its professional and technological resources, notable guest lecturers, WAC network, and user-friendly companion Web site, the Center provides academic support and serves as a successful model of collegiality among faculty and students.

In recent years, Hawisher's focus has shifted toward literacy studies as well as feminism and composition. Her recent book with Selfe, *Literate Lives in the Information Age: Narratives of Literacy from the United States* (Erlbaum, 2004), investigates computer-based literacies acquired by Americans during the last quarter of the 20th century. She continues to research digital literacies as well as new technologies and how they affect the teaching of writing. Currently, she is studying the connection between computer gaming and literacy for young women.

Karen Wright

Sources for Biographical Narrative

▶ *Center for Writing Studies*. UIUC. 1990. 28 Jan. 2003 <http://www.english.uiuc.edu/cws/>.

▶ "Gail Hawisher." Department of English Graduate Faculty home page. University of Illinois, Urbana-Champaign. 3 Dec. 2003. 30 July 2006 <www.english.uiuc.edu/facpages/Hawisher.htm>.

▶ Hawisher, Gail. "Re: Comp Leader Grad Project." Email to Karen Wright. 29 Jan. 2004.

Annotated Bibliography

▶ Center for Writing Studies. UIUC. 1990. 28 Jan. 2004 <http://www.english.uiuc.edu/cws/>.

Founded by director Hawisher in 1990, this Web site is home to a scholarly community of faculty and graduate students from three affiliated departments at the UIUC: English, Education, and Speech Communication. Although too many to enumerate here, the links and resources that can be accessed through the site map include sample syllabi, peer workshop guides, assignments, exercises, literary analyses, faculty and graduate student information, archives of presentations hosted by the Center, and online academic journals. One section is devoted to a Writers' Workshop (tutoring facility), which includes online grammar and writing assistance as well as links to the writing centers of other universities across the country.

▶ Hawisher, Gail E. "Content Knowledge Versus Process Knowledge: A False Dichotomy." *On Literacy and Its Teaching: Issues in English Education.* Ed. Gail E. Hawisher and Anna O. Söter. Literacy, Culture, and Learning: Theory and Practice 1. Albany: SUNY P, 1990. 1-18.

Hawisher presents historical trends in the debate between teaching content and teaching process in the areas of literature, composition, and language (grammar). She concludes that adequate preparation of teachers must involve fusing the two emphases. This is a must-read for fans of theory.

▶ Hawisher, Gail E., and Charles Moran. "Electronic Mail and the Writing Instructor." *CE* 55 (1993): 627-43.

Since freshman writing courses often include letter-writing genres, Hawisher and Moran propose a similar rhetoric of email, which would include structure, language/style, conventions, etiquette, and response time. They describe the benefits of a pedagogy that includes email: collaborative projects, classroom bulletin boards, research capability, tele-apprenticeship (student/teacher interaction/collaboration), and equalization of participants who may be reticent in a traditional classroom setting based on their race or gender. The authors caution about the pitfalls of email, such as "flaming" (anonymity-facilitated offensiveness), students' over-accessibility to professors, and increased homework for teachers, but they ultimately conclude that the benefits, combined with the undeniable, irreversible presence of email, justify its inclusion in the writing class.

▶ ---. "Responding to Writing On-Line." *New Directions for Teaching and Learning* 69 (1997): 115-25.

Drawing on their extensive experience with Web-based and Web-assisted classrooms, Hawisher and Moran discuss ground rules and consequences of responding to writing online, including such potential problems as intimacy, response time, and flaming. The benefits, however, include the natural tendency to collaborate in the on-line environment, the diminishing of teacher authority amid a group of other (peer) reader responses, and the successful transference of effective on-line techniques, such as small group conferences and public responses to student writing, to off-line classrooms. This article should be required reading for any instructor desiring to teach all or partly on-line.

▶ Hawisher, Gail E., and Michael A. Pemberton. "The Case for Teacher as Researcher in Computers and Composition Studies." *Writing Instructor* 10 (1991): 77-88.

Hawisher and Pemberton argue that classroom instructors are in a unique position to investigate the effects of computers on writing because of their close connections to students, their ability to regularly observe classroom activities, and their familiarity with classroom dynamics. Furthermore, the authors suggest areas where research is needed: collaboration studies, writing process studies, and studies in pedagogical theory. Instructors with an eye toward publication may find this article particularly useful.

▶ ---. "Writing Across the Curriculum Encounters Asynchronous Learning Networks or WAC Meets UP With ALN." *Journal for Asynchronous Learning Networks* 1.1 (1997). 28 Jan. 2004 <http://www.aln.org/alnweb/journal/issue1/ hawisher.htm>.

Courtesy of a sizable grant, Hawisher and Pemberton, director and assistant director, respectively, of the Center for Writing Studies at UIUC extended their experiments in Asynchronous Learning Networks (ALN), integrating them into writing-intensive courses from various disciplines. Their analysis of the experiment focuses on their two upper-division English courses (one each) and one electrical engineering course, carefully explaining the effectiveness or failure of the strategies the instructors used. The authors conclude that ALNs can potentially enhance interactions between students and instructors, and they offer specific suggestions for their successful implementation.

▶ Hawisher, Gail E., and Cynthia L. Selfe. "The Rhetoric of Technology and the Electronic Writing Class." *CCC* 42 (1991): 55-65.

Amid the enthusiasm surrounding the use of computers in the writing classroom, Hawisher and Selfe caution instructors to think carefully and critically about integrating electronic technology lest teachers continue to exert authoritative power over their students rather than collaborating with them. The authors take positive comments from writing instructors gleaned from professional journals and questionnaires and decode the information by comparing the verbal feedback of teachers with what actually happens in the classroom based on their research (classroom visits). Teachers concerned about promoting student-centered classrooms would be well advised to consider these warnings about perpetuating the traditional authoritarian model when using computers to teach writing.

▶ ---. "Wedding the Technologies of Writing Portfolios and Computers: The Challenges of Electronic Classrooms." *Situating Portfolios: Four Perspectives*. Ed. Kathleen Blake Yancey and Irwin Weiser. Logan, UT: Utah State UP, 1997. 305-21.

Regarding melding computers and portfolios, *electronic portfolios*, Hawisher and Selfe describe the challenges (ever-changing technology, uneven distribution of technology across schools or campuses), the negative consequences (authoritarian pedagogy, continued oppression of women and minority students), and the positive impacts (inherent collaboration, increased creativity). They conclude with a plea for educators to communicate with each other through conferences and workshops to ensure that technology moves education in a thoughtful, positive direction. This article is useful for instructors in computer-based/assisted classrooms or for those considering portfolio assessment.

▶ --- with Brittney Moraski and Melissa Pearson. "Becoming Literate in the Information Age: Cultural Ecologies and the Literacies of Technology." *CCC* 55 (2004): 642-92.

From over 350 literacy narratives they collected, Hawisher and Selfe select two participants (Moraski and Pearson), whose journeys to digital literacy they describe in various contexts—social, educational, cultural, political, economic, familial, historical, and material. From these contexts, the authors construct the idea of *cultural ecology* and assert that equalizing information literacy among diverse populations can only happen when people have access to technology in a variety of overlapping settings, such as school, work, community, and home. Instructors will appreciate the section directed specifically to English, composition, and communication teachers regarding recognizing our own digital illiteracy, accommodating technologically savvy students, and understanding that students come with different cultural ecologies that inform their digital literacies.

▶ Hawisher, Gail E., and Patricia A. Sullivan. "Fleeting Images: Women Visually Writing the Web." *Passions, Pedagogies, and 21st Century Technologies.* Ed. Gail E. Hawisher and Cynthia L. Selfe. Logan: Utah State UP, 1999. 268-91.

Identified by Hawisher as one of her favorite works, this book chapter briefly discusses and dispels the past hope that a textual emphasis on the Internet would produce a more egalitarian environment for online participants, especially for women. In reality, women have been exposed to as much discrimination and harassment online as they are in the real world, but as women become more technologically savvy, they are beginning to effect a positive change through their online representations. Although these considerations are perhaps most useful to instructors who teach Web-based or Web-assisted courses, this glimpse into the female experience could benefit any instructor.

▶ Selfe, Cynthia L., and Gail E. Hawisher. "A Historical Look at Electronic Literacy: Implications for the Education of Technical Communicators." *Journal of Business and Technical Communication* 16 (2002): 231-76.

In response to academic and workplace demands for electronic literacy skills, the authors investigate the acquisition of those skills from 1978 to 2000. Through a listserv and personal interviews, Selfe and Hawisher compiled autobiographies of 55 participants, which they compare and contrast according to age, race, education, and economic background, and conclude that despite inherent socio-economic indicators, the most important factors in acquiring electronic literacy are willingness and desire to learn. Instructors who are considering teaching with technology will find this discussion useful.

Chapter 22:
Douglas D. Hesse

(b. 1956)

Having worked through most aspects of academic English, Doug Hesse has written numerous articles on diverse topics dealing with writing program administration, the place of literary nonfiction in the composition classroom, and essays and narratives. A first-generation college student, Hesse earned his BA (1978) in Honors English from Iowa State University—the same university where he would later earn both his MA (1980) and PhD (1986) in English. Additionally, he graduated from *Zeugnis* (1978), a German summer course at the University of Vienna, Austria. His dissertation, *"The Story in the Essay,"* analyzes the amalgamation of rhetoric, short prose forms, and British Literature from 1800-1914, in order to examine the use of narration as a means of persuasion. His earliest influence into composition studies was a writing class with Carl Klaus at the University of Iowa, which blended composition, creative writing, literary studies, and rhetoric.

Hesse started as an instructor of English at Findlay College in Ohio (1980-83). At Illinois State University, he has filled numerous positions over the span of the last 19 years: director of Writing Programs (1987-97), director of Graduate Studies

(1997-2000), and his most recent positions as director of both the University Honors Program and Center for the Advancement of Teaching. He has also enjoyed numerous opportunities in the broader academic community, serving as Chair of CCCC (2005) and as president of WPA (1999).

Along with his numerous academic appointments, Hesse has garnered several awards for his efforts. A seven-time recipient of Illinois State research grants, he was awarded the University Outstanding Researcher (2002) and Outstanding College Researcher in the Humanities (2002). Additionally, Hesse was named Distinguished Humanities Teacher, Senior Level (2001), and the Illinois Arts Council awarded Hesse a fellowship in nonfiction prose (2000).

An avid reader of nonfiction, Hesse incorporates this pastime in his approach to the classroom. His earliest writings exhibit concerns with the place of nonfiction, but after just a few years of publications, one sees his assimilation of these studies in his approach to composition instruction. As surprisingly diversified as his teaching and administrative appointments have been, Hesse has remained keenly focused on the place and boundaries of nonfiction (academic vs. non-) and their relationship with the composition classroom.

Hesse is currently at work on a pair of books. Forthcoming from Bedford/St. Martin's, *Creating Nonfiction*, co-authored with Becky Bradway, is scheduled for publication in 2007. Hesse is also working on a historical book which will trace creative nonfiction genres from the late 17th century to the present with close attention paid to the relation of these genres to the academy.

Kristopher Blais

Sources for Biographical Narrative

▶ "Douglas D. Hesse." English Dept. home page. Illinois State University. 24 June 2006.

▶ Hesse, Douglas D. "Re: Seeking Information for a Book."
Email to Kristopher Blais. 29 June 2006.

Douglas Hesse recommends these readings for novice composition instructors:

1. Britton, James. *The Development of Writing Abilities 11-18*. London: Macmillan, 1975.
2. Bizzell, Patricia. *Academic Discourse and Critical Consciousness*. Pittsburgh: U of Pittsburgh P, 1992.
3. Connors, Robert. *Composition-Rhetoric: Backgrounds, Theory, and Pedagogy*. Pittsburgh: U of Pittsburgh P, 1997.

Annotated Bibliography

▶ Hesse, Douglas. "Canon and Critical Thinking: An Inductive Teaching Strategy." *English Journal* 78 (1989): 16-22.

Seeking to move composition students beyond familiar proscriptive analyses of literature, Hesse explicitly encourages instructors to problematize the concept of literature through comparisons of the canonical and noncanonical. He provides a very specific sequence of exercises (with ready-made examples) with frequent justifications for his methods. This can be a tremendous source for the beginning composition instructor who may be seeking a way to engage a class by distorting their familiar high school and collegiate approaches to literature.

▶ ---. "Insiders and Outsiders: A Writing Course Heuristic." *Writing Instructor* 7 (1988): 84-94.

Hesse's assertion here is that the two main approaches to using the "discourse community" concept in composition classrooms lack clear benefits. Thereafter he enumerates a third approach in which students form a discourse community around the issue of the same. Through essay ideas already provided, the students focus on the differences between writing to/as insiders to/as outsiders. This essay is typical for Hesse: straightforward, clearly delineated in the introduction, and followed through in the conclusion. All composition instructors should be familiar with this piece even if not for its heuristic.

▶ ---. "Politics and the WPA: Traveling Through and Past Realms of Expertise." *The Writing Program Administrator's Resource*. Ed. Stuart Brown and Theresa Enos. Mahwah, NJ: Erlbaum, 2002. 41-58.

Hesse's articles dealing with Writing Program Administrators (WPAs) lead one to wonder why he ever moved away from it. This illuminating article is Hesse's attempt to aid other WPAs with their own political entanglements. For each of the four arenas in which WPAs must make their way—departmental, institutional, professional, and the public—Hesse includes up to half a dozen specific maxims to minimize frustration and maximize effectiveness.

▶ ---. "Portfolios and Public Discourse: Beyond the Academic/Personal Writing Polarity." *Journal of Teaching Writing* 12.1 (1994): 1-12.

Again in classifying discourse communities, Hesse argues that freshman composition should be a vehicle for students to write, not what they may need in some imagined future class (as WAC heralds would decree), but rather what they will not get to write elsewhere in the academy—what Hesse calls public discourse, or political/deliberative discourse. Though this essay omits specific examples of such writings and is theoretically heavy at times, Hesse's own deliberative style provides a clear outline for easy navigation.

▶ ---. "Portfolio Standards for English 101." *Strategies for Teaching First-Year Composition*. Ed. Duane Roen, et al. Urbana, IL: NCTE, 2002. 422-31.

While composition portfolios are considered to be passé, in theory if not in practice, this rubric prepared for use by English 101 faculty and adopted by the university writing committee at

Illinois State serves as an eloquent yet practical description of the very qualities to which all academic essays should conform. This is a simple read which clearly and precisely describes the characteristics of essays according to grade level. Included are a coversheet and a student checklist for creating individual portfolios.

▶ ---. "The Recent Rise of Literary Nonfiction: A Cautionary Essay." *JAC* 11 (1991): 323-33. Rpt in *Postmodernism and Composition Studies*. Ed. Gary Olson. New York: SUNY P, 1994. 132-42.

With this essay, Hesse argues that it is not enough to have students bounce along through their composition courses writing merely personal essays. Rather, he suggests that the genre itself be examined to know why it has become so popular as of late, and in what ways can it be defined and then enhanced. Though rhetorically deeper and less practically useful than his other essays about teaching; here, the heart of Hesse, the instructor, is clearly evidenced when he ties the discussion to its application: ideally he proposes that "the power we hold out to students [. . .] is the power to be like other essayists, to write like authors their teachers read in serious leisure" (332).

▶ ---. "Saving a Place for Essayistic Literacy." *Passions, Politics, and 21st Century Technologies*. Ed. Gail Hawisher and Cynthia Selfe. Logan: Utah State UP and Urbana, IL: NCTE, 1999. 34-48.

In light of the rise in computer literacy, and therefore computer compositions, Hesse argues that in both the undergraduate curriculum and the larger culture, essay writing should not necessarily remain foremost, but that it should *not* be removed. By examining the history of the meaning of "the essay," Hesse seeks to prove the importance of essayistic literacy. He sets clear landmarks on his way through this argument to keep the reader in place, and ultimately urges his audience to consider what the essay has meant, and how its traditional aspects can be made applicable in a computer driven society.

Chapter 23:
Rebecca Moore Howard

(b. 1946)

After earning her BA (1977) and MA (1979) at West Virginia
University, Rebecca Moore Howard capped her education with
a PhD (1984) in linguistics and literature. While Howard
analyzed the theories of others in her doctoral dissertation,
"Language Philosophy in Composition Theory and Its
Pedagogical Implications for Native and Nonnative Speakers of
English," she now stands as a composition leader with original
theories on authorship, plagiarism, and pedagogy.

Having focused much of her graduate studies on linguistics and
literature, Howard was well equipped to handle the
responsibilities of her first post-graduate position at Colgate
University where she was an associate professor of Writing in
the Department of Interdisciplinary Writing (1984–97) and the
director of the Writing Program (1984-93). Howard also served
in the position of Department Chair (1993-94) before leaving
Colgate in 1997. She spent the next two years as associate
professor of English and director of Composition for the
Department of English at Texas Christian University (1997-
99). In the summer of 1999, Howard taught as a visiting
associate professor for the John S. Knight Writing Program of

Cornell University before taking on her present position as an associate professor of Writing and Rhetoric in the Writing Program at Syracuse University (1999- present) where she has also served as director of the Writing Program and Faculty Chair (2002-03).

Howard names fellow composition and rhetoric theorist Andrea Lunsford and sociologist, intellectual, and social activist Pierre Bourdieu as her influences, reflecting many of their ideas through her research and civic activities respectively. Howard's interests include composition pedagogy, authorship theory, writing program administration, composition history, and stylistics, although she is most recognized for her innovative theories regarding plagiarism.

Recent academic interest in higher education's policies on plagiarism has resulted in an audience for theories Howard fought hard to publish for over ten years. While many journals refused to consider the theorist's early work because of her focus and innovative ideas on plagiarism, Howard now publishes regularly and addresses audiences at dozens of conferences each year often moving beyond merely defining plagiarism to tackle the complex and awkward issue of educators' responsibilities relative to providing students with the knowledge necessary to avoid becoming plagiarists. Howard admits that "an abiding interest in and opposition to the ways in which advanced literacy instruction preserves and naturalizes social hierarchies" facilitates her work. Not surprisingly, this "opposition" can be divisive, even beyond the walls of academia. This point was made abundantly clear when Howard's article "Forget about Policing Plagiarism: Just Teach", originally titled "Plagiarism, Policing, Pedagogy" and written for an academic audience, was picked up by the popular press. The press, according to Howard, misrepresented her ideas, which led to a small but vocal uprising from the community.

Howard continues her work on plagiarism today while also focusing her attention on the changing definitions of text and, in consideration of the Internet and other advances in technology, the connections between text and information literacy. Never one to shun difficult explorations, Howard began a first-hand examination of technology and learning when, in November 2004, she began her own blog, inviting commentary from scholars and students alike.

Kirsten L. Boatwright and Summer O'Neal

Sources for Biographical Narrative

▶ Eodice, Michele. "Plagiarism, Pedagogy, and Controversy: A Conversation with Rebecca Moore Howard." *Issues in Writing* 13.1 (2002): 6-26.

▶ Howard, Rebecca Moore. Home page. The Writing Program at Syracuse University. 1 Oct. 2004. 12 Oct. 2004 <http://wrt-howard.syr.edu>.

▶ ---. Email interview. 24 Oct. 2004.

▶ ---. Email interview. 13 Nov. 2004.

▶ ---. Telephone interview. 8 Nov. 2004.

Rebecca Moore Howard recommends these readings for novice composition instructors:

1. Jamieson, Sandra. "Composition Readers and the Construction of Identity." *Writing in Multicultural Settings*. Ed. Carol Severino, Juan C. Guerra, and Johnnella E. Butler. New York: MLA, 1997. 150-71.
2. Gilyard, Keith. "African American Contributions to Composition Studies." *CCC* 50 (1999): 626-44.
3. Yancey, Kathleen Blake. "Looking Back as We Look Forward: Historicizing Writing Assessment." *CCC* 50 (1999): 483-503.

Annotated Bibliography

► Howard, Rebecca Moore. "The Binaries of Authorship."
Authorship in Composition Studies. Ed. Tracy Hamler
Carrick and Rebecca Moore Howard. Boston: Thomson
Wadsworth, 2006. 1-12.

Howard's opening chapter offers a review and discussion of the
terms student, writer, and author as well as the connotations
generally applied to each. The author/editor includes a
discussion of ownership and the various ways students,
instructors, and administrators often distort the concept as best
suits their purposes. Instructors looking to start passionate
discussions of authorship in the classroom will find this text a
guaranteed combustible.

► ---. "Collective Pedagogy." *A Guide to Composition
Pedagogies*. Ed. Gary Tate, Amy Rupiper, and Kurt
Schick. New York: Oxford UP, 2001. 54-70.

Howard investigates the benefits and problems of collaboration,
especially in the classroom, noting its difficulty for students to
document and the belief many instructors hold that
collaboration represents an act of plagiarism. Although Howard
does not address solutions, nor advocate or oppose
collaboration, her writing invites readers to join the discussion
and make their own decision.

► ---. "Contextualist Stylistics: Breaking Down the Binaries in
Sentence-Level Pedagogy." *Refiguring Prose Style:
Possibilities for Writing Pedagogy*. Ed. T.R Johnson and
Tom Pace. Logan, UT: Utah State UP, 2005. 42-56.

While Howard erects her thesis on the idea that inherent in
critical value are culturally defined notions of value, her focus
in this historical survey is the status afforded rhetorical style.
Through her analysis of theories crucial to shifts in composition
pedagogy, Howard concludes that sentence-level writing
instruction aimed at rhetorical style is possible. Although she
offers no specific methods for accomplishing this harmony in

this essay, she does note essays, including her own, where readers can find explicit techniques. Students will find this history invaluable, and composition instructors attempting to negotiate today's chasm between sentence-level instruction and textual teaching will find Howard's contribution encouraging.

▶ ---. "Culture and Academic Discourse: Cultivating Authority in Language and Text." Academic Integrity and Plagiarism Seminar. Texas A&M University, College Station. 16 Apr. 2004.

As keynote speaker to Texas A&M's Academic Integrity Week, Howard puts a recognizable face on the plagiarist as she recalls her personal involvement with administering plagiarism policies and underscores the importance of the individual in each case. The address stands as a reminder to students about the risks of plagiarism and to faculty and administrators about the responsibilities beyond identification and enforcement. Most readers are apt to recognize themselves or someone they know in Howard's address, and the result is an engaging piece that requires each person to reassess their own knowledge and beliefs regarding plagiarism.

▶ ---. "Definitions and Epistemologies of Plagiarism." Seminar for the faculty of Bates, Bowdoin, and Colby Colleges: "Engaging Plagiarism: Theory and Practice." Bowdoin College, Brunswick, Maine. 5 Mar. 2004. <http://wrt-howard.syr.edu/presentations.html>.

Howard presents different aspects of plagiarism but also argues that citing the definitions of plagiarism alone does not solve the problem for students. She discusses three epistemologies or approaches to plagiarism: detection and punishment; legislating and enforcing; and a pedagogical basis. The presentation is intriguing, especially the discussion of a patchwriting incident that led to Howard's interest in plagiarism, and novice as well as seasoned instructors will find the presentation beneficial.

▶ ---. "Deriving Backwriting from Writing Back." *Writing Center Journal* 24.2 (2004): 3-18.

Howard describes "backwriting" and the post-colonial concept of writing back in terms of the writing center. While providing clear definitions of these terms, the author does not describe how they function in the writing center. Troubling to many readers will be the definition of writing centers as "no place for 'real' faculty" (5), however, Howard bases much of her backwriting theory on the idea that an absence of academic authorities enables the work most often done in writing centers. Faculty, writing center administrators, and tutors will find this work informative and heartening.

▶ ---. "Grammar: Irrefutable, Irreconcilable Differences." *Reflections in Writing* 23 (2004). 19 Oct. 2004 <http://wrt.syr.edu/pub/reflections/23/howard.html>.

Howard proffers eight theories regarding grammar, the first seven supported through the epigraphs of others, and addresses the unenviable position instructors find themselves in when students, administrators, and professional organizations make demands regarding sentence-level instruction. The author points out that, while solutions may be difficult, it is possible to address teaching at the sentence level. The style applied to this topic offers a fun read while also offering interesting commentary on the necessity of writing inside the box.

▶ ---. "The Great Wall of African American Vernacular English in the American College Classroom." *JAC* 16 (1996): 265-84.

Howard centers her writing on a college course that investigates the usage of African American Vernacular English. As the instructor, she discovers that due to its relaxed tone, not all African Americans take this language style seriously, but makes an argument for AAVE's importance in college education, especially when studying African American literature. Literature instructors as well as those interested in linguistics will find this article enlightening.

► ---. "Plagiarisms, Authorships, and the Academic Death
    Penalty." *CE* 57 (1995): 788-806.

Howard theorizes that academia may too harshly punish
students who plagiarize. She reminds her audience that
ownership of one's own ideas is a relatively new concept and
suggests questions for consideration regarding plagiarism. This
article is vital to an understanding of Howard's definition of
plagiarism, recognizing plagiarism, and creating a personal
technique for approaching the subject and instances of
intentional violations.

► ---. "Selling Out the Writing Program." Council of Writing
    Program Administrators. Park City, UT. 11 July 2002.
    <http://wrt-howard.syr.edu/Papers/WPA2002.html>.

In the written version of Howard's presentation at the WPA
conference, the theorist discusses the need for administrators of
writing programs to include multimedia rhetoric in their efforts
to educate others about their programs. Howard details the
inclusion of a video presentation and human interaction
stations to educate visitors to her university about the writing
program and suggests that, although difficult to create,
multimedia is one way to guarantee inclusion in university
discussions about writing programs and instruction. Writing
center administrators will find this presentation filled with
helpful hints for making the most of their next budget
presentation.

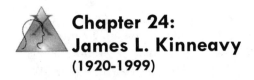

Chapter 24:
James L. Kinneavy
(1920-1999)

Born in Edgewater, Colorado, in 1920, James L. Kinneavy demonstrated his affinity for educating at an early age. At 15, he joined the Christian Brothers, the teaching order within the Catholic Church, and there began a long and illustrious career in education. Kinneavy earned his BA (1942) in English at the College of Santa Fe. Afterwards, he worked as an elementary teacher in Bernalillo, New Mexico, and then he moved on to teach math, sciences, music, languages, and English in secondary schools in Louisiana. Kinneavy returned to college in 1950 and earned his MA and PhD (1956) at the Catholic University of America.

Before he completed his PhD, Kinneavy was made head of the Division of Humanities at the College of Santa Fe. He taught at Western State College of Colorado (1958-63) before moving on to the UT-Austin, where he spent the rest of his career (1963-96) teaching in the Division of Rhetoric and Composition as well as the Departments of English and Curriculum and Instruction. Kinneavy also actively participated in administration, serving as the director of Freshman English (1975-82) and as interim director of lower-division English (1990-92).

Kinneavy was appointed Jane and Roland Blumberg Centennial Professor (1983), a position he maintained until his official retirement in 1990 though he would return to teach as he was needed up until 1996. In 1980, St. Edward's University awarded Kinneavy an honorary doctorate in humane letters in appreciation for helping shape its writing curriculum, and he was honored with the CCCC's Exemplar Award for his contributions to rhetoric and composition (1995). That year, he also received the Pro Bene Meritis Award from the College of Liberal Arts at UT-Austin.

Despite his display of a broad range of interests from ethics to WAC, classical rhetoric to elementary language arts education, rhetorician Timothy Crusius defines Kinneavy's lifelong focus as "the retrieval of the liberal arts tradition within a semiotic framework with practical intent," or, put simply, "the yoking together of history, theory, and practice" (352). This summation well describes Kinneavy's seminal work, his 1971 book, *A Theory of Discourse: The Aims of Discourse* which became the foundation of English programs for Texas and Wisconsin. At its core, the work builds upon Aristotle's rhetorical triangle in order to more clearly depict the varying purposes available to an author depending upon whether his or her focus is on the text, the encoder, the decoder, or reality. Kinneavy is careful to subordinate the modes in favor of emphasizing the writer's aims, aims that he makes clear are dependent upon the audience of the rhetoric, thereby foreshadowing the post-process movement.

Kristopher Blais

Sources for Biographical Narrative

▶ Crusius, Timothy W. "James L. Kinneavy." *Encyclopedia of Rhetoric and Composition*. Ed. Theresa Enos. New York: Garland, 1996. 376.
▶ Faigley, Lester. "Report of the Memorial Resolution Committee for James L. Kinneavy." *CCC* 51 (2000): 154-55.

Annotated Bibliography

▶ Crusius, Timothy W. *Discourse: A Critique and Synthesis of Major Theories*. New York: MLA, 1989.

Though difficult to read at times and densely referential, this work performs a necessary role as a critical examination of several theories of rhetoric. For the student seeking to read criticism of Kinneavy's theories, experiencing the soundness of Crusius's discussion proves indispensable. Most of his

Kinneavy chapter deals with the concept of aim, which is central to Kinneavy's seminal work. Crusius's primary concern with Kinneavy lies in the latter's adherence to structuralism.

▶ Kinneavy, James L., John Q. Cope, and J. W. Campbell. *Aims and Audiences in Writing*. Dubuque, IA: Kendall/Hunt, 1976.

This resource strongly supports Kinneavy's theories of language and discourse by providing chapters based upon six primary aims: persuading audiences, exploring problems, proving a thesis, conveying information, making poems and stories, and expressing oneself. Each chapter introduces a particular aim followed by numerous examples and an analysis of the aim's construction before concluding with a liberal amount of exercises covering both analysis and composition. Even without the detailed examples, this book is a tremendous resource for the assignments alone.

▶ Kinneavy, James L. "The Basic Aims of Discourse." *CCC* 20 (1969): 297-304.

This essay captures Kinneavy's primary theory of discourse. Included are two graphs that serve as tremendous sources for discussion and thought. The first plots the standpoints of great thinkers in the area of rhetoric (Aristotle to Bühler, Jakobson, and Kinneavy) and the relation of their terms to Kinneavy's own. The second lays out his modification to Aristotle's rhetorical triangle. Specifically, Kinneavy renames the primary points and lists examples of how a focus on one or another demonstrates a bent toward particular genres and purposes.

▶ Kinneavy, James L., and Catherine R. Eskin. "*Kairos* in Aristotle's *Rhetoric*." *Written Communication* 11 (1998): 131-42.

This article argues the importance of the word *kairos* as it is used in Aristotle's *Rhetoric*. Kinneavy translates the word as "the right or opportune time to do something, or right measure" (132). Representative of Kinneavy's concern with classical concepts of rhetoric, there is little of use to the composition instructor as the implementation of the idea lies beyond the scope of most freshman English students. However, teaching appropriateness and moderation make useful goals for instructors.

▶ Kinneavy, James L. Interview with Roger Thompson. "*Kairos* Revisited." Virginia Military Institute. Aug. 1998. 6 Oct. 2003 <http://academics.vmi.edu/ENG_rt/ kairos_revisited.html>.

Roger Thompson, working on his dissertation involving *kairos* and American literature, interviewed Kinneavy on the importance of this word and its implications. This theory of the opportune time to do something with the right measure serves to guide Kinneavy through thoughts on rhetorical theory and practice, politicization of the origins of the word, and ethics. This interview does a phenomenal job integrating the whole body of Kinneavy's thoughts and studies.

▶ ---. "The Process of Writing: A Philosophical Base in Hermeneutics." *JAC* 7 (1987): 219-30.

Kinneavy begins this essay praising the inherent focus that the process approach to composition yields to students, calling it one of the two most important innovations in the field of composition. However, Kinneavy speaks out against some of the weaker tendencies he sees such as the too frequent neglect and disregard of the product and a narrowness of conception where he accuses writers such as Emig, Macrorie, Flower and Hayes, and Elbow of taking too narrow a view of the process of writing.

▶ ---. *A Theory of Discourse: The Aims of Discourse.* 1971. New York: Norton, 1980.

No doubt Kinneavy's crowning achievement in the area of composition and rhetoric, *A Theory of Discourse* embellishes the rhetorical triangle to support his notions that discourse is always purposeful and that the purpose is directly related to a text's emphasis on the encoder (expressive), decoder (persuasive), signal (literary), or reality (referential). This book, an outgrowth of his earlier essay, "The Basic Aims of Discourse," allows him to add a great many examples to support his divisions and the uses of discourse.

▶ ---. "Translating Theory into Practice in Teaching Composition: A Historical View and a Contemporary View." *Essays on Classical Rhetoric and Modern Discourse.* Ed. Robert J. Connors, Lisa S. Ede, and Andrea A. Lunsford. Carbondale, IL: SIUP, 1984. 69-81.

In this brief article, Kinneavy constructs an intensive analysis of three classical thinkers and the application of their epistemologies to their rhetoric from Plato's focus on *theoria*, a level of certainty in knowledge; Isocrates' *praxis*, emphasizing exercises and a preference for probability over certainty; and Aristotle's synthesis of the two. This discussion of ancient pedagogies is strongly supported with a series of figures demonstrating the application of each method to composition. In fact, it is difficult to understand the differences apart from these figures.

▶ ---. "Writing Across the Curriculum." *ADE Bulletin* 76 (1983): 14-21.

Described by Kinneavy as the second of the two most important innovations in the field of composition, this concept encapsulates two notions of practicality. First, he sees the inherent benefit in writing-intensive courses in all departments where the instructor is an expert in the discipline, knowing both its genres and vocabulary. Second, he sees the importance of English trained instructors teaching students of all majors in order to impart a greater sense of nuance and for opening a large academic conversation. As with his other essays, this one shares Kinneavy's straight-forward approach and language.

► Odell, Lee. "Teachers of Composition and Needed Research in Discourse Theory." *CCC* 30 (1979): 39-45.

Odell's captivating article addresses two troublesome aspects of Kinneavy's work: it is based primarily on examinations of written products over writers' processes, and when analyzing a written work, it does not often address the writer's reasoning. Primarily, Odell is concerned that an examination of a product reveals too little about the writing process. Odell proposes methods by which teachers/rhetoricians/researchers study student answers to the question of what reasons they give for the choices they make. This is a tremendous essay not only for the subject but for the questions it asks.

Chapter 25:
Ilona Leki

(b. 1947)

As a leader in researching second language learners, Ilona Leki is best known for her analyses of second language pedagogical theories and practices as well as contributing to ESL studies by promoting the fusion of evolving linguistic and composition theories with evolving practices. Having served as the director of the Self-Instructional Language Program in Asian Studies at the University of Tennessee from 1978 to 1982, Leki has been the director of the University of Tennessee's English as a Second Language (ESL) Program since 1980, and she also serves as chair of the Interdisciplinary Linguistics Program.

After pursuing both a BA (1968) and an MA (1970) in French language studies at the University of Illinois, Leki completed her PhD (1974), also at Illinois, in philosophy and French literature. Leki continued her studies at Washington University (St. Louis), Georgetown University (Washington D.C.), and at the TESOL Summer Institute in Barcelona, Spain. Her teaching experience includes course instruction in French, English as a Foreign Language (Centro Colombo American, Medellin, Colombia), and English at Lycèe de Saint-Cloud, Paris. With additional experience in translation for government services, computer-based language instruction, and adult literacy instruction, Leki has developed a keen and dynamic interest in teaching composition to students who are second language learners (L2).

Leki has received numerous honors and awards: she was twice nominated for the University of Tennessee's National Alumni Association Outstanding Teacher Award (2001, 1999), received the Tennessee TESOL award for best conference presentation in the Higher Education category (1999), and also received the prestigious TESOL/Newberry House Distinguished Research Award (1996). Leki has also been the recipient of multiple Hodges Research Grants (1991, 1995, 1996, University of Tennessee Department of English), as well as a Fulbright Grant for travel to Brazil (1997).

In addition to Leki's service on many professional boards relating to second language learning, such as the Newbury/TESL Distinguished Research Award Committee (1998-99) and both the *TESOL Journal* and *TESOL Quarterly* editorial boards, she is the founder and co-editor, along with Tony Silva, of the primary academic journal for second language composition studies, *Journal of Second Language Writing*.

Because Leki's research focuses on second language learners and writing English for Academic Purposes (EAP), she has published extensively on topics related to the intersections of linguistic theory, pedagogical practices, and the real-world experiences of students who find themselves at those junctures. Representative articles include "Cross-talk: ESL Issues and Contrastive Rhetoric," in *Writing in Multicultural Settings* (MLA, 1997) and "Broadening the Perspective of Mainstream Composition Studies: Some Thoughts from the Disciplinary Margins" with Silva and Joan Carson in *Written Communication* (1997). She has also authored texts aimed at aiding instructors of second language learners such as *Academic Writing: Exploring Processes and Strategies* (Cambridge), *Understanding ESL Writers: A Guide for Teachers* (Boynton/Cook Publishers 1992), and *Academic Writing* (St. Martin's 1989).

Elizabeth McDaniel

Sources for Biographical Narrative

▶ "Ilona Leki." English Dept. home page. University of
    Tennessee . 20 Nov. 2004
    <http://web.utk.edu/~english/gf_leki.php>.

▶ Leki, Ilona. "About the Editors." *On Second Language
    Writing.* 10 Nov. 2004
    <web.ics.purdue.edu/~silvat/jslw/editors.html>.

▶ Leki, Ilona. Email to Elizabeth McDaniel. 4 Nov. 2004.

▶ Washington Area Teachers of English to Speakers of Other
    Languages 2003 Fall Convention home page.
    WATESOL Fall Convention 10 nov. 2004
    <http://www.watesol.org/Convention%202003/keynote.html>

Ilona Leki recommends these readings for novice composition instructors:

1. Casanave, Christine Pearson. *Controversies in Second
   Language Writing: Dilemmas and Decisions in Research
   and Instruction.* Ann Arbor: U of Michigan P, 2003.
2. ---. *Writing Games: Multicultural Case Studies of
   Academic Literacy Practices inHigher Education.*
   Mahwah, NJ: Erlbaum, 2002.
3. Hyland, Ken. *Second Language Writing.* Cambridge:
   Cambridge UP, 2003.

Annotated Bibliography

▶ Leki, Ilona. "Coaching From the Margins: Issues in Written
    Response." Ed. Barbara Kroll. *Second Language
    Writing: Research Insights for the Classroom.* New
    York: Cambridge UP, 1990. 57-68.

In this article, Leki offers valuable suggestions for written feedback to student writers. Leki argues that previous studies on teacher responses have been limited due to the lack of analysis of the ongoing dialogues that take place between students and instructors. She promotes using a more holistic approach that provides for the consideration of classroom contexts and procedures. This article supplies accessible food for thought to those considering a thorough examination of their teaching practices.

▶ ---. "Coping Strategies of ESL Students in Writing Tasks across the Curriculum. *TESOL Quarterly* 29 (1995): 235-60.

By following the experiences of five English as a Second Language (ESL) students in their university courses, Leki identifies a variety of coping strategies which students use to satisfy, or sometimes escape, the requirements of their instructors. The study describes strategies, such as intentionally misinterpreting assignments, avoidance, and the ways which students seek out assistance and who they seek it from. Overall, this article sheds much needed light on the real practices of some second language learners and points to important areas of concern to students that may need greater attention from second language educators.

▶ ---. "Cross-talk: ESL Issues and Contrastive Rhetoric." Ed. Carol Severino, Juan C. Guerra, and Johnnella E. Butler. *Writing in Multicultural Settings: Research and Scholarship in Composition.* New York: MLA, 1997. 234-44.

This article recognizes the ways that contrastive rhetoric allows for differences of expectations for second language students' writing as well as the degree to which it may be limiting. While Leki promotes an awareness of contrastive rhetorical theories, she also warns against allowing it to dictate expectations for particular students. Critical of the ideological implications of imposing predetermined, and often prejudicial, expectations of students, Leki promotes the use of contrastive rhetoric to study the very particular responses of students in certain circumstances.

▶ ---. "Good Writing: I Know It When I See It." Ed. Diane
  Belcher and George Braine. *Academic Writing in a
  Second Language: Essays on Research and Pedagogy.*
  Norwood, NJ: Ablex, 1995. 23-46.

This very interesting, and eyebrow-raising, study describes the
practices of both second language teachers' and students'
practices concerning the evaluation of writing. Twenty students
were asked to rank essays, and 29 instructors were asked to do
the same. The highly varied and inconsistent results reveal the
lack of consensus, and perhaps confidence, that both
instructors and students maintain about writing standards.
The data and the references to texts used in the ranking
provide a clear picture of the circumstances of the study and
explanations are thorough.

▶ ---. Introduction: "Accessing Communities and Disciplines
  through L2 Writing Programs." Ed. Ilona Leki.
  *Academic Writing Programs: Case Studies in TESOL
  Practice.* Alexandria, VA: TESOL Publications, 2001.
  1-4.

In her introduction to this casebook of TESOL practices, Leki
advocates teaching second language writing as a means rather
than an end in order to fully integrate the language skills
necessary to succeed in an academic setting as well as other
social environments. By merging high quality content with
challenging exercises, such as long-term projects that stimulate
the intellect, Leki asserts that students will be better served so
that they may engage competently and effectively in various
arenas.

▶ ---. "Living Through College Literacy: Nursing in a Second
  Language." *Written Communication* 20 (2003): 81-98.

As she does in other publications, Leki provides a case study of
a Chinese nursing student who is struggling to learn academic
English. Leki demonstrates how the student's experiences in
her discipline, and the writing demands specifically, contribute
to her educational experience in a more direct and relevant way
than academic writing courses or exercises. The student's need

for discipline-related knowledge of practices provides a reminder to instructors of L2 writers that there are great demands yet to be met while in the writing classroom.

► ---. "A Narrow Thinking System: Non-Native English Speaking Students in Group Work Projects across the Curriculum." *TESOL Quarterly* 35 (2001): 39-67.

In this article, Leki traces the experiences of two Non-native English speaking (NNES) students as they partake in group projects assigned in university-level courses. While collaborative learning is often touted as highly beneficial to students, Leki aims to remind instructors of the potential drawbacks of using such projects with NNES students who often find themselves deterred from fulfilling their duties adequately and effectively due to social relationships that develop between students.

► ---. "Reciprocal Themes in ESL Reading and Writing." Ed. Tony Silva and Paul Kei Matsuda. *Landmark Essays on ESL Writing*. Mahwah, NJ: Erlbaum, 1993. 173-90.

Leki asserts here the importance of merging the reading and writing skills of second language learners in order to provide the most effective learning opportunity to these students. Arguing that the teaching practices of ESL reading and ESL writing are often not in accord with each other, Leki uses pedagogical theories, including cognitive and social epistemic, to promote a system of practices that allow for meaning making rather than product development.

► ---. "Research Insights on Second Language Writing Instruction." ERIC Bulletin, CAL EDO-FL 3 (2004): 6.

In this accessible read aimed at generating more valuable classroom experiences for L2 writers, Leki advocates a re-examination of L2 writing programs in the higher educational system. Based on her research, Leki argues that second language writers, like many native writers, have expectations that must be met in order for writing classes to prove effective: classes should facilitate more efficient processes and writing should serve an academic purpose. Because of the L2 writers' association of writing with stress, Leki promotes projects where writing is the means rather than an end of classroom curriculum. This enables students to develop ideas as they develop the skills to express those ideas.

▶ Silva, Tony, and Ilona Leki. "Family Matters: The Influence of Applied Linguistics and Composition Studies on Second-Language Writing—Past, Present, and Future." *Modern Language Journal* 88 (2004): 1-13.

This article provides an excellent, but highly academic, genealogy of second language studies' influences: applied linguistics and composition studies. After briefly tracing the histories of rhetoric and linguistics, the authors focus on the ways that applied linguistics and composition studies have created internal strife within second language studies due to theoretical tensions and operational differences. Leki and Silva suggest that second language studies should develop its own distinct position in the academy, a middle ground, just as other cross-disciplinary studies have successfully accomplished.

Chapter 26:
Neal Lerner

(b. 1960)

Co-author of *The Allyn & Bacon Guide to Peer Tutoring*, Neal
Lerner is a leader in writing center assessment, Writing Across
the Curriculum (WAC), and history of composition. Lerner
earned his BA (1982) in American Literature from SUNY,
Purchase, his MA (1989) in English and Creative Writing from
San Jose State University, and his EdD (1996) in Literacy,
Language, and Cultural Studies from Boston University School
of Education, with an emphasis in writing center theory.

Lerner began his teaching career at San Jose State University
where, in addition to his one-to-one teaching in the writing
center (1986-90), he worked as the assistant to the composition
director (1986-88) and the computer network manager (1988-
90). After completion of his MA, he accepted a position as TA
(1994-95) at Boston University (BU) and as Senior Writing
Fellow in the BU Writing Center. Following completion of his
PhD, Lerner joined the faculty of the Massachusetts College of
Pharmacy and Allied Health Sciences (MCP) where he served
as the Writing Center Coordinator (1996-97), Writing Programs
Coordinator (1997-02), and Coordinator of First-Year
Experience (1999-02). Throughout the period between 1989 and

1997, Lerner also served as a composition instructor at his various institutions. Lerner currently lectures in WAC at MIT where he supports communication-intensive classes and has developed FYC classes focusing on literacy, rhetoric, and technology.

Beyond teaching, Lerner has served professionally on IWCA's Executive Board, Northeast Writing Center Association's Executive Board, Writing Centers Research Project, and CCCC's Research Committee. Lerner was one of eight invited leaders at the first Summer Institute for Writing Center Directors and Professionals at the University of Wisconsin, Madison (2003) and served as co-chair for the second Summer Institute at Clark University in Worcester, Massachusetts (2004).

Lerner's research has earned him numerous awards: the IWCA's Outstanding Scholarship Award (2003), the Learning Assistance Association of New England Outstanding Research Publication (2001), the National Writing Centers Association Outstanding Scholarship Award (1999, 2000), and the Boston University School of Education Graduate Scholar Award (1993-94). His dedication to student mentoring earned him three awards from the MCP Student Government Association for Student Organization Advisor of the Year (1999-01).

Lerner has garnered several grants for his research, including the dean of Humanities Arts and Social Sciences Faculty Development Grant at MIT for the last four years (2003-06) and the IWCA Research Grant (2001, 2004).

Throughout his career, Lerner has worked closely with professors and students in the sciences, administering writing centers and WAC programs. Also, he continues to further writing center historical research and writing center assessment. In addition to co-editing *The Writing Center Journal* with Beth Boquet, Lerner has presented at over 30 conferences and published 16 journal articles, ten book chapters, two essays, and two short stories.

Lerner exhibits his dedication to writing center work through his willingness to conduct workshops for writing center administrators, faculty, and students. He has conducted workshops at the IWCA Annual Conference (2002, 2005 with Mary Wislocki), CCCC's (1996-99, 2000 with Paula Gillespie, and 2004), and the NWCA Conference (1997, 1999, 2000).

Currently, Lerner's book chapter "Situated Learning in the Writing Center" is due to appear in the forthcoming publication *Marginal Words, Marginal Work? Tutoring the Academy in the Work of Writing Centers,* and *CCC* will be publishing his article "Rejecting the Remedial Brand: The Rise and Fall of the Dartmouth Writing Clinic." In addition, he is working with Beth Boquet on a book chapter entitled "Moving Past North" and individually on an article entitled "Laboratory Lessons for Writing and Science."

Tanya McLaughlin

 Sources for Biographical Narrative

▶ Lerner, Neal. "Re: Bio for New Book." Email to Tanya McLaughlin. 21 June 2006.

▶ Lerner, Neal. "Re: Bio for New Book." Email to Tanya McLaughlin. 4 July 2006.

▶ "Neal Lerner: Brief Bio Statement." Norman H. Ott Memorial Writing Center, Department of English home page. Marquette University. 30 June 2006 <www.marquette.edu/~writing/NealLerner.htm>.

Neal Lerner recommends these readings for novice composition instructors:

1. Boquet, Elizabeth. *Noise from the Writing Center*. Logan, UT: Utah State UP, 2002.
2. Ede, Lisa. "Writing as a Social Process." *Writing Center Journal* 16 (1989): 111-30.
3. North, Stephen. "Idea of a Writing Center." *CE* 46 (1984): 433-46.

Annotated Bibliography

▶ Gillespie, Paula, and Neal Lerner. *The Allyn & Bacon Guide to Peer Tutoring*. 2nd ed. Boston: Allyn & Bacon, 2003.

Lerner and Gillespie walk peer tutors through every aspect of tutoring sessions from introductions to goodbyes, intermingling theory, practical advice, and mock sessions. Topics include the purpose of peer tutoring, the writing process, the tutoring process, cultural influences on tutoring, the value of observing sessions, note-taking during sessions, reading in the center, working with ESL students, discourse analysis, online tutoring, writing center ethics, and dealing with difficult sessions. This must-have work offers new tutors a top notch how-to guide and an invaluable reading list.

▶ Lerner, Neal. "Choosing Beans Wisely." *Writing Lab Newsletter* 26.1 (2001): 1-5.

A follow-up to his 1997 article, this article examines the flaws in his earlier study, particularly the weak correlation between SAT verbal scores and performance in FYC courses, the inability of grades to indicate writing ability, and an incorrect assumption that students would receive the same grades from different professors. Lerner continues to call for quantitative research methods but warns that such research must be statistically and logically sound. This article, combined with his earlier article, offer essential advice for writing center administrators.

▶ ---. "Confessions of a First-Time Writing Center Director." *Writing Center Journal* 21.1 (2000): 29-48.

Winner of the 2000 NWCA Outstanding Scholarship Award, this article explores the attempts of writing center directors to obtain professional status and respect within writing programs, desiring to be seen not just as administrators but also as teachers and scholars. Lerner fears that the divide among writing center directors who have such status within their institutions and those who do not will increase over time and make achieving such status more difficult for those still struggling, believing the answer lies in furthering writing center research and theory. This article presents a frank look at the role of writing centers within the institution through the inclusion of ads for writing center directors and Lerner's personal journal entries.

▶ ---. "Counting Beans and Making Beans Count." *Writing Lab Newsletter* 22.1 (1997): 1-4.

This well-known article recounts Lerner's initial efforts to track the effectiveness of his writing center using SAT scores, first semester grades, and writing center attendance statistics. Lerner asserts that in order to survive, writing centers must be willing to use quantitative research methods to produce statistical results for institutional administrators. Although Lerner's study contains serious statistical flaws addressed in later works on assessment, the theory behind the study is sound and a worthwhile read for writing center professionals charged with assessing writing center effectiveness.

▶ ---. "Drill Pads, Teaching Machines, and Programmed Texts: Origins of Instructional Technology in Writing Centers." *Wiring the Writing Center*. Ed. Eric H. Hobson. Logan: Utah State UP, 1998. 119-36.

Winner of the 1999 NWCA Outstanding Scholarship Award, this book chapter examines the role of instructional technology, particularly drill and practice methods, teaching machines, and programmed learning, in writing centers, laboratories, and clinics over the course of writing center history. Although Lerner admits technology can offer substantial assistance to writing centers, he remains skeptical of the overuse of technology in writing centers and agrees that a tutorless center does not adequately meet student needs. Lerner offers writing center professionals an in-depth, well-researched look at theories behind the use of such technologies and an honest look at their appropriate uses in writing centers.

► ---. "Punishment and Possibility: Representing Writing
      Centers, 1939-1970." *Composition Studies* 31.2 (2003):
      53-72.

Breaking down writing center history into four periods (1939-
49, 1950-59, 1960-70, and post-1970), Lerner examines the
tensions between the writing center as punishment for
underprepared students and the writing center as possibility
for the improvement of all writers, which he asserts define both
writing center history and its present day-to-day existence.
Lerner argues that trends in one direction or the other reflect
trends in composition theory, pressures of increased
enrollment, and budgetary constraints and that the pre-1970
writing clinics and labs were far more than simple fix-it shops.
Similar to many of Lerner's historical works, this article
challenges the misconception that writing centers had a bleak
history and a hopeful future, presenting a far more complex
and complete view of writing center reality.

► ---. "Searching for Robert Moore." *Writing Center Journal*
      22.1 (2001): 9-32.

In this article, Lerner challenges the tendency of writing center
professionals to ignore the early history of writing centers and
the belief that writing centers before 1970 were nothing more
than remedial, fix-it shops based on Robert Moore's 1950 article
in *CE*. Lerner argues that Moore's Writing Clinic at UIUC,
which reflected trends in both UIUC policies and the field of
composition, exceeded its mission statement in order to meet
student needs and serves as a survival story in writing center
history. Lerner's article offers an insightful examination of
Robert Moore's work and writing centers history prior to 1970.

► ---. "The Teacher-Student Writing Conference and the Desire
      for Intimacy." *CE* 68 (2005): 186-208.

Lerner presents research regarding the popularity of teacher-
student writing conferences in the 20th century, examining the
constant struggle between the desire to teach and the
constraints of administrative reality, and addressing how such
attitudes have shaped writing center theory. Lerner explores
the interaction and influence of various historical trends,
including the relationship between prevalent theoretical views

in composition theory, increases in enrollment, preparedness of students, and teacher workloads. Based on extensive research, this article is an interesting look at the past of composition theory.

▶ ---. "Writing Center Assessment: Searching for the 'Proof' of Our Effectiveness." *The Center Will Hold: Critical Perspectives on Writing Center Scholarship.* Ed. Michael A. Pemberton and Joyce Kinkead. Logan, UT: Utah State UP, 2003. 58-73.

Winner of the 2003 IWCA Outstanding Scholarship Award, this book chapter examines writing center research and assessment, calling for collaboration across institutions and more advanced quantitative research. Lerner outlines the eight-part assessment framework of Upcraft and Schul (2000) and the ways in which writing centers can successfully employ each aspect. His inclusion of his personal successes and mishaps in quantitative writing center research and assessment provide a practical framework for this follow up to his "Counting Beans and Making Beans Count" and "Counting Beans Wisely."

▶ Lerner, Neal, and Eric H. Hobson. "Writing Centers/WAC in Pharmacy Education: A Changing Prescription." *Writing Centers and Writing Across the Curriculum Programs: Building Interdisciplinary Partnerships.* Ed. Robert W. Barnett and Jacob S Blumner. Westport, CT: Greenwood, 1999. 155-75.

Lerner and Hobson explain the ways in which changes in the health care industry are changing pharmacy education and creating opportunities for writing center and composition professional to create and administer writing centers and WAC programs as pharmacy education attempts to develop higher-order critical thinking skills, decision-making skills, and mature communication skills in students. Hobson shares his experiences in running the relatively large and well-established writing center at St. Louis College of Pharmacy, and Lerner shares his experiences in administering the writing center at MCP during its inception and first two years of existence. This book chapter offers writing center and WAC program administrators practical advice in responding to the needs of pharmacy education.

Chapter 27:
Erika Lindemann

(b. 1946)

A noted bibliographer and specialist in teacher training, Erika Lindemann has contributed significantly to the areas of teaching composition instructors and writing program administration. Lindemann earned her BA (1968) in English from the University of Georgia, Athens. She completed her graduate work in English, earning an MA (1969) and a PhD (1973) at the University of North Carolina, Chapel Hill. Major influences on her career include Edward P. J. Corbett, Win Horner, James Kinneavy, and Gary Tate, who devoted scholarly attention to composition despite their training in literary fields.

Lindemann began her teaching career in 1972 at the University of South Carolina, Columbia, where she eventually became the director of the freshman English program. Since 1980, she has held various assignments at UNC, Chapel Hill, including professor of English, associate dean of the Graduate School (1991-95), director of the Composition Program (1980-85; 1986-90; 1995-98; 1999-02), and Interim Chair, Department of Romance Languages (2003-05). Her professional service includes positions on MLA's Advisory Committee on the *MLA International Bibliography* and on the editorial boards of *Written Communication* and the *Journal of Basic Writing*. Furthermore, she has acted as CCCC's Bibliographer and NCTE's Parliamentarian.

Lindemann's leadership qualities have made her a favorite at Chapel Hill, where she has won the Outstanding Faculty Woman Award (1996), the University Distinguished Teaching Award for Post-Baccalaureate Instruction (2001), and the Association of English Graduate Students award for mentoring MA students (2004). Nationally, she has been recognized by CCCC with the Exemplar Award (2005) and the John Gerber 20th Century Leadership Award for exemplary service (2000).

Lindemann has garnered numerous grants for instructional development and research in writing. She received IBM Course Development Project grants (1983-88) to develop materials for computer-assisted instruction as well as Mellon Foundation grants (1984-86) to offer internships and summer workshops for high school teachers. More recently, she received a Library Services and Technology Act Grant to build the Web site for *True and Candid Compositions: The Lives and Writings of Antebellum Students at the University of North Carolina* (2004).

Writing program administration has been integral to Lindemann's career. Building a writing program requires effective training of writing instructors, often graduate TAs, who teach a large percentage of composition courses. As director of the composition program at Chapel Hill, Lindemann developed in-house training manuals to assist new graduate students. Moreover, she has reached instructors beyond Chapel Hill with her comprehensive book *A Rhetoric for Writing Teachers*, now in its fourth edition.

Lindemann has continually sought a respectable place for composition in a field traditionally dominated by literature. Her now-famous debate with sometime collaborator Gary Tate over the inclusion of literature in first-year composition courses sparked heated reactions on both sides of the argument. Lindemann maintains that teaching students to write about literature in their composition courses does not prepare them for writing in other disciplines. Despite their opposite views, Lindemann and Tate emphasize discussion, not judgment, among writing teachers.

Currently, Lindemann is researching the language spoken by teachers in writing and literature classrooms and is documenting student writing at Chapel Hill from 1795 to 1870. She continues to deliver invited papers and workshops on issues related to teaching composition.

Karen Wright

 Sources for Biographical Narrative

▶ "Erika Lindemann." Dept. of English Faculty and Staff home page. University of North Carolina, Chapel Hill. 10 Sept. 2003. 29 July 2006 <http://english.unc.edu/faculty/lindemanne.html>.

▶ Flora, Joseph M., and Erika Lindemann. "Department Chairs and Writing Program Administrators: An Antiphonal Reading." *ADE Bulletin* 100 (1991): 35-40.

▶ Lindemann, Erika. "Re: Comp Leader Grad Project." Email to Karen Wright. 21 Sept. 2004.

▶ ---. "Three Views of English 101." *CE* 57 (1995): 287-302.

▶ Tate, Lyndsey. "Nation's Largest Professional Organization of Writing Teachers Honors Outstanding College Educators." *NCTE*. 21 Mar. 2005. 29 July 2006 <http://www.ncte.org/about/press/rel/ 120052.htm?source=gs>.

> **Erika Lindemann recommends these readings for novice composition instructors:**

> 1. Bizzell, Patricia. *Academic Discourse and Critical Consciousness.* Pittsburgh: U of Pittsburgh P, 1993.
> 2. Corbett, Edward P.J., Nancy Myers, and Gary Tate. *The Writing Teacher's Sourcebook.* 4th ed. New York: Oxford UP, 2000.
> 3. Lindemann, Erika. *A Rhetoric for Writing Teachers.* 4th ed. New York: Oxford UP, 2001.

 Annotated Bibliography

▶ Lindemann, Erika, ed. *CCCC Bibliography of Composition and Rhetoric.* 4 vols. Carbondale, IL: SIUP, 1990-92.

This resource contains annotations of scholarship on writing and teaching writing that are divided into five major categories—bibliographies, theory and research, education, curriculum, and assessment—which are further subdivided. Entries are drawn from four primary sources: scholarly journals, publishers, DAI, and ERIC. Although these entries were published several years ago, writing teachers will still find these volumes a valuable research tool when balanced with more current investigation.

▶ ---. "Erika Lindemann's Assignment." *What Makes Writing Good: A Multiperspective.* Ed. William E. Coles, Jr. and James Vopat. Lexington, MA: Heath, 1985.

This chapter appears in a textbook designed for both students and teachers of composition: each contributor has submitted a sample student essay, the corresponding assignment, and follow-up explanation of why the writing is good. Lindemann's contribution is a descriptive essay assignment that uses comparison and contrast to make a point. Instructors and students alike will find her commentary on the merits of the sample essay helpful, and the assignment itself is one that new teachers could easily adapt for their own purposes.

▶ ---. "Freshman Composition: No Place for Literature." *CE* 55 (1993): 311-16.

In the first half of the now-famous debate with Gary Tate, Lindemann argues that a first-year writing course should train students to read and write critically in a number of academic discourses. She refutes several claims for including literature: the focus becomes consuming rather than creating texts; humanistic content is covered by other required courses; writing about literature does not teach the writing style that it is intended to model; recent critical theories can be applied to texts other than literature; and it will not help graduate students (teachers in training) become better writing teachers. Unlike literature, readings from the humanities, sciences, and social sciences highlight the processes used by writers to contribute knowledge, such as collaborating, problem-solving, and critical analysis, and are more appropriate for writing students.

▶ ---. "Playing in the Archives: Pleasures, Perils, and Possibilities for Teaching." CCCC Convention, Minneapolis, MN. 14 Apr. 2000. *ERIC*. 15 July 2006 <http://www.eric.ed.gov/ERICDocs/data/ericdocs2/ content_storage_01/0000000b/80/10/ef/2d.pdf>.

Lindemann describes three assignments designed to introduce unconventional research methods to students: transcribing and annotating historical student documents; describing and tracing the history of a museum artifact; and researching and contextualizing similar local and national historical events. Using UNC, Chapel Hill's own historical collections engages her students, connecting them to their past and emphasizing student voices and experiences. These assignments can be modified easily according to course level, available institutional collections, or field of study.

▶ ---. *A Rhetoric for Writing Teachers.* 4th ed. New York: Oxford
    UP, 2001.

In this guide first published in 1982, Lindemann provides
overviews of key figures in composition, ranging from ancient
rhetoricians to modern theorists, and consistently applies them
to classroom practices and stages of the writing process.
Practical considerations include assignments, assessment,
course design, and components of writing, such as paragraph
development and grammar. New teachers especially can benefit
from this comprehensive, easily navigable text of teaching
concepts.

▶ ---. "Teaching as a Rhetorical Art." *CEA Forum* 15 (1985): 9-12.

Lindemann theorizes that skilled writing teachers are effective
rhetoricians who can balance subject, audience, and voice
(writing, student needs, and teacher objectives). This balance is
achieved through class activities, assignment design, and
comments on student writing, all of which must emphasize
writing as a process requiring practice rather than as a set of
facts to be learned. As Lindemann asserts, this rhetorical view
transcends differences in institutions, students, and teaching
styles; therefore, this article is appropriate for writing teachers
of all levels.

▶ ---. "Three Views of English 101." *CE* 57 (1995): 287-302.

Lindemann argues that the place of literature in freshman
composition courses is determined by the instructor's
pedagogical approach. In product-centered courses, the
instructor requires students to read and imitate models of good
writing that are typically taken from traditional literary forms;
process-centered courses emphasize student voices, so assigned
readings (literature or other texts) serve as prompts for self-
discovery rather than models to adopt; and the goal of system-
centered courses is functionality in the academic community,
which involves collaboration and communicating in various
disciplines. Lindemann clearly outlines the benefits and
drawbacks of each approach, including instructor personalities,
types of reading and writing assignments, and audience
considerations.

▶ Lindemann, Erika, and Gary Tate, eds. *Introduction to Composition Studies.* New York: Oxford UP, 1991.

Lindemann and Tate present a collection of invited essays on the emergent field of rhetoric and composition, with such notable contributors as Andrea Lunsford and Robert Connors. Rather than discuss practical teaching methods, the essayists focus instead on theory and call for more research. Although more specialized study is currently available, this book offers a solid introduction for beginning composition scholars.

▶ "Professor Erika Lindemann on 'Writing to Learn.'" *For Your Consideration* 4 (1989): 1-4. *Center for Teaching and Learning.* 4 Dec. 2004 <http://ctl.unc.edu/fyc4.html>.

In interview format, Lindemann answers questions regarding how instructors from any discipline can incorporate writing into their courses successfully. She explains the connection between writing and learning, provides several examples of effective assignments (short and long), suggests ways to encourage revision, and offers strategies for responding to student writing. Although this article appears in a campus newsletter at UNC, Chapel Hill, its content is relevant for instructors at other schools and at any level.

▶ Tate, Gary. "A Place for Literature in Freshman Composition." *CCC* 55 (1993): 317-21.

In his response to Lindemann, Tate bemoans the loss of literature in the first-year writing course due to its prior perceived misuse, the quiet ascension of rhetoric, and the recent interdisciplinary goals of writing courses. He claims that the goal of competence in academic discourse across disciplines has not only turned education into merely a job-training program, but also it is an unrealistic goal considering the diversity of career fields represented in a typical freshman composition class. In asserting that literature enriches student lives outside the academy, Tate prompts writing teachers to consider carefully their course designs.

Chapter 28:
Min-Zhan Lu

(b. 1946)

Born in Shanghai, China while her father was still in the
United States studying medicine at John Hopkins University,
Min-Zhan Lu was two years old before she met her father.
Growing up during the Cultural Revolution, she saw him
imprisoned for his political affiliations. She left China in 1981
for post-graduate studies in the US. Lu received her MA (1983)
in English and her PhD (1989) in Cultural and Critical Studies
from the University of Pittsburgh with a dissertation that
discussed literary practice in Chicago in the 1890s.

She began her professional career at Drake University in Des
Moines, Iowa where she held numerous positions: visiting
assistant professor (1989-90) assistant professor (1990-95),
director of the Writing Workshop (1992-95), associate professor
(1995-01) and Endowment Professor of the Humanities (1998-
2001). Lu then moved to the University of Wisconsin-
Milwaukee as professor of English and coordinator of the
graduate program in rhetoric and composition (2001-06).
During that time her research and teaching focused on the use
of cultural dissonance in all of the following areas: composition
theory and pedagogy, life writing, critical and cultural theory,

postcolonial pedagogy, creative nonfiction, critical ethnography, and translation theory. In 2006, Lu joined the composition/rhetoric faculty at the University of Louisville in Kentucky as professor of English and University Scholar, where she will be teaching classes in writing about literature.

While still in graduate school, Lu won Pittsburgh's An Apple for the Teacher Award twice (1986, 1987) as well as the Andrew W. Mellon Predoctoral Fellowship (1987). At Drake she was award the International Students Association Teacher of the Year Award (2000). In addition to her teaching, Lu has served on the editorial boards of *CE, CCC, JAC,* the *Asian Journal of English Language Teaching,* and the *Writing Center Journal.* She has served on the NCTE College Section Steering Committee (1998-2002) and the CCCC Executive Committee (1991-94) as well as numerous award and proposal review committees for CCCC.

Lu's publication credits include three books and over 29 journal articles and book chapters. Awards include the Richard Braddock Award (2005) and the MLA's Mina P. Shaughnessy Prize (1992) for her seminal article, "Conflict and Struggle: The Enemies or Preconditions of Basic Writing?". The article, which challenged three of composition's most renowned pioneers (Kenneth Bruffee, Thomas Farrell, and Mina Shaughnessy), became a controversial publication often cited in works critiquing Lu's arguments. Influenced by her personal experiences and struggles, Lu believes that reading and writing take place "at sites of political as well as linguistic conflict" (888). In her argument, she addresses past attempts to underplay this conflict with a softer approach to teaching the academic discourse. Lu criticizes Bruffee, Farrell, and Shaughnessy for having an essentialist view of language that does not give proper attention to the cultural dissonance that arises when a student is attempting to learn one discourse and at the same time seeing the differences, both positive and negative, between the new and his/her old (home) discourse.

Although Lu has often criticized well-revered composition theorists, such as Shaughnessy, for what their work lacks, in many of her other works, including "Redefining the Legacy of Mina Shaughnessy: A Critique of the Politics of Linguistic

Innocence," she recognizes the work Shaughnessy and others have done for the study of composition. Lu clearly does not believe that her attempts to shine a light on the cultural dissonance and conflicts that are a natural component of learning a new discourse in any way diminish the foundations of composition theory upon which her theory is built. For the field of composition to move forward, Lu believes theorists and practitioners must develop of an awareness of the contradictions inherent in the academy's view of literacy, as well as the way we explain to students the effects a new discourse can have on their identities.

Erica Marsh and Sara Sweitzer

 Sources for Biographical Narrative

► Jensen, Geeta Sharma. "Midwest Passages: Min-Zhan Lu." 2 Feb. 2003 *Milwaukee Journal Sentinel*. 16 Nov. 2004 <http://www.jsonline.com/Enter/books/jan03/114761.asp>.

► Lu, Min-Zhan. "Conflict and Struggle: The Enemies or Preconditions of Basic Writing?" *CE* 54 (1992): 887-913.

► ---. "An Essay on the Work of Composition: Composing English against the Order of Fast Capitalism." *CCC* 56 (2004): 16-50.

► ---. "From Silence to Words: Writing as Struggle." *CE* 49 (1987): 437-48.

► ---. "Professing Multiculturalism: The Politics of Style in the Contact Zone." *CCC* 45 (1994): 442-58.

► ---. "Redefining the Legacy of Mina Shaughnessy: A Critique of the Politics of Linguistic Innocence." *Journal of Basic Writing* 10.1 (1991): 26-40.

► ---. *Shanghai Quartet: The Crossings of Four Women of China*. Pittsburgh: Duquesne UP, 2001.

▶ ---. *Curriculum Vitae*. Email to Tanya McLaughlin. 21 Aug. 2006.

▶ "Min-Zhan Lu." English Dept. home page. University of Lousiville. 2003. 15 Aug. 2006 <http://coldfusion.louisville.edu/webs/a-s/english/people_2.cfm?id=75>.

▶ "Min-Zhan Lu." English Dept. home page. University of Wisconsin. 22 May 2006. 15 Aug. 2006 <http://www.uwm.edu/Dept/English/faculty/facultyjm.html>.

Min-Zhan Lu recommends these readings for novice composition instructors:

1. Canagarajah, A. Suresh. *A Geopolitics of Academic Writing*. Pittsburgh: U of Pittsburgh P, 2002.
2. Corbett, Edward P. J., Nancy Myers, and Gary Tate, eds. *A Writing Teacher's Sourcebook*. 4th ed. New York: Oxford UP, 2000.
3. Horner, Bruce. *Terms of Work for Composition: A Materialist Critique*. Albany: SUNY P, 2000.

 Annotated Bibliography

▶ Haswell, Richard H., and Min-Zhan Lu. *Comp Tales: An Introduction to College Composition Through Its Stories*. New York: Longman, 2000.

The compilation offers individual anecdotes from various stages of a composition teacher's life: colleagues, the classroom, the writing, students, the public, professional dilemmas, and mentors. Haswell and Lu offer practical dos and don'ts in the form of oral narratives from many of the major composition leaders in the 1990s: Cynthia Selfe, Muriel Harris, Wendy Bishop, and others. New teachers especially can benefit from this comprehensive, easily navigable text covering all ranges of teaching experiences.

▶ Lu, Min-Zhan. "Conflict and Struggle: The Enemies or Preconditions of Basic Writing?" *CE* 54 (1992): 887-913.

Lu criticizes Kenneth Bruffee, Thomas Farrell, and Mina Shaughnessy for having an essentialist view of language that does not give proper attention to the cultural dissonance that arises when a student is attempting to learn one discourse and at the same time seeing the differences, both positive and negative, between the new and his/her old (home) discourse. Lu argues that reading and writing take place at a site of linguistic and political conflict, but her argument can be a bit daunting for those not familiar with linguistic analyses. This article can be very beneficial to teachers new to the field of Teaching English Speakers of Other Languages (TESOL).

▶ ---. "An Essay on the Work of Composition: Composing English against the Order of Fast Capitalism." *CCC* 56 (2004): 16-50.

This article attempts to define what being a responsible and responsive user of English means. Lu suggests a change of assumptions with the relationship between English and its users, the language needs and purposes of individual users of English, and the relation between the work we do and the work done by users of English. This essay relies heavily on composition and linguistic theories, and new teachers unfamiliar with this discourse may find the article difficult.

▶ ---. "From Silence to Words: Writing as Struggle." *CE* 49 (1987): 437-48.

Through her educational experiences, Lu illustrates how the languages of formal discourse and everyday life can create an inner conflict for students. She uses her own teaching experiences to show the dangers of not confronting the differences and argues the need for educating students on how to handle this conflict. This article clearly presents a recurring problem and calls for teachers of every background, especially new teachers, to aid students with this inner conflict.

▶ ---. "Professing Multiculturalism: The Politics of Style in the
    Contact Zone." *CCC* 45 (1994): 442-58.

Lu illustrates a method of teaching composition in the context
of cultural differences and acknowledgements. This article
provides examples of her assignments and students' responses
or reactions from both native and non-native English speakers.
New teachers, especially ESL teachers, can benefit from the
real-life examples and student responses presented.

▶ ---. "Reading and Writing Differences: The Problematic of
    Experience." *Feminism and Composition Studies: In
    Other Words.* Ed. Susan C. Jarratt and Lynn Worsham.
    New York: MLA, 1998. 239-51.

Lu argues that readers and writers often do not see past their
own gendered experience so a critical consideration of those
biases could lead to a more fruitful analysis. This article,
although helpful, relies heavily on feminist and composition
theories rather than providing strategies or models. New
teachers may find this article beneficial when diversifying
expository writing.

▶ ---. "Redefining the Legacy of Mina Shaughnessy: A Critique
    of the Politics of Linguistic Innocence." *Journal of Basic
    Writing* 10.1 (1991): 26-40.

Lu recognizes the work that Mina Shaughnessy and others
have done for the study of composition and attempts to show
how her desire to shine a light on the cultural dissonance and
conflicts she considers necessary when learning a new
discourse are created from their foundations. Directed at basic
or developmental writing instructors, this article highlights the
conflicts writers experience and brings contact zone theory into
the discourse. While this article is especially helpful to basic
and developmental writing instructors, new instructors can
find this article beneficial but may want to familiarize
themselves with the works of Shaughnessy before reading Lu.

► ---. "Redefining the Literate Self: The Politics of Critical
       Affirmation." *CCC* 51 (1999): 172-94.

Lu defines the literate self in the interest of social justice and
discusses the insights and difficulties personal narratives can
bring. Lu argues that more focus on the difficulty of finding
one's identity is needed to combat the theories that claim
personal experience is a self-evident thing that should be
written off if it does not fit into a simplistic notion of culture.
This article relies heavily on theory while providing few
practical models or examples; however, new teachers strongly
interested in exploring the personal narrative in class will find
it beneficial.

► Lu, Min-Zhan, and Bruce Horner. "Expectations,
       Interpretations, and Contributions of Basic Writing."
       Journal of Basic Writing 19.1 (2000): 43-52.

Lu and Horner address issues in which universities promote
their abilities to serve diverse student populations and how
Basic Writing assists and leads the charge in that service. The
writers argue that basic students have been viewed as needing
acculturation into the academy while those elite members of
the academy are attempting to diversify their voice. Easily
understood, this article can be beneficial to new teachers of
both freshman and developmental English.

► ---. "The Problematic of Experience: Redefining Critical
       Work in Ethnography and Pedagogy." *CE* 60 (1998):
       257-77.

Lu and Horner raise the question of defining and negotiating
the issue of experience within critical ethnography and
pedagogy. They analyze approaches taken to counter the
problem of experience and map possibilities and obstacles
facing those committed to teaching and research. This article
can be very beneficial to new teachers planning to conduct
further research in pedagogy while simultaneously negotiating
teaching responsibilities.

Chapter 29:
Andrea A. Lunsford

(b. 1942)

A notable researcher in composition and rhetoric, Andrea A. Lunsford has published on several topics including women and writing, collaboration, intellectual property, and technologies of writing. Lunsford received her BA (1963) and her MA (1965) degrees in English at the University of Florida and her PhD (1977) in English at The Ohio State University. In a career that has spanned four decades, her academic appointments have included the University of British Columbia (1977-86), where she also served as director of Writing (1981-86), and The Ohio State University (1986-00), including the roles of center director for the Study of Teaching and Writing (1998-00) and Distinguished professor of English (1990-00). She has also been the director of the Bread Loaf Graduate School of English, Santa Fe (1990-01). Lunsford is currently professor of English and director of the Program in Writing and Rhetoric at Stanford University (2000-present).

In addition to serving as an active committee member for many academic and professional associations, Lunsford has also held leadership positions, such as Chair of the MLA Division on

Writing (1987), Chair of CCCC (1989-90), and Co-Chair of the Alliance of Rhetoric Societies International Conference (2002-03).

Lunsford has received numerous awards for her work, including the Richard Braddock Award (2005) for the best essay published in *CCC*, the MLA/ADE Francis Andrew March Award (2002), the University Distinguished Scholar Award, Ohio State (1998), the CCCC Exemplar Award (1994), and the MLA Mina Shaughnessy Prize (1985).

Lunsford readily acknowledges influences from other composition leaders including Wayne Booth, Edward P. J. Corbett, Janet Emig, James Moffett, Walter Ong, and, collaborative writing partners Lisa Ede, Robert J. Connors, and John J. Ruszkiewicz. The key ideas for which these leaders are remembered reflect Lunsford's wide-ranging interests as an author and educator. She has authored 14 books, many book chapters, and numerous articles. Perhaps Lunsford is best known to composition teachers for *The St. Martin's Handbook*, now in its fifth edition. Additional undergraduate composition texts include *Everything's An Argument* and *The Everyday Writer*.

Lunsford has a longstanding association as a collaborator with fellow composition leader Lisa Ede. Their work includes *Singular Texts/Plural Authors: Perspectives on Collaborative Writing*. Though other collaborative writing partnerships have been successful and longstanding, including that with Robert J. Connors (*St. Martin's Handbook*) and John Ruszkiewicz (*Everything's an Argument*), the collaboration of Ede and Lunsford has been particularly rich for composition studies.

Recently, Lunsford contributed the book chapter "Toward Delivering New Definitions of Writing" to Delivering College Composition: The Fifth Canon (Boynton/Cook, 2006). She is currently working on another book chapter regarding women's rhetorics.

Katherine Haynes

Sources for Biographical Narrative

▶ Clark, Carlton L. "The Work of Andrea A. Lunsford: An Annotated Bibliography of Journal Articles and Book Chapters." 1 Feb. 2004. 5 May 2000 <http://webpages.charter.net/carlton.clark/ lunsford.htm>.

▶ "Lunsford, Andrea A. Curriculum Vitae, Recent Publications, Syllabi, Email." English Dept. home page. Stanford University. 1 Feb. 2004. 27 Mar. 2004. <http://www.stanford.edu/~lunsfor1/ >.

Annotated Bibliography

▶ Connors, Robert J., and Andrea A. Lunsford. "Frequency of Formal Errors in Current College Writing, or Ma and Pa Kettle Do Research." *CCC* 39: (1988): 395-409.

Connors and Lunsford analyzed about 3,000 graded US college student essays from a pool of more than 21,000 to determine the most common error patterns of the 1980s. Although local error patterns have changed over 50 years, the number has not increased, and the authors believe that the shift in patterns can probably be attributed to the oral, electronic nature of modern communication. While the research is somewhat dated, it is helpful for beginning composition instructors who feel insecure about current grading patterns.

▶ ---."Teachers' Rhetorical Comments on Student Papers." *CCC* 4 (1993): 200-23.

This article analyzes what kinds of global comments teachers give on college students' essays, and the results show that 77 percent of the papers did contain some global comments, the most common beginning with praise and ending with negative commentary. The article is quite revealing of actual practice and provides lucid commentary on the conflicting messages composition teachers send. Composition teachers learning about assessment methodology should refer to this article.

► Connors, Robert J., Lisa S. Ede, and Andrea A. Lunsford, eds. *Essays on Classical Rhetoric and Modern Discourse*. Carbondale, IL: SIUP, 1984.

This collection of essays is especially cognizant of the role that Edward P. J. Corbett played in reviving interest in rhetoric as a vibrant field of research for composition studies. Contributions from other composition leaders, such as Lunsford and James Kinneavy, make this a good source for identifying major themes in contemporary rhetoric. Though it is now over twenty years old, it does provide a beginning scholar with historical, philosophical, theoretical, and pedagogical foundations for pursuing the discipline.

► Ede, Lisa, and Andrea Lunsford. "Audience Addressed/Audience Invoked: The Role of Audience in Composition Theory and Pedagogy." *CCC* 35 (1984): 155-71. Rpt. in *The Writing Teacher's Sourcebook*. 4th ed. Ed. Edward P. J. Corbett, Nancy Myers, and Gary Tate. New York: Oxford UP, 2000. 320-34.

This essay responds to two extreme interpretations of the dialogue between writer and reader, attempting a more balanced perspective between those who overemphasize the power of the external reader to shape discourse, and those who place too much emphasis on the power of the writer to create the audience. Ede and Lunsford insist upon mutually creative roles for writer and audience. Level-headed and informative for the new instructor, the article highlights some ethical and practical implications of teaching a balanced role for the writer-audience dialogue.

► ---. *Singular Texts/Plural Authors: Perspectives on Collaborative Writing*. Carbondale IL: SIUP, 1990.

More than a review of collaborative writing, this is a history and philosophy of the continuously evolving definition of authorship. With the increasing controversy over the ownership of published and copyrighted materials, this book should be read and considered by all composition instructors, not just those interested in collaborative authorship. Composition teachers especially would benefit from the analysis of collaborative efforts on improving student writing and the pedagogical questions raised at the end of chapter four.

▶ Lauer, Janice M., and Andrea Lunsford. "The Place of Rhetoric and Composition in Doctoral Studies." *The Future of Doctoral Studies in English*. Ed. Andrea Lunsford, Helene Moglen, and James F. Slevin. New York: MLA, 1989. 106-10.

The authors provide a rationale for the existence of doctoral programs in rhetoric and composition, citing the varieties of specialization: historical, rhetorical or theoretical, and empirical research. They point to its interdisciplinary context-rich value for English studies, its pedagogical importance, and its politically astute responsiveness to socio-economic issues, such as illiteracy and the future of English education at all levels. For students who think they may be interested in specializing in this field, but need a clearer definition, this is the text.

▶ Lunsford, Andrea A. "Collaboration, Control, and the Idea of a Writing Center." *Writing Center Journal* 12.1 (1991): 3-10. Rpt. in *The Allyn and Bacon Guide to Writing Center Theory and Practice*. Ed. Robert W. Barnett and Jacob S. Blumner. Boston: Allyn and Bacon, 2001. 92-99.

Three philosophies of writing centers are presented here in relationship to one another: positivism, expressionism, and social constructivism. Like all of Lunsford's work, this shows a canny appreciation for practical solutions to present circumstances and a breathtaking capacity to inspire. The essay is essential reading for writing center tutors and quite helpful for the beginning classroom instructor who is not aware of these different perspectives.

► ---. "Intellectual Property in an Age of Information: What Is at Stake for Composition Studies?" *Composition in the Twenty-First Century: Crisis and Change.* Ed. Lynn Bloom, Donald A. Daiker, and Edward M. White. Carbondale, IL: SIUP, 1996. 261-72.

This chapter provides a follow-up to questions posed in her earlier book, *Singular Texts / Plural Authors.* Lunsford complicates matters by raising more questions, highlighting social, political, and economic ramifications that the romantic construct of copyrighting intellectual property has produced. This is a serious discussion of a complicated issue, which has enormous significance for writers and teachers of writing.

► ---. *The St. Martin's Handbook.* 5th ed. Boston: Bedford/ St. Martin's, 2003.

With its invitingly simple style and rejection of prescriptive fallacies, Lunsford explores issues important to her, such as audience, intellectual property, and collaboration. Addressed to college writing students, this handbook has much to recommend it with its wide layout, reliable commentary, and emphasis on improved written (and oral) communication for specific rhetorical purposes, rather than abstract correctness. Readable, practical, and very well organized, it truly is required for today's composition instructor.

► Lunsford, Andrea, Helene Moglen, and James F. Slevin. eds. *The Future of Doctoral Studies in English.* New York: MLA, 1989.

This slim book turned out to be as much retrospect as prediction. Though the overall mood of the times did not exude optimism or enthusiasm for bright prospects, the book does present a group of thoughtful, caring mentors who willingly persevere for the next generation. For those who seek a historical framework, the essays provide some helpful advice concerning the field.

Chapter 30:
Ken Macrorie
(b. 1918)

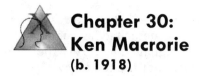

Ken Macrorie's academic success in high school earned him a two-year scholarship to Oberlin College, Ohio. Though Macrorie struggled with grades and nearly lost his scholarship, he eventually earned his BA (1940) after three years of study. He then served four years in the United States Military before returning to his studies at the University of North Carolina at Chapel Hill where he worked as an instructor while earning his MA (1948). Macrorie also worked as an assistant professor of communication skills at Michigan State University in the years prior to earning his PhD (1955) from Columbia University.

Macrorie served as editor of *CCC* for three years (1962-64) before becoming an associate at Western Michigan University, Kalamazoo. Two years after obtaining the rank of professor, Western Michigan honored Macrorie with their Teaching Excellence Award (1968), an award celebrating teachers who exhibit superior teaching skills. The Michigan Council of Teachers of English presented Macrorie with the Charles Carpenter Fries Award (1982) for his faithful service to the teaching of English, distinguished leadership within his community, and his positive impact on colleagues and students. In addition to his professorship at Western Michigan, Macrorie served for 13 summers as a staff member of the Bread Loaf School of English in Middlebury, Vermont.

Macrorie's work has been immortalized in seven books and numerous journal articles and book chapters. Although his work includes classics such as *Uptaught, Writing to Read, Telling Writing,* and *Twenty Teachers,* he is most known for his concept of the I-search paper, which is a response to study aids that advise students to use "clear and competent prose. Be restrained, impersonal, objective, and factual, Avoid expressing personal opinion and feeling" (*I-search* 55). Macrorie believes that the academy's emphasis on formal aspects of paper writing destroys students' natural curiosity, which then encourages their use of lifeless prose. Students, in an effort to impress their teachers, prepare papers with the same detached language found in many of their textbooks, a language Macrorie calls Engfish. In addition, Macrorie asserts that the tendency of instructors to focus on grammar rather than content leads students to believe that the content of their papers is inconsequential or that their teachers don't care what they write. To revive students' curiosity and their writing style, Macrorie urges educators to encourage students to write about their interests with the hope that this freedom will engage students, consequently producing better writing and better writers.

Macrorie's pedagogical approach, known as the Third Way, involves a four-step process that (1) exposes the student to Engfish, (2) has freewriting sessions on topics that interest the students, (3) has students share their essays with the class, and (4) ends the process by publishing the best works. Though publishing may only mean posting the paper in the hall or on classroom bulletin boards, the purpose is to encourage students to take pride in their writing.

Jessica McKee

 Sources for Biographical Narrative

▶ "The Bulletin." *English Department Western Michigan.* Dec. 2002. 20 Nov. 2004 <http://wmich.edu/english/bulletin/bulletin64.pdf>.

▶ "Heinemann Authors." *Heinemann Books.* 2006. 15 Aug. 2006. <http://books.heinemann.com/authors/117.aspx>.

▶ "Ken(neth) Macrorie." *Contemporary Authors Online.* 19 Apr. 2002. 16 Nov. 2004 <http://galenet.galegroup.com>.

▶ Lindemann, Erika. "Ken Macrorie: A Review Essay." *CE* 44 (1982): 358-367.

► Macrorie, Kenneth. *The I-search Paper*. Portsmouth, NH: Boynton/Cook, 1988.

► *WMU Alumni Association*. 28 Sept. 2004. 20 Nov. 2004. <http://www.wmich.edu/alumni/awards.html#teaching>

Annotated Bibliography

► Macrorie, Ken. "The Circle of Implication." *CE* 28 (1967): 435-38.

In this brief essay, Macrorie discusses the limitations and implications of language, reminding his audience that the inclusion and omission of words evokes judgment. Thus, Macrorie concludes, writers must recognize themselves as judges, so they may write honest, meaningful prose. Informative and well written, this essay reminds novice and experienced writers to be aware of their own circle of implication.

► ---. *The I-search Paper*. Portsmouth, NH: Boynton/Cook, 1988.

Rejecting the traditional methods of composition textbooks, Macrorie ends each chapter of his "contextbook" with writing exercises intended to cultivate the students' natural curiosity and encourage them to write freely and creatively. Appropriate for students at any grade level, this book provides an alternative approach to the traditional research paper.

► ---. "A Literature Without Criticism." *CE* 22 (1961): 565-78.

Macrorie responds to the accusation that English classrooms should stop teaching mass communication. While Macrorie agrees with the criticism made by opponents of the study of mass communication, he maintains that some analysis of mass communication should remain in the academic discourse of English departments. Persuasive and informative, this essay reminds educators of the need for communication studies in the English classroom and may be read as a defense of pop culture in the field of composition studies.

▶ ---. *Searching Writing: Making Knowledge Personal.*
        Videocassette. Portsmouth, NH: Boynton/Cook, 1994.

In this 40-minute video, Macrorie explains to teachers from
various academic disciplines how the I-search process
illuminates students writing. Macrorie also shows ways to help
students engage in the I-search process while satisfying the
traditional goals and expectations of the academy.

▶ ---. "Teach Listening?" *CE* 12 (1951): 220-23.

Macrorie tells communication instructors who are waiting for a
scientific method for teaching listening to stop waiting and use
the world around them for instruction. He blames   the fast
paced, multi-tasking nature of our culture for the demise of
listening and urges educators to seek out good listeners and
employ their techniques in the communication classroom.

▶ ---. *Telling Writing.* New York: Hayden, 1970.

Macrorie blames the diligent correction of students' grammar
for the lifeless prose produced by students. He encourages
students to avoid using the flat language of the academy by
warning them of the poison fish, known as Engfish. Each
chapter ends with practical advice for the free writing that
encourages students to write about their own experiences.

▶ ---. *Twenty Teachers.* New York: Oxford UP, 1984.

In this book, Macrorie presents profiles of twenty teachers who
exceed the traditional expectations of pedagogy by enabling
their students to produce good works. Macrorie condenses the
advice of these enablers into 43 tips for teachers. He concludes
with an "Open Letter About Schools," which criticizes schools
for promoting methods of instruction that contradict the work
of their best teachers.

▶ ---. *Uptaught.* New York: Hayden, 1970.

Macrorie accuses the academic faculty of asking students to
express themselves meaningfully while denying them a voice
with which to say what they want to say. Macrorie advocates

the "The Third Way," a method of teaching that embodies mutual respect among students and faculty and invites the two to engage in instructive dialogue.

▶ ---. *Writing to be Read*. New York: Hayden, 1968.

In this high-school version of *Telling Writing*, Macrorie maintains his criticism of academic writing while offering students advice on writing freely and truth telling. He argues that schools teach students to lie in their attempt to write acceptable academic prose. Macrorie provides many entertaining exercises that he believes will enable the student to avoid lifeless writing.

▶ ---. "Writing's Dying." *CCC* 11 (1960): 206-10.

In this short story, Macrorie relays a conversation between Ed, "The World's Best Direction Writer," and George, a teacher of composition. The two discuss the impact of increased images and technology on the writing process, citing electronic advancements as writing's cause of death. Their discussion evolves to include the role education plays in the death of writing and ends with Ed providing George with practical pedagogical advice.

Chapter 31:
Paul Kei Matsuda

(b. 1970)

Paul Kei Matsuda is renowned for his contributions to second language (L2) writing and has written and edited several books and articles that have advanced the field. Matsuda earned his BA (1993) in Communication from the University of Wisconsin-Stevens Point; his MA (1995) in English with a concentration in Composition and Rhetoric from Miami University, Ohio; and his PhD (2000) in English with a primary emphasis in Rhetoric and Composition and secondary concentration in Applied Linguistics from Purdue University.

Matsuda began his teaching career in 1994 while a graduate student at Miami-Ohio, where he served as a visiting instructor in the Department of German, Russian, and East Asian Languages. After receiving his doctorate, Matsuda returned to Miami-Ohio as an assistant professor of Composition, Rhetoric and Linguistics, and, in 2001, he took a position as assistant professor of Composition Studies at UNH, where he currently serves as director of Composition and teaches various undergraduate and graduate writing courses for both native and nonnative English speakers. Outside of teaching, Matsuda has chaired the CCCC Committee on Second Language Writing since 1998, and, also in 1998, with Tony Silva, he co-founded the Symposium on Second Language Writing, a biennial gathering of L2 writing specialists.

In addition to his professional service, Matsuda has been recognized for his research on Teaching English as a Second Language (TESL) and rhetoric and composition. In 2001, he received honorable mention for the *Journal of Second Language Writing*'s (*JSLW*) Award for the Best Article Published, and while a graduate student at Purdue, Matsuda won numerous awards for his essays. Matsuda was also awarded a CCCC Research Initiative Grant (2004) for his project "Composition, Rhetoric, and Literacy—What We Know, What We Need to Know."

Early in his career Matsuda discovered the limitations of the historical disciplinary division of labor wherein L2 writing was relegated exclusively to the field of L2 studies, despite the number of L2 writers in first language (L1) composition classes; as a non-native English speaker, this was even more relevant to his work. Concerned that composition programs and their instructors were not prepared to meet the special needs of L2 writers, Matsuda proposed the need for an open dialogue among all disciplines where L2 students are situated in order to create more democratic teaching practices. Matsuda has conducted extensive research on the interdisciplinary relationships among composition studies, L2 studies, and L2 writing, specifically within the context of the United States. His historical narratives about L2 writing and its evolution reveal the field's progress and look forward to future developments in the field.

Currently, Matsuda serves on several editorial boards including the *Journal of Basic Writing*, the *Journal of Second Language Writing*, and *TESOL Quarterly* and is the series editor for the Parlor Press Series on Second Language Writing. He is also presently working on a special issue of *WPA* and an edited collection entitled *Politics of Second Language Writing: In Search of the Promised Land*, both forthcoming in 2006.

Keri L. Mayes

Sources for Biographical Narrative

▶ Matsuda, Paul Kei. "About Me." University of New
    Hampshire. 6 June 2006
    <http://webster.unh.edu/~pmatsuda/aboutme.html>.

▶ ---. "L2 Writing." Email to Keri Mayes. 6 June 2006.

▶ ---. Paul Kei Matsuda home page. 7 May 2006. 6 June 2006
    <http://pubpages.unh.edu/~pmatsuda/vita/vita.html>.

Paul Kei Matsuda recommends these readings for novice composition instructors:

1. Casanave, Christine Pearson. *Controversies in Second
   Language Writing: Dilemmas and Decisions in Research
   and Instruction.* Ann Arbor: U of Michigan P, 2003.
2. Matsuda, Paul Kei, Michelle Cox, Christina Ortmeier-
   Hooper, and Jay Jordan, eds. *Second Language Writing
   in the Composition Classroom: A Critical Sourcebook.*
   Boston: Bedford/St Martin's, 2006.
3. Silva, Tony, and Paul Kei Matsuda, eds. *Landmark
   Essays on ESL Writing.* Mahwah, NJ: Erlbaum, 2001.

Annotated Bibliography

▶ Matsuda, Paul Kei. "Composition Studies and ESL Writing:
    A Disciplinary Division of Labor." *CCC* 50 (1999): 699-
    721. Rpt. in *Cross-Talk in Comp Theory: A Reader.* Ed.
    Victor Villanueva. 2nd ed. Urbana, IL: NCTE, 2003.
    773-96.

In his seminal work Matsuda presents the historical context
surrounding the emergence of the metaphoric "disciplinary
division of labor" wherein components of first language (L1)
and second language (L2) writing became divided between

213

composition studies and Teaching English as a Second Language (TESL), respectively. Matsuda contends that the professionalization of TESL institutionalized this division, and he argues the need for an open dialogue between the two fields. Rather than eliminating the division, Matsuda proposes instead multiple ways for the two disciplines to work together to improve the conditions for ESL writers in composition classrooms.

▶ ---. "Contrastive Rhetoric in Context: A Dynamic Model of L2 Writing." *Journal of Second Language Writing* 6.1 (1997): 45-60. Rpt. in *Landmark Essays on ESL Writing*. Ed. Tony Silva and Paul Kei Matsuda. Mahwah, NJ: Erlbaum, 2001. 241-55.

In this study Matsuda discusses early contrastive rhetoric and its limitations in teaching organization in L2 writing, which he calls static theory. Focusing more broadly on the interaction between the writer and reader and their backgrounds as well as multiple other influences, Matsuda proposes a dynamic model of L2 writing as an alternative to this early static theory, which has restricted the pedagogical application of contrastive rhetoric research. This article's use of comprehensible diagrams and clear headings throughout provides an easy-to-follow organization, and Matsuda's call for more empirical research with this proposed model serves to incite readers to pursue further inquiry in the construction and organization of L2 texts.

▶ ---. "Process and Post-Process: A Discursive History." *Journal of Second Language Writing* 12 (2003): 65-83.

This article provides a thorough, informative historical timeline of the genesis of process and post-process pedagogy in both L1 and L2 composition studies that all composition instructors should read. Cautioning against the uncritical acceptance of terms like process, current-traditional rhetoric, and post-process, Matsuda aims to scrutinize closely each and, in particular, consider their implications for L2 writing. Instead of completely rejecting process and replacing it with post-process, Matsuda argues for multiple L2 writing theories and pedagogies that recognize other key elements of writing besides process and warns L2 researchers not to overlook the complexity of these nuanced terms.

▶ ---. "Second Language Writing in the Twentieth Century: A
Situated Historical Perspective." *Exploring the
Dynamics of Second Language Writing.* Ed. Barbara
Kroll. New York: Cambridge UP, 2003. 15-34. Rpt. in
*Second Language Writing in the Composition
Classroom: A Critical Sourcebook.* Ed. Paul Kei
Matsuda, Michelle Cox, Christina Ortmeier-Hooper,
and Jay Jordan. Boston: Bedford/St. Martin's, 2006.
14-30.

This highly informative chapter traces the development of the field of L2 writing specifically within the context of the United States and from an interdisciplinary perspective. In this useful resource for newcomers to the field, Matsuda illustrates, in narrative form, how L2 writing has evolved over the last 50 years due to influential relationships with both composition studies and L2 studies. After examining the historical progression of the field, Matsuda calls L2 teachers and researchers to continue to play a role in influencing the field's relationship with other programs and departments that affect L2 writing instruction so that L2 writing will develop into a symbiotic field.

▶ ---. "Situating ESL Writing in a Cross-Disciplinary Context."
Written Communication 15 (1998): 99-121.

In this study of the field of ESL writing, Matsuda critiques three interdisciplinary models of L2 writing: the disciplinary division of labor model, the disciplinary intersection model, and the symbiotic model. After presenting an historical account of the development of research in L2 writing, Matsuda examines the field's situation in the context of TESL and composition studies and calls L2 researchers and instructors to address the special needs of ESL students, which have been overlooked and neglected over the years. Underlying the text is a concern for the welfare of ESL writers, which, Matsuda exclaims, should be the driving force behind future developments in the field of ESL writing.

▶ Matsuda, Paul Kei, and Jeffrey Jablonski. "Beyond the L2 Metaphor: Towards a Mutually Transformative Model of ESL/WAC Collaboration." *Academic Writing* 1 (2000) 6 June 2006   <http://wac.colostate.edu/aw/articles/ matsuda_jablonski2000.htm>.

In response to the invocation of the L2 metaphor by WAC specialists, Matsuda and Jablonski critique and consider the implications of its use in composition studies and L2 studies in an effort to prevent further marginalization of L2 writers. Although beginning with an investigation of the beneficial uses of the metaphor, the article focuses primarily on its problems and offers a mutually transformative model of interdisciplinary collaboration between ESL and WAC to enhance the relationship between the two. The article concludes with a call for more dialogue between ESL and WAC specialists in order to promote more democratic practices for L2 writers in the disciplines.

▶ Matsuda, Paul Kei, Michelle Cox, Christina Ortmeier-Hooper, and Jay Jordan, eds. *Second Language Writing in the Composition Classroom: A Critical Sourcebook*. Boston: Bedford/St. Martin's, 2006.

This compilation of 21 scholarly articles is an excellent, user-friendly resource for graduate students in L2 studies and composition instructors who work with multilingual writers. Divided into five parts including historical perspectives of L2 writing, the complexities of L2 writers, theoretical frameworks, curriculum designs, and response to and assessment of L2 writing, this book addresses the major issues in the field, and the introduction to each part provides insightful background information. Due to the increasing number of L2 writers in first-year composition courses, all instructors would benefit from reading this collection and revising their pedagogies to accommodate this diverse student population.

▶ Matsuda, Paul Kei, and Tony Silva. "Cross-Cultural
   Composition: Mediated Integration of US and
   International Students." *Composition Studies* 27.1
   (1999): 15-30. Rpt. in *Second Language Writing in the
   Composition Classroom: A Critical Source Book*. Ed.
   Paul Kei Matsuda, Michelle Cox, Christina Ortmeier-
   Hooper, and Jay Jordan. Boston: Bedford/St. Martin's,
   2006. 246-59.

In this essay Matsuda and Silva suggest the creation of a cross-
cultural first-year composition course as an alternative
placement option for ESL and NES students in order to address
two major challenges university writing instructors and
administrators face: providing classroom instruction ideal for
ESL students and helping ESL and NES students develop the
communication skills necessary for living and working in a
globalized world. Matsuda and Silva offer both the advantages
and disadvantages of this course, illustrating the pedagogical
strategies implemented in an actual class taught at Purdue
University. From the practical, useful writing projects and
activities described, which have helped students develop
cultural sensitivity and eased anxieties, to actual student
comments praising the class, Matsuda and Silva present a
convincing argument for the cross-cultural composition course
as a plausible solution to meeting the needs of both ESL and
NES students.

▶ Silva, Tony, and Paul Kei Matsuda, eds. *Landmark Essays
   on ESL Writing*. Mahwah, NJ: Erlbaum, 2001.

An anthology of the seminal essays in the field of L2 writing,
Silva and Matsuda's edited collection is an invaluable tool for
current and future ESL teachers and researchers. Organized in
chronological order, the reader can trace the development of the
emerging field of L2 writing from linguistic theory and
contrastive rhetoric to ESL writing process research, textual
analysis, and different approaches to the curriculum as
separate and distinct from L1 composition. Even though many
of the theories and pedagogies presented have been challenged

and refuted by more current research, these articles
demonstrate how the field of L2 has evolved over time and
point to the future of ESL writing scholarship.

▶ ---. *On Second Language Writing*. Mahwah, NJ: Erlbaum,
    2001.

This edited collection of papers presented at the first
Symposium on Second Language Writing in 1998 addresses the
major issues in the field of ESL composition including research,
theory, pedagogy, assessment, ideology and politics, and the
relationships between L2 writing and other disciplines. A broad
survey of the most recent scholarship in the field of L2 writing,
this text is particularly useful for novice L2 teachers and
researchers and should be read by anyone who works with ESL
writers, including L1 composition instructors. Engaging and
readily accessible, readers are not overwhelmed with the
theoretical as the focus of the entire text is developing a field
that will best serve the needs of the L2 writing student.

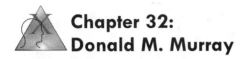

Chapter 32:
Donald M. Murray

(1924-2006)

Donald M. Murray is a highly respected leader in the arena of composition theory, research, and pedagogy; however, as a public-school student, he had a very difficult time due to his boredom with the curriculum. Murray was a child with a gift for writing, yet he dropped out of high school twice before deciding to finish his high school degree and attend college. Murray completed his BA (1948) at UNH and his MA (1951) at Boston University (BU). Murray never entered a doctoral program; however, he has been awarded honorary doctorates from UNH (1990) and Fitchburg State College (1992) for his contributions in the field of composition theory.

Murray suggests that the greatest influences in his life have been the negative ones: "They gave me the materials for my writing but more than that, gave me the emotional hunger, the needs, the drive to express myself, to discover myself, to exist, to influence, to shout I AM HERE" (Smith 308). Murray admits that he was blessed with positive role models as well, including his physician, his uncle, and two public school teachers who recognized his potential and encouraged him to express his individuality. In college, he encountered another role model,

English professor Mortimer Howell, who supported Murray and inspired him to excel in his writing.

Murray had a busy professional life outside of his work in academia, and he is probably most remembered for being the youngest journalist to win a Pulitzer Prize (1954) for his editorial writing with the *Boston Herald* about the changes in the American Military. Prior to winning this award, Murray served as a paratrooper in the U.S. Army (1943-46). After leaving the service, he finished his bachelor's degree and started working for the *Boston Herald* where he held several positions, including copyboy, full-time reporter, and editorial writer. In 1953 he became a journalism instructor at BU, and in 1954 he took a job on the editorial staff of *Time* magazine. From 1956 until 1963, Murray earned his living solely as a freelance writer until he accepted a professorship in English at UNH. Through the years he has written scholarly essays, magazine articles, editorials, and over 20 books. Up to his recent passing, he was a correspondent for *The Boston Globe.*

Murray taught writing at UNH for over 30 years. During that time, he maintained memberships in NCTE and AAUP, and he acted as English Department Chairperson and as director of the Freshman English Program. Murray has received many awards, including the New England Award from the associated Press (1951) and the Yankee Quill Award (1981), and he was selected best columnist (1996) in Boston by *Improper Bostonians* magazine. In 2004, UNH established the Donald Murray Visiting Journalist Program in order to fund professionals who complete a one-week lecturing residency.

Due to his difficulty with the educational system of his youth, Murray always questioned rigid teaching methods and the reasons behind them, and this scrutiny of methodology carried over into his contributions in the area of composition theory and research. Murray's composition theory is organized around the process approach and expressivism, both focusing more on writers and the experience of writing than on the final text. Until his recent death, Murray wrote daily for his "Over Sixty" newspaper column for fellow retirees, and, true to his expressivistic approach to writing, Murray claimed that every day he set out "to write what I do not expect. I invite, encourage, cultivate, welcome, and follow surprise" (307).

Chris Greer

Sources for Biographical Narrative

▶ *Biographies Plus Illustrated.* 20 Jan. 2004 <http://vnweb.hwwilsonweb.com/hww/ emailprintsave/emailprintsave_results.jhtml>.

▶ "Donald M(orison) Murray." *Literature Resource Center.* MTSU, James E. Walker Lib., Murfreesboro, TN. 2004. 20 Jan. 2004. <http://80galenet.galegroup.com.ezproxy.mtsu.edu/>.

▶ Mantz, Erika. "UNH Announces New Visiting Journalist Program." 14 Oct. 2004. *UNH Media Relations.* 14 Aug. 2006 <http://www.unh.edu/news_releases/2004/ october/em_20041014journalist.htm>.

▶ Smith, Jeanne Jacoby. "Anatomy of a High School Dropout." *The World and I* 13 (1998): 306-12.

▶ *University of New Hampshire.* 20 Jan. 2004 <http://www.unh.edu/general/awards/murray.htm>.

Annotated Bibliography

▶ Murray, Donald M. *A Writer Teaches Writing.* Boston: Houghton Mifflin, 1985.

Murray uses personal examples and stories from his own teaching experience throughout the text, as he offers other instructors practical advice about his successful method of teaching process writing. Murray introduces his theory of response teaching, which functions in tandem with his individual conferencing method and discusses helpful techniques for conducting workshops by sharing actual examples of writing course assignments. Murray concludes this hands-on tutorial by providing readers with a bibliography of sources for writing teachers.

▶ ---. *Crafting a Life in Essay, Story, Poem*. Portsmouth, NH: Boynton/Cook, 2000.

In this encouraging text, Murray provides his secrets of success as a Pulitzer Prize winning author, as he motivates writers to practice their craft on a regular basis. Murray opens by suggesting that all writers must give themselves permission to write. Then, writers must learn to listen to their own creative voices and invite surprise into their work. After presenting this practical theory of writing, Murray describes how he applies his method to different kinds of writing, like essays, stories, and poems.

▶ ---. *Learning by Teaching*. Portsmouth, NH: Boynton/Cook, 1982.

In this instructive book, Murray compiles 29 articles that he wrote about the writing process between the years 1969 and 1982. The first portion of the text focuses on the writing process and why writers write. The middle part discusses ways to make research writing creative and interesting to read. And, the last segment contains essays about teaching writing using the process approach. Murray handily draws all of these articles together and interjects personal comments about the essays prior to introducing each group of papers, which makes this a very enjoyable and instructional read.

▶ ---. "One Writer's Curriculum." *English Journal* 80 (1991): 16-20.

This article instructs all writers to practice their writing every day. Murray breaks down the writing process into three stages. Stage one introduces the need for writers to embrace solitude, experience, and faith. Secondly, Murray suggests that writers must identify need, tension, pattern, and voice in their writing. Lastly, writers must learn to write with ease; they must produce daily, and they must be aware of their audience. Murray provides readers with great tips for writing success in this eloquent, creative, and practical article.

▶ ---. "Reading for Surprise." *Expecting the Unexpected.* Portsmouth, NH: Boynton/Cook, 1989. 12-18.

Murray begins this chapter by describing how writers should learn to read for surprise. He believes that reading for surprise goes hand in hand with writing for surprise, which he advocates heartily. Murray claims that often he does not know where his writing will take him. He suggests that this openness to surprise in reading and writing is one key to creativity, and he advises his students to read ahead, read backwards, question failure, and read for what isn't written yet. Murray closes this educational essay by reminding his readers to remain open to the lessons that their writing will reveal to them as they read and write for surprise.

▶ ---. "Teaching the Other Self: The Writer's First Reader." *CCC* 33 (1982): 140-47.

Murray suggests in this article that, "The act of writing might be described as a conversation between two workmen muttering to each other at the workbench" (140). Murray explains that every writer has two selves. The first self acts as the writer, while the second self performs as the reader. Murray discusses the important task of listening as a composition teacher and describes how he allows his students to explain their words to him before he responds to what they have to say about their work. True to form, Murray provides his readership with several practical ideas to use in the innovative composition classroom.

▶ ---. "The Interior View: One Writer's Philosophy of Composition." *CCC* 21 (1976): 21-26.

In this educational essay, Murray strives to "capture the essential process of writing in one sentence" (21). Murray claims, "A writer is an individual who uses language to discover meaning in experience and communicate it" (21). Murray is suggesting that all good writing starts inside the mind of the writer. In other words, good writing arises when writers seek to discover meaning through their writing. Initially, writers may not know what needs to be said, but through the process of bringing their thoughts to the page, the significance of what they have to say starts to become clear. Murray believes "that the writing course should have one central purpose: to allow the student to use language to explore his world" (24). Murray reminds his readers that content is always more important than form in this very readable and entertaining essay.

▶ ---. "Writing After a Career of Writing." *Nieman Reports* 44 (1990): 16-17, 22.

In this instructive journal article, Murray offers aspiring writers handy tips that he has used over the years to help him along the path to being a productive writer. Initially, Murray advises readers to write every day, and he remarks, "Writing allows me to reflect on where I have been and what it all means" (16). Murray finds that he pays close attention to details as he moves through his day because often he will use that material as he writes his next story. Murray believes that all good writing in inherently personal: "To write, to really write, is to expose yourself to yourself and to your reader" (17). Finally, Murray advises writers to write in small chunks in order to complete large projects, but mainly he helpfully instructs writers to write every day.

▶ ---. *Writing to Deadline: The Journalist at Work*. Portsmouth, NH: Heinemann, 2000.

Murray applies his practical classroom teaching methods in the field of writing to the practice of professional journalism. Murray has worked as a journalist for most of his adult life, and he brings his ideas about reading and writing for surprise to the realm of news-writing. Murray includes examples of stories that were produced by actual news-writers, and he traces their methods for keeping up with the steady rhythm of newspaper production. Murray has produced another practical book that is a beneficial resource to anyone considering a career in the field of journalism.

► Romano, Tom. "The Living Legacy of Donald Murray."
　　English Journal 89 (2000): 74-79.

In this inspiring article, Tom Romano recalls moments from a
1997 convention that was held "to honor Don's life and work"
(74). Romano refers to Murray's process-oriented approach;
"His was a rhetoric of dialectic, not unity—a rhetoric of tension,
not taxonomy. Tradition valued certainty, predictability;
Murray valued surprise" (74-5). Romano suggests that the roots
of Murray's process approach are probably linked to the
author's own struggles with the formal educational system.
This article includes excerpts from the letters of many of
Murray's colleagues and friends, who have all learned a great
deal from him. The central message of this article is that
Murray is much more than a good writer; he is a good man,
who has carried his love for humanity into the classroom, and
this is what makes him a great writer, teacher, and friend.

Chapter 33:
Stephen M. North

The defining moment in Stephen North's career came in 1976 when he attended the *CCCC* in Philadelphia. At the height of a national literacy crisis, he listened intently to Carl Klaus's grim proposition that to this point there were "no professional teachers of writing" (North ii). Nearly three decades later, few would question the tenacity with which Stephen North answered this call.

North completed his DA (1979) in Composition at SUNY, Albany. Just two years later, he returned to his alma mater where he continues to serve as a tenured professor. North also spent two years teaching overseas both as visiting professor at Shandong University in China (1988-89) and as Fulbright Professor at Turku University and Abo Akademi in Finland (1996-97). At SUNY, Albany he was chosen as the recipient of the Excellence in Teaching Award (2001). Recognized as founder of the NCTE's *Refiguring English Studies* book series, North served as its first editor (1992-96). He has also published several books, articles, and book chapters.

Early in his professional endeavors, North was troubled by a sense of ambiguity and division within the field of composition that he, in turn, attributed to two essential causes: 1) the absence of an established model to synthesize the various discourses of the discipline, and 2) the lack of solidarity amongst faculty and theorists in the field. North channeled these frustrations into two monumental works that are now regarded as foundational pieces in writing center and composition theory. In both his seminal article "The Idea of a Writing Center" (1984) and *The Making of Knowledge in Composition: Portrait of an Emerging Field* (1987), North calls for a unified vision amongst faculty—one that places student writers above the goals of the institution and encourages the development of a community of learners based upon shared goals and perspectives.

North argues in "The Idea of a Writing Center" that the aim of writing instruction should be to produce better writers, rather than better texts. He promotes an expressivist approach to teaching and tutoring in which knowledge derived from the composing process lies entirely within the writer. As participant-observer, the goal of the tutor is to oversee the sacred ritual of writing unfold and ultimately to stimulate conversation. North's theory that the writing center's only reason for existence is to provide a space to converse with writers outlines a fundamental objective for the practice of peer tutoring that continues to be utilized in writing programs across the nation.

Most recently, North has extended his knowledge of composition into the realm of popular culture, examining the images of writing and the writer that have transformed American writers into celebrity icons for commercialized purposes. Appropriately, North views himself as both a teacher of writing and a teacher of teachers of writing. Reflecting upon his career, he states that the most rewarding part of his job is that "I write about what I do, and I do what I write about" ("Stephen North").

Cristy Hall

Sources for Biographical Narrative

▶ "The 2001 Excellence in Teaching Awards." University at
   Albany, SUNY. 2006. 22 June 06
   <www.albany.edu/feature2001/excellence_awards>.

▶ North, Stephen. "The Idea of a Writing Center." *CE* 46
   (1984): 433-46.

▶ ---. Preface. *The Making of Knowledge in Composition:
   Portrait of an Emerging Field.* Upper Montclair, NJ:
   Boynton/Cook, 1987. i-v.

▶ "Stephen North, Distinguished Teaching Professor." English
   Dept. home page. University of Albany, SUNY. 2006. 20
   June 06
   <http://www.albany.edu/english/faculty/north_s.html>.

Annotated Bibliography

▶ Carlton, Susan Brown. "Composition as a Postdisciplinary
   Formation." *Rhetoric Review* 14.1 (1995): 78-88.

Carlton refers to North's fear in *The Making of Knowledge in
Composition: Portrait of an Emerging Field* that the lack of
agreement concerning how knowledge is made has led to
feelings of ambivalence within the field. Carlton maintains that
ambivalence is both productive and healthy because it signifies
a resistance to conform to disciplinarity. Her essay offers a
valuable, fairly recent discussion that is pertinent to beginning
composition instruction. She discusses how researchers
continue to grapple with North's dilemma of wanting
composition to be an independent field and yet recognizing the
importance of strong disciplinary ties.

▶ Cawelti, Scott. "Five Difficult Truths about Composition."
   Iowa English Bulletin 39 (1991): 47-55.

Cawelti breaks down five of the principle arguments of *The
Making of Composition: Portrait of an Emerging Field* and
applies a validity test based upon his own knowledge and

experience of the discipline. Though Cawelti questions North's somewhat hackneyed depiction of the different communities that comprise Composition Studies, he agrees that many of North's grim projections are relevant and demand attention. His article offers new instructors with a fascinating springboard for discussing the manner in which present academic settings are shifting in the direction that North predicts in his book.

▶ Ede, Lisa. "Writing Center and the Politics of Location: A Response to Terrance Riley and Stephen M. North." *Writing Center Journal* 16.2 (1996): 111-21.

In assessing the reconfigured SUNY writing sequence program outlined in "Revisiting the Idea of a Writing Center," Ede argues that North merely resituates, rather than solves, the conflict between the grade-driven pressures of the university and the process-based, student-centered objectives of the writing center. Her discussion offers a stimulating analysis concerning the incongruity between theory and practice in writing center pedagogy that is quite useful for newcomers to the field.

▶ North, Stephen M. "On Book Reviews in Rhetoric and Composition." *Rhetoric Review* 10 (1992): 348-61.

On the surface, North appears to be merely arguing against current book review practices, which unfairly place a text completely in the hands of an isolated reviewer. However, on a deeper level, he offers an interesting parallel of the way the university limits the power of the student-writer by imposing a distorted judgment of what constitutes good or bad writing. Thus, a close reading of the text provides an in-depth look into North's attitudes concerning the power agencies who control the writing process. The hope is that this newfound awareness will aid instructors in shifting the power from institutions to individuals.

► ---. "The Death of Paradigm Hope, the End of Paradigm Guilt, and the Future of (Research in) Composition." *Composition in the Twenty-First Century*. Ed. Lynn Z. Bloom, Donald A. Daiker, and Edward M. White. Carbondale, IL: SIUP, 1996. 194-207.

North predicts that future research in composition will be positively impacted by a dramatic shift away from paradigmatic control. He envisions composition studies branching out of the classroom setting—a move that will entail reassessing what qualifies as research. Moreover, he foresees that as online communication replaces print sources, the public will have the ultimate responsibility of deciding what to read and what not to. North's fascinating essay is a must-read for anyone interested in the future vision of composition.

► ---. "Designing a Case Study Method for Tutorials: A Prelude to Research." *Rhetoric Review* 4 (1985): 88-99.

In this brief, but thought-provoking essay, North discusses the extent to which research in composition influences the actual practice of tutoring and teaching. He concludes that for all his theoretical knowledge, the essence of what he does on a daily basis is merely talk with writers. Overall, this piece is most beneficial to beginners in the field in that it provides composition instructors with a personal mission statement of North's goals and objectives for writing instruction.

► ---. "The Idea of a Writing Center." *CE* 46 (1984): 433-46.

Since its publication in 1984, North's article continues to be referred to as the foundational model of writing center instruction. North addresses his landmark essay to English faculty who, in his opinion, abuse the writing center to promote their own objectives. He expresses his sharp opposition to the fix-it-shop mentality of writing centers as remedial services and argues instead for an expressivist, student-centered approach to tutoring that aims to improve writers rather than the texts. Considered by writing programs across the nation as the landmark essay of writing center instruction, this article is a must for all teachers and students of composition.

▶ ---. *The Making of Knowledge in Composition: Portrait of an Emerging Field*. Upper Montclair, NJ: Boynton/Cook,1987.

In an expansive work that North admits was approximately ten years in the making, he provides a useful commentary of the three basic communities that comprise the field of composition: practitioners, researchers, and scholars. At present, he claims that each of these communities is competing for control. He closes the book with a grim vision of the future of composition studies unless the various groups can resolve their differences and unite together. His discussion of the politics of writing instruction provides a pertinent foundation for all instructors who should be well-versed in the struggles that continue to plague the discipline.

▶ ---. "Revisiting the Idea of a Writing Center." *Writing Center Journal* 15.1 (1994): 7-18.

Ten years after publishing "The Idea of a Writing Center," North writes this essay to clarify that the principles outlined in his earlier piece, which were addressed to faculty rather than tutors, were designed to outline the internal vision of the writing center rather than to govern tutoring practices. This article is most beneficial in that it reveals to new teachers and researchers the more pragmatic side of North—one who understands the day-to-day frustrations and concerns that occur in the writing center. Coupling this article with North's earlier piece provides practical application of North's philosophies, which strengthens, rather than diminishes, his spirited belief in the value of writing center instruction.

▶ Rankin, Elizabeth. "Taking Practitioner Knowledge Seriously: An Argument with Stephen North." *Rhetoric Review* 8 (1990): 260-67.

A teacher of composition, Rankin points out discrepancies in North's argument of practitioner inquiry. She argues that the definition he assigns to practitioners is too theoretical and does not properly recognize that their knowledge is acquired through a dialectic community of shared experiences. For those closely involved with the inner-workings of teaching composition, Rankin offers a fascinating examination of North's views on writing instruction.

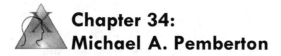

Chapter 34:
Michael A. Pemberton

(b. 1954)

With his diverse body of published work—including four books, several book chapters and over 50 articles—research, teaching experience and scores of conference presentations relating to the process of writing instruction, writing centers, WAC and technology, Michael A. Pemberton has distinguished himself as a leader in the field of composition studies.

Pemberton earned a BA (1975) in Motion Picture/TV Production at UCLA, and his MA (1984) in English at California Polytechnic State University. After earning his PhD (1990) in English and American Literature/Composition Studies at the UC, San Diego, where he studied under Charles Cooper and was influenced by cognitivists (the work of Flower and Hayes, in particular). Pemberton's contributions to the teaching of writing include his body of work on WAC and pedagogical, theoretical, social, psychological, ethical, scholarly, administrative, technological and professional issues as they relate to university writing centers and composition studies.

Pemberton became assistant professor of English at UIUC (1990), where he simultaneously began as associate director of the Center for Writing Studies and director of the Writers' Workshop; Pemberton held all three positions until 1999. Also at the UIUC, Pemberton served as director of Instructional Computing (1996-98), director of Outreach Programs (1996-99) and acting director of Programs in Professional Writing (1998-99). He was assistant professor of English at Georgia Southern University (1999-03), where he is currently associate professor of English (2003-present), member of the graduate faculty (2000-present) and director of the University Writing Center (1999-present). Pemberton has served in various offices for the IWCA: Past President (2001-03), President (1999-01), Vice President (1997-99), Treasurer (1995-97), and most recently as At-large Member (2004-present). He is active on both the governing and editorial boards of the *Writing Center Research Project* (2000-present), *Computers and Composition* (1990-present), *NWCA Press* (1995-present), *Academic Writing*, the *Writing Center Journal* (1995-present), *Language and Learning Across the Disciplines* (founding co-editor, 2001-04) and *Across the Disciplines* (editor, 2005-present). He is also a member of the Publishers and Professionals Committee of the NCTE.

Pemberton has received numerous scholarly awards, including the WPA Best Book Award (2004) and the IWCA Best Book Award (2004), for his work, *The Center Will Hold: Critical Perspectives on Writing Center Scholarship.* He earned the CLASS Award for Distinction in Service (2002) from the College of Liberal Arts and Social Sciences at Georgia Southern and received a Distinguished Scholarship Award (1994) from the NWCA for his "Writing Center Ethics" series of columns in the *Writing Lab Newsletter.*

Pemberton's recent works include *Bookmarks: A Guide to Research and Writing, 3rd Ed.* (Longman 2004, with John Ruszkiewicz and Janice Walker); "Working with Faculty Consultants in the Writing Center: Three Guidelines and a Case History" and "Critique or Conformity?: Ethics and Politics in the Writing Center," chapters in *The Writing Center Director's Resource Book* (Erlbaum 2005). Upcoming works include *Points of Contact: Readings Across the Curriculum* (Longman 2006); *Shifting the Center of Africanism: Language,*

Economic Regionalism, and Globalization; Proceedings of the 36th Annual Conference on African Linguistics (with Olaoba Arasanyin); and *The Best of the Writing Lab Newsletter* (with Muriel Harris).

Chris Driver

 Sources for Biographical Narrative

▶ Pemberton, Michael A. *Curriculum Vitae.* 9 Sept. 2004.

▶ ---. Home page. Writing and Linguistics Dept., Georgia Southern University. 20 Aug. 2006 <http://www.georgiasouthern.edu/~michaelp/>.

▶ ---. "Re: Class Project at MTSU." Email to Chris Driver. 22 Sept. 2004.

Michael Pemberton recommends these readings for novice writing center staff:

1. Murphy, Christina. "The Writing Center and Social Constructionist Theory." *Intersections: Theory-Practice in the Writing Center.* Ed. Joan Mullin and Ray Wallace Urbana: NCTE, 1994. 25-38. "Actually, this whole book would be an excellent resource."
2. Shamoon, Linda, and Deborah Burns. "A Critique of Pure Tutoring." *Writing Center Journal* 15.2 (1995): 134-51.
3. Carino, Peter. "Theorizing the Writing Center: An Uneasy Task." *Dialogue: A Journal for Writing Specialists* 2.1 (1995): 23-27.

Annotated Bibliography

▶ Pemberton, Michael A. "Grammar Redux, Redux, Redux." *Writing Lab Newsletter* 20.1 (1995): 5-6.

Pemberton continues his series on ethics, this time diving into the grammar debate that continues to rage within the composition departments of many universities. He concludes with a call for prioritization, though he emphasizes the fact that grammar is often the least important of the writing problems that appear in most student texts. Anyone interested in the intricacies of issues related to teaching grammar in first year composition classes and writing centers should take note.

▶ ---. "Ignorance and the Unethical Writing Center." *Writing Lab Newsletter* 19.6 (1995): 13-14.

Pemberton continues his series on ethics in the writing center by particularly addressing two of his previously-mentioned unethical accusations leveled at centers: the opinions that centers are unethical because tutors both tell students exactly how they should write papers, and that they write papers for students. Pemberton highlights the social nature of the writing process, and he asserts that teachers who make these unethical claims are clearly not accepting the social definition of writing itself. This column is rife with both amusing and effective ammunition for writing center devotees who are eager to vocally defend their ground.

▶ ---. "Modeling Theory and Composing Process Models." *CCC* 44 (1993): 40-58.

Pemberton begins by drawing lines of equity between epistemological models of scientific research and models that seek to map out the composing or writing process for scholars of composition and teachers alike. He concludes with a call for future researchers to carefully consider their own assumptions and goals when creating research and writing models. Though this article begins as a dense, historical overview, it moves into very practical points for researchers of the composition process.

▶ ---. "Preparing for Hypertext in the Writing Center. . . Or
    Not." *Writing Center Journal* 24 (2003): 9-24.

Pemberton is concerned with the rapidly approaching advances
in technologies available to the student and writer, particularly
hypertexts and web design. He notes that while new
technologies offer new pathways for the writing process to
become redirected, challenged and redefined, he also cautions
the reader to consider the implications on the evolving
structure of rhetoric. Pemberton makes a case for centers to
carefully consider and evaluate individual approaches to
evolving technology based on their circumstances; any
researcher involved in the intersection between technology and
the writing center would find this work helpful.

▶ ---. "Questioning Our Own Existence." *Writing Lab
    Newsletter* 19.5 (1995): 8-9.

With this, his first in a series of columns concerning ethics in
the writing center, Pemberton begins by greeting the "Newt
Year," reminding readers of the current (1995) political climate
in Washington D.C., one of promised budget cuts and
widespread, panic-induced attempts to justify social and
educational programs. Wishing to prepare those of us
concerned with protecting our writing centers, Pemberton
outlines the ten main arguments he predicts said budget
assassins will likely use when grinding their axes on writing
centers. All ten arguments focus on how the work that occurs in
writing centers is often deemed unethical, and those interested
in the writing center's ongoing battle for funding and respect
will be both engaged and find Pemberton's synopsis useful for
defense of writing centers and their methodologies.

▶ ---. "Rethinking the WAC/Writing Center Connection."
    Writing Center Journal 15.2 (1995): 116-33.

An often-cited piece on the connections, benefits and problems
that occur when WAC programs and writing centers intersect,
this article brings both enthusiasm and caution to the merging
of the two pedagogies. Pemberton reminds the reader that
writing centers are certainly not equipped, in most cases, to

instruct these specifics in every discipline, but, invoking Paulo Freire, Pemberton advocates the mutually beneficial learning that can occur between a tutor and a student of another discipline when they come together to work on writing. This article is essential for any researcher of the intersections between WAC and writing centers.

▶ ---. "Teaching, Learning, and Problem-Solving." *Writing Lab Newsletter* 19.8 (1995): 15-16.

With this installment of his ethics in the writing center series, Pemberton lowers his sights on the argument that writing center tutors "short circuit" the processes that students go through in order to learn how to write. He proceeds by making an effective argument that tutors can even be more effective at instilling a true understanding of the writing process than classroom teachers can, at times. Researchers of the teacher/tutor dichotomy and writing center ethics would benefit much from this article.

▶ ---. "Undermining the System." *Writing Lab Newsletter* 19.7 (1995): 15-16.

In this issue of his *Writing Lab Newsletter* series, Pemberton resumes his assault on the "unethical" accusations leveled at the writing center. While dissenting with each point, Pemberton relies on his previously argued point that teachers who still manage to view the writing process as a completely solitary and individual act are deliberately blinding themselves to the way most writers actually create. This article provides the writing center researcher/advocate with more useful defensive ammunition.

▶ Pemberton, Michael A., and Muriel Harris. "Online Writing Labs (OWLs): A Taxonomy of Options and Issues." *Computers and Composition* 12 (1995): 145-60.

Another popular source for contemporary scholarship in writing center and technology intersections, Pemberton and Harris's article offers a broad overview of issues and concerns for the then rapidly-growing rate of technological change in writing centers. The changes inherent in adapting face-to-face tutoring to the online environment are explored in depth, and the multitudinous options for administrators hoping to adopt new technology in their centers are thorough. Though some of the material is outdated, the social/instructional issues that technology and its various opportunities entail is certainly still relevant; this article is a great place to start for any study of the places where technology and the writing center meet.

▶ Pemberton, Michael A., and Joyce Kinkead, eds. *The Center Will Hold: Critical Perspectives on Writing Center Scholarship.* Logan: Utah State UP, 2003.

This collection of articles about ten seminal issues pertaining directly to today's writing centers was written in honor of Muriel Harris and her invaluable contributions to the field. The various authors, current leaders in the writing center community, discuss the issues that both challenge and contribute to the evolution of writing center theory and practice, including history, research, assessment, tutoring, writing center design, and administration. Pemberton and Kinkead have achieved both an historical introduction to writing center administration scholarship and a focused, helpful overview of some of the most current issues facing centers today. This book should be required reading for anyone researching any aspect of the contemporary writing center.

Chapter 35:
Mike Rose

(b. 1944)

Mike Rose entered the educational system in South Central Los Angeles where he attended, at various times, both public and parochial schools. At the private high school Our Lady of Mercy, he discovered what it was like first-hand to be labeled remedial. The exam he took to gain entrance was accidentally switched with another student named Rose, and he found himself on the vocational track rather than college bound. Once the mistake was uncovered, the school placed him in the college prep program, but he was far behind other students in many areas and struggled to maintain good grades.

With the help of his high school English teacher, Rose gained entrance to Loyola University of Los Angeles where he earned his BA (1966) in English. During his senior year, he received an honorable mention from the Danforth Foundation and, a month later, was offered a three-year full scholarship to UCLA. He attended UCLA as a graduate student for one year and then requested a leave of absence from his graduate program to pursue undergraduate studies in Psychology. After a year, Rose quit UCLA altogether and entered the University of Southern California (USC) under the Teacher Corps program where he received his MS (1970) in Education. He returned to UCLA and earned his MA (1970) in English and his PhD (1981) in Psychology, majoring in Educational Studies Counseling.

His teaching career actually began when he entered USC under the Teacher Corps program. He spent two years getting to know the educational system in Los Angeles from the teacher perspective, which gave him great insight into remedial studies and the effect such a label has on students. He held various counseling and consulting jobs before gaining a position at UCLA in 1971 where he has been a professor in the Graduate School of Education and Information Studies since 1996.

Rose has received many grants, awards, and fellowships for his achievements. Some of the grants received include those from the NCTE's Research Foundation (1988, 1994), the McDonnell Foundation Program in Cognitive Studies for Educational Practice (1988), and the Spencer Foundation (1991, 1998, 1999, 2000). He has received such awards as the MLA's Mina P. Shaughnessy Prize (1989), the Spencer Foundation Mentor Program Award (1998), and the David H. Russell Award for Distinguished Research in the Teaching of English from NCTE (1989).

In addition to his research and teaching, Rose has published numerous articles on rhetoric, literacy and instruction, schooling and society, cognition and work, program administration, program evaluation, and opinion pieces on educational policy. His best known book, *Lives on the Boundary: The Struggles and Achievements of America's Underprepared* (1989), focuses on the remedial, illiterate and intellectually deficient students as labeled by society. Another of his popular books is *Possible Lives: The Promises of Public Education in America* (1995), which deals with the educational system in under-funded school districts across America. Rose's work dealing with the psychology of writer's block and his research into the effectiveness of textbooks are major contributions to the theory and practice of writing.

Rose's current interest is the study of thinking and learning and how they are affected by such factors as what enhances or inhibits a person's interaction with written language, pedagogies and materials developed to aid with critical reading and writing, and effective teaching. These studies complement and build on the work he has accomplished.

Rose's most recent book, *An Open Language: Selected Writing on Literacy, Learning, and Opportunity* is a retrospective of his career and work from 1980 to 2005 and illustrates exactly what he has accomplished. Rose introduces each article or selection with the story of its origins as well as commentary on what he likes about the article or wants to highlight for readers. This text truly exemplifies the span of an important career while also chronicling a personal journey.

Dianna Baldwin

 Sources for Biographical Narrative

▶ "Mike Rose." Graduate School of Education and Information Studies home page. U of California, Los Angeles. 29 Jan. 2004 <http://www.gseis.ucla.edu/faculty/pages/rose.html>.

▶ Rose, Mike. Email to Dianna L. Baldwin. 27 Jan. 2004.

▶ ---. Email to Dianna L. Baldwin. 26 Jul. 2006.

▶ ---. *Lives on the Boundary: The Struggles and Achievements of America's Underprepared.* New York: Free Press, 1989.

▶ ---. *An Open Language: Selected Writing on Literacy, Learning, and Opportunity.* Boston: Bedford/St. Martin's, 2006.

Mike Rose recommends these readings for novice composition instructors:

1. Shaughnessy, Mina P. *Errors and Expectations: A Guide for the Teacher of BasicWriting.* New York: Oxford UP, 1977.
2. Ede, Lisa, ed. *On Writing Research: The Braddock Essays, 1975-1998.* Boston: Bedford/St. Martin's, 1999.
3. Villanueva, Victor, Jr., ed. *Cross-Talk in Comp Theory: A Reader.* 2nd ed. Urbana, IL: NCTE, 2003.

 Annotated Bibliography

▶ Hull, Glynda, and Mike Rose. "'This Wooden Shack Place': The Logic of an Unconventional Reading." *CCC* 41 (1990): 287-98.

This article explores the possibility that interpretation of literary works is dependent on the reader's personal history as well as his cultural background. It focuses on one of Rose's students in a remedial composition class who interprets a poem in a way that appears unconventional. The student uses his knowledge of "life" to interpret the poem, which is quite different from the standard reading. Hull and Rose suggest a "pedagogical model that places knowledge-making at its center" (296). This clear, concise article makes apparent the need for academia to understand that not all readers are the same.

▶ Peck, David, and Elizabeth Hoffman. "A Comment on 'Remedial Writing Courses.'" *CE* 46 (1984): 302-04.

Peck and Hoffman criticize Rose for minimizing the effectiveness of personal writing in his article entitled "Remedial Writing Courses: A Critique and a Proposal." They feel that he equated "personal" with "simple," and they argue that not only is writing from personal experience "'relevant and motivating' (which Rose denies) but that it allows remedial students to draw from the well of their own lives – their own experiences and culture." (303). Although Peck and Hoffman make a valid argument for using the personal essay, it must not be overlooked that they agree with Rose's article overall and validate much of what he says. It is an effective article at reminding readers to scrutinize what they read.

▶ Rose, Mike. "The Language of Exclusion: Writing Instruction at the University." *CE* 47 (1985): 341-59.

In this article Rose exposes the attitudes held by many in academics and the related politics concerning the college writing course. He advocates that until the language used to discuss writing changes, the attitudes will remain the same. This is a source that should be read by all who are involved with academia, not just by those concerned with writing courses. Rose does an outstanding job of explaining why the language used in the late 1800s is still in use today.

▶ ---. "Language Story: A Serial for Radio." *Rhetoric Review* 5 (1986): 48.

This is an interesting poem by Rose that depicts a young professor grading essays. The professor's pen has become his sword he uses to defend the art of writing. Yet try as he may, the battle is too much for him, and he succumbs to the "babies babies babies / tumbling to gum the edge of his tongue" (48). This poem contains important advice for any professor, TA, or adjunct grading the written word.

▶ ---. *Lives on the Boundary: The Struggles and Achievements of America's Underprepared.* New York: Free Press, 1989.

This in-depth look at the life and studies of Mike Rose, begins with the story of his family's relocation to California and his early school years and progresses to his studies at UCLA and his budding career. He spends one chapter relating the story of being in remedial classes in high school and what the attitudes often are toward students and classes. This is an easy, yet profound reading experience that anyone associated with teaching should learn from and enjoy. Professors could even recommend it to students who need a boost in confidence and morale.

► ---. *Possible Lives: The Promise of Public Education in America.* Boston: Houghton, 1995.

Rose takes the reader on an incredible journey from coast to coast through America's public schools. He focuses on school systems that have limited to modest funding to prove that good education takes place regardless of financial support. Education is not about money or who is in office at the time; it is about the teachers, the students and their families, and the community. With so much negative talk drowning our public school systems, his book is like coming up for air: we know we will have to go down again, but at least we have seen a glimpse of how it can be.

► ---. "Remedial Writing Courses: A Critique and a Proposal." *CE* 45 (1983): 109-28.

In this article, Rose discusses remedial courses: he reviews the effectiveness of UCLA's based on analyses performed on essays generated in these courses, and he explores why they failed. Based on his studies, he proposes a "four-tiered plan" for developing effective remedial courses. Anyone involved with developmental writing will find this article interesting, although sometimes difficult to follow.

► ---. "Speculations on Process Knowledge and the Textbook's Static Page." *CCC* 34 (1983): 208-13.

Rose questions the effectiveness of composition textbooks and argues that "students learn about the process of writing from a textbook less frequently and less effectively than many of us think" (208). He illustrates that writing is a complex, open-ended procedure that cannot be simply reduced to a series of problem solving steps as many disciplines can. This is a source that anyone teaching composition should read; however, some of the examples might require a second reading to gain a full understanding and appreciation for what Rose is saying.

▶ ---. "Sophisticated, Ineffective Books. The Dismantling
of Process in Composition Texts." *CCC* 32 (1981): 65-74.

This article, like "Speculations on Process Knowledge and the
Textbook's Static Page," takes to task the usefulness of
composition textbooks. Rose believes that the use of textbooks
often hinders, rather than helps, a student's ability to write
because the student believes what is written in the text to be
hard and fast rules for writing that must not be deviated from.
He suggests that composition should be taught "through a
program that acknowledges both the complexity of the
composing process and the dilemma of the student as a
stranger in a strange land of academic discourse and academic
audiences" (73). Compared with "Speculations," this one is
easier to read, but both should be read to gain a full
understanding of Rose's ideas concerning the inefficiency of
composition textbooks.

▶ ---. "When Faculty Talk about Writing." *CE* 41 (1979):
272-79.

This article—the result of a UCLA writing conference for its
own faculty including representatives from every discipline as
well as TAs, learning skills specialists, and Educational
Opportunity Program tutors—investigates solutions to the
problem of student writing, looking specifically at the
evaluation of writing, organization of writing instruction, who
would teach these classes, and how they should be taught. Any
university considering a WAC program should consult the
findings in this article.

▶ Rose, Mike, and Karen A. McClafferty. "A Call for the
Teaching of Writing in Graduate Education."
Educational Researcher 30.2 (2001): 27-33.

Rose and McClafferty discuss the issues of "the interrelation of
formal and rhetorical elements of writing; writing as craftwork;
writing as a method of inquiry; audience; becoming a critic; and
writing and identity" (28) as they pertain to the graduate
professional writing course began at UCLA in 1996. An
interesting, easy-to-read discourse for those concerned with the
state of scholarly writing at the graduate level and how this
type of course might be perceived, remedial or not.

Chapter 36:
Jacqueline Jones Royster

(b. 1950)

A nationally recognized scholar and educator, Jacqueline Jones Royster has devoted her career to advocating for the voices of the Other, especially in terms of literacy and academia. Royster's scholarship addresses issues of African American women's literary tradition and historical contributions, and issues in composition rhetoric and pedagogy. She earned her BA (1970) in English from Spelman College and completed graduate work in English Language (1971) from the University of Michigan, where she also earned her DA (1975) in English Language.

Royster's career began at Northern Illinois University (1972), followed by appointments at the University of Michigan and Clayton Junior College in Morrow, Georgia. Royster taught at Spelman College (1976-92), where she held various assignments, including associate professor of English, assistant dean for Freshman Studies, and director of the Comprehensive Writing Program. She served on the Faculty of the Breadloaf School of English, Middlebury College in Middlebury, Vermont (1991). Since 1992, Royster has served on the faculty of The Ohio State University, where she was director of the Writing Center (1992-94), before becoming a full professor in English

(2000). She has also served as associate Faculty in the Departments of Women's Studies and African American and African Studies and has held various administrative positions at Ohio State, culminating in her current position as Executive Dean of the College of the Arts and Sciences. Royster has served professionally as Chair of CCCC (1995) and held advisory positions with the College Board, NCTE, and MLA.

Royster's book *Traces of a Stream: Literacy and Social Change among African American Women* earned her the MLA's Mina P. Shaughnessy Prize (2001), and "History in the Spaces Left: African American Presence and Narratives of Composition Studies," co-authored with Jean C. Williams, won the Braddock Award for Best Article in *CCC* (2000). *Profiles of Ohio Women: 1803-2003* earned First Place Awards from both the Ohio Professional Writers and the National Federations of Press Women (2004). Additionally, Royster earned the CCCC Exemplar Award (2004) for her professional contributions and has received numerous awards of distinction from Ohio State, including being named one of its 2003 Distinguished Lecturers of the Year.

Royster insists that academia become more inclusive, in both the classroom and in scholarship, and she maps out a means by which teachers can accomplish this task. She claims that the voices of the marginalized must be given not merely respect but room to flourish, which is accomplished as much by how we listen to these voices as by how they communicate. Such inclusivity also requires knowledge of and respect for the histories that inform these voices. Royster's own voice is a powerful testament to this inclusiveness, both in her writing, which is often personal and engaging, and in her public speaking, which is noted for its power to excite audiences.

Lori McClure-Wade

Sources for Biographical Narrative

▶ "2003 University Distinguished Lecturer." The Ohio State University. 2003. 17 June 2005 <http://www.osu.edu/facultystaff/university_awards/ lecturer.html#royster>.

► "Jacqueline Royster." Colleges of the Arts and Sciences home
   page. The Ohio State University. 2005. 16 June 2006
   <http://artsandsciences.osu.edu/contact/
   contact_bio.cfm?Email=royster.3.@osu.edu>.

► "Jacqueline Jones Royster Tapped to Lead the Colleges of
   the Arts and Sciences." *Humanities Express* 1.4 (2005).
   The Ohio State Univesity. 15 June 2005
   <http://humanities.osu.edu/news/express/yr2005/
   may_article01.cfm?HEID=archive>.

► "Royster, Jacqueline Jones. "RE: Composition Leaders."
   Email to Lori McClure-Wade. 14 June 2006.

**Jacqueline Jones Royster offers this advice for novice
composition instructors:**

"Subscribe to the journals in the field (e.g., *CCC*, *CE*, *Pedagogy*,
JAC, *Journal of Basic Writing*, etc.) and keep up with the cutting
edges of our quite multiply defined discipline."

 Annotated Bibliography

► Jacqueline Jones Royster. "In Search of Ways In: Reflection
   and Response." *Feminine Principles and Women's
   Experience in American Composition and Rhetoric*. Ed.
   Louise Wetherbee Phelps and Janet Emig. Pittsburgh:
   U of Pittsburgh P, 1995. 385-91.

Royster responds to both the editors of this volume and the
other writers in it, explaining that her perspective as an
African American woman is not really represented here. This is
not an indictment but a reminder of the need for more
attention to be paid to inclusivity in studies-based rhetoric and
is targeted more towards editors and authors than it is to
teachers. She calls for inclusiveness in all arenas of composition
studies and offers useful insights to anyone working in
composition rhetoric.

▶ ---. "Issues of Tolerance and College Writing Courses." *ADFL Bulletin* 31.1 (1999): 38-42.

Royster outlines the challenges that introductory writing teachers face in helping students make the transition into the multicultural landscape of academia. She presents methods for shifting classroom paradigms so that the classroom becomes a site of mediation for students as they learn to use language to speak across communities. This article can remind teachers in gen-ed writing courses of the broader role they play in helping students become citizens of the academic community.

▶ ---. "On Writing Centers: Reflections of a Wanderer about Time, Space, and Variable Fortune." *Focuses* 7.1 (1994): 18-26.

This essay presents a two-fold hypothesis on why writing centers are important in university communities and challenges writing center staffs to answer four questions that should serve to support that hypothesis. Personal and engaging, Royster uses Homer's *Odyssey* as a metaphor for her writing center experiences, which becomes a springboard for her challenge to writing center staffs to engage in some detailed self-examination. This may initially seem a bit dated, as Royster contemplates whether or not writing centers will still be viable in 21st century universities, but the problems and challenges she outlines are not outdated and are still worth considering.

▶ ---. "Perspectives on the Intellectual Tradition of Black Women Writers." *The Right to Literacy*. Ed. Andrea A. Lunsford, Helene Moglen, and James Slevin. New York: MLA, 1990. 103-12.

Royster argues that more room must be made for African American women's intellectual tradition and scholarship, asserting that this will only happen when that tradition's history is fully acknowledged; she then offers a brief delineation of that history. She details a rich history of literature, scholarship and intellectualism that stretches as far back as most other American literary traditions. This argument is useful for composition and literature instructors as they consider texts and authors for classroom use, reminding them that classroom inclusivity begins with texts.

▶ ---. "Shifting the Paradigms of English Studies: Continuity and Change." *PMLA* 115 (2000): 1222-28.

This essay outlines problems, realities and challenges facing PhD candidates in composition and rhetoric and calls for graduate programs to deal with some harsh realities. Among these realities are an increasingly distrustful public, a potentially glutted job market, and students who may not be prepared for either. While this may sound bleak in tone, Royster's intention is to call for a re-imagining of English studies that places importance on teaching as a primary component of the profession rather than considering it a burden placed upon scholars.

▶ ---. *Traces of a Stream: Literacy and Social Change Among African American Women.* Pittsburgh: U of Pittsburgh P, 2000.

In this award-winning text, Royster establishes in three sections—A Rhetorical View, A Historical View, and An Ideological View"—the rhetorical tradition of African American women writers of the 19th century, asserting that these women were engaged in making meaning and developing authority to address the white patriarchal establishment both politically and academically. This writing, Royster asserts, is sophisticated and counters the idea that the African American literary tradition is somehow new; however, she contends that this thesis is met with the resistance of "deep disbelief" in academia (254). In instructional and powerful prose, Royster offers scholars in composition and rhetoric an opportunity to move past this deep disbelief and into a deeper understanding of the traditions in which they operate.

▶ ---. "When the First Voice You Hear Is Not Your Own." *CCC* 47 (1996): 29-40.

In a first-person narrative detailing Royster's own experiences as an Other, she seeks to examine the significance of subject position in both the classroom and the field of composition and rhetoric. Royster advocates the importance of respecting and listening to myriad voices, both as rhetoricians and instructors, calling for a paradigm shift that does away with notions of primacy. This narrative serves as an excellent primer for white teachers who may face classrooms filled primarily with white faces, which may prevent them from considering how to reach out to their non-white students and encourage them to develop their voices as writers.

▶ Royster, Jacqueline Jones, and Rebecca Greenberg Taylor. "Constructing Teacher Identity in the Basic Writing Classroom." *Journal of Basic Writing* 16.1 (1997): 27-50.

Inspired by a CCCC workshop that Royster and Taylor created in which writing teachers examine their identities from both personal and student perspectives, this article presents information from that workshop along with excerpts from Taylor's teaching journal and reflections on both. As Taylor struggles to locate her own authority as a TA among a varied group of students, she reminds teachers of the often disregarded role they play in creating classroom cultures. Engaging and thought-provoking, this could be quite useful for all first year writing instructors as it challenges them to be conscious of how their own sense of self informs and shapes their conceptions of their students' varied identities and how that impacts what occurs in the writing classroom.

▶ Royster, Jacqueline Jones, and Jean C. Williams. "History in the Spaces Left: African American Presence and Narratives of Composition Studies." *CCC* 50 (1999): 563-84.

Royster and Williams call for a more inclusive history of composition studies by reviewing landmark works in the field and examining their inclusion and treatment of (or lack thereof) African American voices; they then highlight the history of African American intellectual traditions and contributions to the field. This work challenges the trend in composition studies to conflate African American students with basic writers and reminds us that the history of composition studies is in fact multicultural in nature.

▶ ---. "Reading Past Resistance: A Response to Valerie
    Balester." *CCC* 52 (2000): 133-42.

Royster and Williams respond to Balester's article "The
Problem of Method: Striving to See with Multiple
Perspectives," published in the same issue of *CCC*. Balester
takes issue with Royster and Williams' assessment of her book
Cultural Divide (in "History in the Spaces Left") and the way it
represents African American students as outsiders and basic
writers who are hindered by their use of AAVE. Royster and
Williams welcome Balester's response and use it as an
opportunity to further clarify their position and to again
advocate for teachers and scholars to read past their resistance
and make multiple viewpoints operational in the classroom.

Chapter 37
Cynthia L. Selfe

(b. 1951)

Although she did not set out to change the worlds of computers and composition, Cynthia L. Selfe, along with her frequent co-author Gail E. Hawisher, has done just that. The author and co-author of more than ten books, Selfe has based her career on encouraging and promoting a changing view of technology and computers in composition studies. In 1989, she and Hawisher founded the Computers and Composition Press based out of their respective universities, Michigan Technological University and the UIUC. Selfe graduated with her BS (1973) from the University of Wisconsin, Madison, and went on to UT-Austin, to get her MEd (1977) and her PhD (1981). Prior to receiving her MEd, Selfe was already a teaching professional as the Supervisor of Student Teachers at the UT-Austin, a position she held until 1978.

Upon earning her PhD, Selfe accepted a position at Michigan Tech as an assistant professor where she taught as wide range of courses such as Hypertext Theory, Computers in Writing, Technical Writing, Grammar and Editing, Literature and Lore of the Upper Peninsula, and Science Fiction. In 1991, she accepted, a full Professorship of Humanities at Michigan Tech, and in 2006, Selfe became the Humanities Distinguished professor in the Department of English at The Ohio State University.

In 1983, the same year that she was awarded a $26,000 development grant for process-based computer-assisted instruction in composition at Michigan Tech, Selfe published her first work on computers and composition, "The Benevolent Beast: Computer-Assisted Instruction for the Teacher of Writing," in *The Writing Instructor*. Then, in 1996, Selfe was the first composition leader and the first woman to win the EDUCOM Medal award for innovative computer use in higher education, an award granted by a consortium of higher education institutions interested in the use of information resources for educational purposes. Selfe's theories about computers focus on her plea for teachers to incorporate them into the classroom and their own lives because their students' lives are increasingly tied up with technology, and the teacher who is unwilling to give computers a chance in the classroom is doing a disservice to his or her students by further widening the gap between teacher and student. Since she first began working with computers and composition, she has published many more works in these fields and received several grants, the most recent being a CCCC Research Initiative Grant (2004) for her project entitled, "Composition, Rhetoric, and Literacy: What We Know, What We Need to Know," with co-researchers Cheryl Ball, Anthony Atkins, Richard Selfe, Daniel Anderson, and Krista Homiez Miller. Also in 2004, Selfe was named the Distinguished Watson Professor in the Department of English at the University of Louisville.

In 1989, Selfe began her collaboration with Hawisher as co-editor of *Critical Perspectives on* Computers and Composition. Together, they serve as co-authors and editors of numerous books and articles and as co-editors of Computers and Composition: An International Journal for Teachers of English. They have also been the recipients of the NCTE Research Foundation Grant (2000-01), the Society for Technical Communications Special Opportunities Grant (2000-01), and the Outstanding Technology Innovator award by the CCCC Committee on Computers (2000).

Selfe's most influential contributions to composition theory, research, and pedagogy obviously center on the inclusion of computers and technology in the composition classroom and in writing instruction, but her interests also overlap into the fields of feminist theory in composition, literacy, alternative texts, educational reform, and writing apprehension. Recently, Selfe's work has examined the innovative role of visual rhetoric. She claims that images and words influence each other and the ways that humanity understands each. Selfe, along with Lester Faigley, Diana George, and Anna Palchik, presents her findings on images and words in the book *Picturing Texts* (2004). In addition to visual rhetoric, Selfe is currently exploring the video game culture in her forthcoming book *Gaming Lives in the 21st Century* as a place for young people to learn a variety of literacies. Selfe is also continuing her work on providing resources for teachers with another soon-to-be-published work *Resources in Technical Communication: Approaches and Outcomes,* in which she lays out a specific approach for teachers of technical communication courses.

It is because of Selfe's work with technology, composition, and cutting-edge views on literacy that she has become one of the forerunners not only in the field of composition, but also in the field of technology.

Rachel Robinson

 Sources for Biographical Narrative

▶ Hawisher, Gail, Paul LeBlanc, Charles Moran, and Cynthia L. Selfe. *Computers and the Teaching of Writing in American Higher Education: 1979-1994: A History.* Assoc. Ed. Sibylle Gruber and Margaret Faler Sweany. Norwood, NJ: Ablex, 1996.

▶ Selfe, Cynthia L. Humanities Dept. home page. Michigan Technological University. 26 November 2004 <http://www.hu.mtu.edu/~cyselfe/>.

► ---. "RE: Book Chapter." Email to Rachel Robinson. 26 July
2006.

► ---. "RE: Composition Project." Email to Rachel Robinson.
28 Nov. 2004.

► ---. "Technology and Literacy: A Story about the Perils of Not
Paying Attention." *CCC* 50 (1999): 411-36.

Cynthia Selfe recommends these readings for novice composition instructors:

1. Certeau, Michel de. *The Practice of Everyday Life.*
   Trans. S. Randall. Berkeley: U Cal P, 1984.
2. Cope, Bill, and Mary Kalantzis. *Multiliteracies:
   Literacy Learning and the Design of Social Futures.*
   London: Routledge, 2000.
3. Giddens, Anthony. *The Constitution of Society:*
4. *Outline of a Theory of Structuration.* Berkeley: U Cal P,
   1984.

 Annotated Bibliography

► Faigley, Lester, Diana George, Anna Palchik, and Cynthia
Selfe. *Picturing Texts.* New York: Norton, 2004.

Because of the growth in the use of the Internet and other graphic-intensive technology, the authors argue that increasingly, visual information can be regarded as texts. They claim that the power relationship between words and pictures is one that is not co-dependent so much as it is co-inspirational—words inspire pictures (Paris=Eiffel Tower) just as pictures inspire words (golden arches=McDonald's). Anyone interested in the newest aspect of rhetoric should read this book.

▶ Hawisher, Gail E, and Cynthia L. Selfe. *Literate Lives in the Information Age: Narratives of Literacy from the United States*. Mahwah, NJ: Erlbaum, 2004.

Begun as a way to track technological literacy, *Literate Lives* showcases 20 case studies of a widely varied group of people, all of whom have become proficient in the literacy of technology to their own degree. Hawisher and Selfe argue that the lack of knowledge of these literacies today is stifling to education, and a more familiar understanding of these workings is imperative, especially among students and educators. Both broad in scope and subject, the book aptly presents a multitude of different cases with subjects ranging in age from their 60s to age eight, each providing his or her own snapshot of cultural ecology, while not overloading the reader with too much information.

▶ Hawisher, Gail E., Paul LeBlanc, Charles Moran, and Cynthia L. Selfe. *Computers and the Teaching of Writing in American Higher Education, 1979-1994: A History*. Assoc. Ed. Sibylle Gruber and Margaret Faler Sweany. Norwood, NJ: Ablex, 1996.

This book is an extensive history of how scholars have adapted the computer to fit into their work in the field of composition between the years of 1979 and 1994. The authors claim that the use of computers is two-fold in the lives of people: computers advance and change us, and we change computers to fit our needs. With side panels on every page giving extra details on the progression of computers and interesting tidbits about the authors, this book is a quintessential piece to any composition scholar's library.

▶ Selfe, Cynthia L., *Computer-Assisted Instruction in Composition, Create Your Own!* New York: NCTE, 1986.

This book, written in manual style, gives practical advice and instruction in creating a personal computer-assisted instruction (CAI) course with chapters that include everything from pedagogical decision making about CAIs to screen displays. Selfe claims that CAIs have become more popular because of an increasing desire to motivate students, move toward paperless classrooms, and decrease teacher workload. Although some of her instruction seems a bit dated today, for the beginning CAI developer, this book provides a useful resource.

▶ ---. "Lest We Think the Revolution is a Revolution: Images of Technology and the Nature of Change." *Passions, Pedagogies, and 21st Century Technologies.* Ed. Gail E. Hawisher and Cynthia L. Selfe. Logan: Utah State UP, 1999. 292-322.

Selfe argues that although technology is advancing, teachers are actually harming their students by reinforcing old stereotypes and prejudices by teaching them to be technology indulgers and not technology scholars. While she never says that technology is outright bad, Selfe claims that American cultural values are reflected in our advertisements, and therefore, subliminally instilled in those people who have not been taught ways to identify this, causing the worldly American cultural view to change little over time and to capitalize on the oppression of different cultures and the suppression of different voices. This, Selfe's seminal article, provides a very clear look at some of the lingering ugly aspects of American culture and is particularly useful for anyone interested in teaching cultural awareness.

▶ ---. "Redefining Literacy: The Multilayered Grammars of Computers." *Critical Perspectives on Computers and Composition Instruction.* Ed. Gail E. Hawisher and Cynthia L. Selfe. New York: Teachers College P, 1989. 3-15.

In this article, Selfe defines the term "grammars" in light of their work with computers as rules that govern arrangement, structure, form and appearance. After explaining how we perceive reality through the use of traditional literacy, Selfe outlines the different ways that grammars add to the way that computer-supported communication environments can be examined, and in so doing, we are able to visualize text and construct meaning and understanding from this visualization. Written simply and concisely, this article is imperative for scholars wanting to know more about computers and literacy but not wanting to become bogged down with many computer terms.

▶ ---. "Technology and Literacy: A Story about the Perils of Not Paying Attention." *CCC* 50 (1999): 411-36.

In this article, Selfe points out that it is a growing trend among Humanists to ignore modern technology, computers, in favor of a much more accessible and understandable mainstream technology, books. Because of this, Humanists are lacking the knowledge to accurately teach growing populations of students whose lives are almost entirely computerized, and as a result, they tend toward teaching how to use technology while still refusing to think about technology. Readers interested in computers, but not savvy with computer language, may find this article tedious, but Selfe's wit and passion make it an interesting, enjoyable, and informative read.

▶ Selfe, Cynthia L., and Sue Rodi. "An Invention Heuristic for Expressive Writing." *CCC* 31 (1980): 169-74.

Selfe and Rodi present a heuristic for expressive writing that centers on three perspectives of the individual—how the individual defines himself or herself, how the individual is defined by others, and how the individual is defined by the things he or she uses to achieve certain goals in his or her life. They claim that the hardest part of writing for students is that of invention, where the student must find something interesting in his or her experiences and figure out the best way to write about these experiences. By examining past, present, and future within the students' perceptions of themselves, Selfe and Rodi present an interesting model for the teacher looking for a way to engage reluctant writers.

▶ Selfe, Cynthia L., and Richard J. Selfe, Jr. "The Politics of the Interface: Power and Its Exercise in Electronic Contact Zones." *CCC* 45 (1994): 480-504.

After presenting an anecdote in which an Indian professor at an American university is held up at the Mexican border on his way back into the U.S. from a day trip, Selfe and Selfe examine the borders that computer-based English composition courses inherently provide and the colonialism and oppression that results from these borders. Using computers in the classroom, the authors argue, can create a space that appears to be safe for people of all races, ages, genders, and sexual preferences, but it also creates a belief that all students have the same access to computers, which, studies prove, is not the case. Anyone ready to be challenged by the arguments presented in the link between oppression, colonialism, liberation, and technology should read this article.

▶ Selfe, Cynthia L., and Billie J. Wahlstrom. "Computer-Supported Writing Classes: Lessons for Teachers." *Computers in English and the Language Arts.* Ed. Cynthia L. Selfe, Dawn Rodrigues, and William R. Oates. Urbana, IL: NCTE, 1989. 257-68.

In this article, Selfe and Wahlstrom outline the basics for teachers wishing to incorporate computers into their classrooms, and in so doing, present the positive and negative aspects of teaching with computers. They conclude that although choosing to incorporate a classroom with computers will be a burden for the overworked and underpaid teacher, teachers need to understand that students are living in a world rapidly growing with technology, and leaving it out of the curriculum would be a disservice to students. Any teacher wishing to weigh the pros and cons of a computer-assisted classroom should read this article.

Chapter 38:
Mina P. Shaughnessy

(1924-1978)

Known for her compassionate and innovative work in the field of basic writing, Shaughnessy served as dean and director of the Instructional Resource Center at CUNY from 1975 until her death in 1978. As director of CUNY's basic writing program, she was a powerful advocate for basic writers when open admissions challenged educators to look beyond traditional teaching methods in order to meet the needs of under-prepared students. Shaughnessy's analysis of the logic behind student error in her landmark text *Errors and Expectations: A Guide for the Teacher of Basic Writing* validated the texts of basic writers and legitimized the work of basic writing instructors. Even though she published only one book and a handful of articles, Shaughnessy's work continues to be a seminal source for current research in the field.

Shaughnessy received her BA (1946) from Northwestern University and her MA (1951) from Columbia University. She worked as a research assistant (1951-54), spent a year in Rome helping a pastor write his memoirs (1955), and supervised the editor training program at McGraw Hill (1956-61) before taking a part-time position teaching evening courses in Hunter

College's General Studies division. Shaughnessy's determination to help non-traditional, under-prepared students succeed stood in stark contrast to the conviction of many academicians who argued that these students did not belong in college. This opposition only steeled her resolve, and Shaughnessy continued teaching evening classes at Hunter College even after she accepted a full-time faculty position at Hofstra University (1964).

In 1967, Shaughnessy became the director of CUNY's Pre-Baccalaureate Program called SEEK (Search for Education, Elevation, and Knowledge). When CUNY adopted its open admissions policy in 1970, the SEEK population grew by almost 600 percent, and Shaughnessy was faced with the challenge of integrating thousands of non-traditional students into the traditional halls of academia. In 1975, as director of the Instructional Resource Center, Shaughnessy founded the *Journal of Basic Writing* in order to promote scholarship and raise awareness. Two years later, she published *Errors and Expectations*. As the first person to conduct a scholarly inquiry into the field of basic writing, Shaughnessy quickly became the most respected and influential spokesperson in what was just beginning to be recognized as a legitimate field of study.

In recent years, critics including Bruce Horner, Min-Zhan Lu, John Rouse, and Ira Shor have argued that Shaughnessy's formalistic methods deprive students of their own language by emphasizing skill over expression. However, Shaughnessy's followers would counter that without skill, students are unable to use language to express themselves. This ongoing debate is indicative of the impact Shaughnessy's work continues to make in the field of basic writing.

In 1978, Shaughnessy was honored by a proclamation signed by President Jimmy Carter in recognition of her work on behalf of literacy. Later that year, the NCTE presented her with the prestigious David H. Russell Award for Distinguished Research. Shortly after her death in November of 1978, the Mina P. Shaughnessy Prize was established by the MLA Executive Council as a memorial to one of the most widely respected scholars and teachers in the field of writing. Other memorials include the Mina P. Shaughnessy Writing Award given to outstanding articles published in the *Journal of Basic Writing* and the Mina Shaughnessy Scholars Program designed to support practitioners in their efforts to improve teaching and learning at the post-secondary level.

Victoria Knierim

Sources for Biographical Narrative

▶ Maher, Jane. *Mina P. Shaughnessy: Her Life and Work.* Urbana, IL: NCTE, 1997.

▶ Patterson, Amy. "Mina Shaughnessy." *Encyclopedia of Rhetoric and Composition: Communication from Ancient Times to the Information Age.* Ed. Theresa Enos. New York: Garland, 1996.

▶ Reeves, LaVona L. "Mina Shaughnessy and Open Admissions at New York's City College." *The NEA Higher Education Journal* 24 Sept. 2003 <http://www.nea.org/he/heta01/w01-02p117.pdf>.

Annotated Bibliography

▶ Allen, Michael. "Writing Away from Fear: Mina Shaughnessy and the Uses of Authority." *CE* 41 (1980): 857-67.

Written as a rebuttal to an attack on Mina Shaughnessy's *Errors and Expectations,* this article gives insight into the tension between academics who see themselves as guardians of the culture and those who see themselves as servants of the students. Allen clarifies and supports Shaughnessy's views by describing how her principles work in his own classroom. Allen's practical, easy-to-read, and entertaining style makes this article a great place to begin an examination of the complex issues surrounding basic writing.

► Bartholomae, David. "Released into Language: Errors, Expectations, and the Legacy of Mina Shaughnessy." *The Territory of Language.* Ed. Donald A. McQuade. Carbondale, IL: SIUP, 1986. 65-88.

Bartholomae offers an excellent summary of Shaughnessy's contributions to the field of basic writing. He then builds on Shaughnessy's foundation by exploring the connection between a literary education and a basic writer's concept of style. He calls for the development of a new basic writing curriculum that uses a literary canon to engage basic writers in the work of the university. Bartholomae's engaging style makes this article an easy read. Scholars interested in the connection between reading and writing will find plenty to ponder in these pages.

► Emig, Janet. "Mina Pendo Shaughnessy." *CCC* 30 (1979): 37-38.

This memorial written by Mina Shaughnessy's friend and colleague is only one of the many that were published in various newspapers, journals, and magazines after Shaughnessy's death. It describes the profound impact Shaughnessy had on those who knew her. Emig's challenge to academia to continue Shaughnessy's work with under-privileged and under-prepared students is a challenge worthy of any English scholar's consideration. Emig's comments will remind composition instructors why they spend their weekends reading student essays.

► Laurence, Patricia. "The Vanishing Site of Mina Shaughnessy's *Errors and Expectations.*" *Journal of Basic Writing* 19.2 (2000): 22-43.

This article, originally presented as an address at the 4th National Basic Writing Conference in 1992, argues that Shaughnessy's *Errors and Expectations* cannot be evaluated outside of the political and historical context that helped to shape it. This argument is being made in response to two reassessments of the book that fail to consider the audience for whom *Errors* was written: Min-Zhan Lu's "Redefining the

Legacy of Mina Shaughnessy: A Critique of the Politics of Linguistic Innocence" and Steven North's *The Making of Composition: Portrait of an Emerging Field.* Laurence's warning against historic retrospective accounts of the basic writing movement and her scholarly discussion of the theories and practices surrounding legitimate research and analysis will prove invaluable to students pursuing a career in composition.

▶ Lu, Min-Zhan. "Redefining the Legacy of Mina Shaughnessy: A Critique of the Politics of Linguistic Innocence." *Journal of Basic Writing* 10.1 (1991): 26-40.

This article is an example of the kind of discourse generated by Mina Shaughnessy's *Errors and Expectations.* Lu argues that basic writing programs make an essentialist assumption about the meaning of language. She asserts that while Shaughnessy's pedagogical intentions help students gain control of the conventions of language, they don't allow students to address the "the potential dissonance between academic discourses and their home discourses" (27). Lu's argument is representative of those who protest the use of Standard American English as a measure of literacy. This article will help beginning composition instructors determine where they stand on that controversial issue.

▶ Maher, Jane. *Mina P. Shaughnessy: Her Life and Work.* Urbana, IL: NCTE, 1997.

In this biography of Mina Shaughnessy, Jane Maher traces the remarkable life of the first person to begin a scholarly inquiry into the field of basic writing. Mina Shaughnessy's life story not only contributes to an understanding of the events that took place in the open admissions environment of the late sixties and early seventies, but it also serves as an inspiration to anyone who desires to make a difference in the lives of his or her students. With the help of Mina's friends and family, Maher creates a biography that is personal, warm, and entertaining. This book will affirm any student planning a career in composition.

▶ Reeves, LaVona L. "Mina Shaughnessy and Open
     Admissions at New York's City College." *The NEA
     Higher Education Journal*. 24 Sept. 2003
     <http://www.nea.org/he/heta01/w01-02p117.pdf>

Reeves discusses the role Shaughnessy played in establishing a
basic writing program at CUNY during the sixties and
seventies when open admissions was challenging the way
academics approached higher education. Reeves continues her
discussion by tracing the changes that have occurred in the
field since that time and speculates as to what Shaughnessy's
reaction might be to current plans for phasing out remedial
programs at four-year colleges. This informative article is a
must-read for anyone interested in pursuing a career in
beginning composition.

▶ Shaughnessy, Mina P. "Basic Writing." *Teaching
     Composition: 10 Bibliographical Essays*. Ed. Gary Tate.
     Fort Worth: Texas Christian UP, 1976. 137-68.

This comprehensive article prepared as a bibliographical essay
begins by discussing the implications of being labeled a basic or
remedial writer. It goes on to explore who basic writers are,
why they write the way they do, how they have been taught in
the past, and how they should be taught in the future.
Shaughnessy addresses each topic and then provides names,
dates, resources, and publications that support or challenge her
ideas. Some of the resources mentioned are out-of-date, and
some of the theorists have moved on to other things, but there
is so much historical information in this article that all basic
writing teachers should be aware of what it has to offer. It will
serve as a rich source of information for researchers.

▶ ---. "Diving In: An Introduction to Basic Writing." *CCC* 27
     (1976): 234-39.

This article, originally presented as an address to the MLA
Convention in 1975 in San Francisco, suggests that students
are not the only ones who need remedial help in an open
admissions environment—English teachers who have been
trained in traditional methods of teaching need remedial
training in order to meet the needs of beginning students.

Using a developmental scale similar to the ones teachers use to evaluate students, Shaughnessy categorizes the willingness of teachers to undertake this challenge, noting that it takes professional courage for a teacher to remediate himself. As an address, "Diving In" had a profound impact on those present at the MLA in 1975; the article continues to inspire composition teachers by challenging them to move up the developmental scale so that they can meet the needs of their students.

▶ ---. "The English Professor's Malady." *Journal of Basic Writing* 13.1 (1994): 117-24.

Originally delivered as an address at the ADE Conference in June, 1977, in Albany, New York, this article does what Shaughnessy does best—gets to the heart of the problem. Shaughnessy boldly suggests that English professors really don't know much about writing—the psychology of writing, the history of writing, the cultural part of writing, or even the functions and forms of academic writing. She observes that writing is often used in academia to separate the privileged from the underprivileged and cautions that literateness should not be confused with intelligence. Her challenge to those who seek to become truly altruistic teachers makes this an important work for beginning teachers to read.

▶ ---. *Errors and Expectations: A Guide for the Teacher of Basic Writing.* New York: Oxford UP, 1977.

One of the most important books ever written in the field of English composition, *Errors and Expectations* not only reveals the logic of student errors, but also offers suggestions for the teacher on how to help students reduce those errors. Shaughnessy studied more than 4,000 student essays to provide a practical, compassionate, and intelligent analysis of the problems student writers face. Her research demystifies the writing process so that teachers can empower their students by helping them gain control over language. Every composition teacher should have a copy of this book in her own library so that she can return to it again and again. The comprehensive index in the back of the book serves as a direct link to practical suggestions for helping students learn what they need to know about grammar so that they can express themselves through their writing.

Chapter 39:
Tony Silva

(b. 1953)

Internationally recognized for his research and scholarship in second language writing, Tony Silva has become a leader in his field with five books and over 30 journal articles and book chapters. Silva received his BA (1977) in Spanish from Kutztown State College in Pennsylvania, his MA (1981) in TESL from UIUC, and his PhD (1990) in English with a concentration in rhetoric and composition and linguistics from Purdue.

Upon completion of his doctorate, Silva began his professional career at Auburn University where he served as assistant professor of English and director of the ESL program (1990-91). In 1991, he returned to Purdue as assistant professor of English and the ESL Writing Program director (1991-97), and he has since been promoted to associate professor of English (1997-05) and full professor of English (2005-present). Currently, Silva is a professor of English as a Second Language and teaches undergraduate and graduate courses for ESL students and teachers. In addition to teaching, he has also served as chair or a member on over 120 doctoral and master's committees at Purdue and currently serves on the editorial boards of *Assessing Writing, Journal of Basic Writing, Journal of Writing Assessment, TESL Canada Journal*, and *WPA*.

Silva has received the Excellence in Teaching Award from the Department of English at Purdue for nine consecutive academic years (1996-05). He also won the School of Liberal Arts Departmental Excellence in Teaching Award at Purdue (2003-04). In addition to his pedagogical achievements, Silva has garnered numerous grants for his research in second language writing including a Research Grant-in-Aid at Auburn (1990), Humanities Fund Grant at Auburn (1990), Faculty Incentive Grant at Purdue (1992), Global Initiative Faculty Grant at Purdue (1992), Purdue Research Foundation Grant (1998), Purdue Research Foundation International Travel Grant (1999), dean of School of Liberal Arts International Travel Grant at Purdue (2002), and Research Incentive Grant at Purdue (2003). He has also served professionally as a member of the CCCC's Executive Board, Committee on Second Language Writing, and Special Interest Group on Second Language Writing; chair of the CCCC Committee on ESL; member of TESOL's Steering Committee of the Second Language Writing Interest Section; and associate chair of the NCTE/TESOL Committee.

Silva's major contributions to composition theory, research, and pedagogy involve his tireless efforts and visionary work in second language writing. Most notably, in 1993, he co-founded with Ilona Leki the *Journal of Second Language Writing*, a refereed journal published quarterly that he also currently co-edits with Leki. Also, beginning in 1998, Silva and Paul Kei Matsuda co-founded and began hosting the Symposium on Second Language Writing. In addition, since 1993, Silva has collaborated with colleagues, including Matsuda, to compile the *Selected Bibliography of Recent Scholarship in Second Language Writing*, a bibliography of essays and research reports in second language writing, which is published biennially in the *Journal of Second Language Writing*.

Keri L. Mayes

Sources for Biographical Narrative

▶ Silva, Tony. "Composition Project." E-mail to Keri Mayes. 22 July 2006.

▶ ---. *Curriculum Vitae.* 16 Mar. 2006.

▶ ---. "Re: Composition Project." E-mail to Keri Mayes. 26 July 2006.

▶ "Tony Silva." College of Liberal Arts home page. Purdue University. 2006. 13 July 2006 http://www.cla.purdue.edu/english/directory/personid27>.

Annotated Bibliography

▶ Matsuda, Paul Kei, and Tony Silva, eds. *Research on Second Language Writing: Perspectives on the Construction of Knowledge.* Mahwah, NJ: Erlbaum, 2005.

This edited collection of essays based on presentations at the 2002 Symposium on Second Language Writing focuses on the complex nature of L2 writing research and serves to represent the range of methodological approaches to knowledge construction. Both novice and experienced L2 writing researchers as well as graduate students in applied linguistics and TESOL would benefit from reading about the discursive process of research and the methods used by 18 world-renowned L2 writing scholars as they reflect on the difficulties they have encountered in their own research projects. Matsuda and Silva acknowledge that this text is not a comprehensive survey of L2 writing research; however, this volume provides useful insights into primary issues and assumptions in an honest, sophisticated manner.

▶ Silva, Tony. "An Examination of Writing Program Administrators' Options for the Placement of ESL Student in First Year Writing Classes." *WPA* 18 (1994): 37-43.

In this article Silva presents research on the distinct differences between ESL and native-English speaking writers and addresses four options for ESL students in first year writing programs, including mainstreaming, basic writing classes, ESL writing classes, and cross-cultural composition classes. A thorough, readily accessible presentation of the advantages and disadvantages of each, WPAs and L2 writing instructors can assess which placement options are best for their ESL writers. While promoting the cross-cultural composition and ESL writing classes, Silva encourages the adoption of as many options as possible for ESL students.

▶ ---. "From the Working Class to the Writing Class: A Second Generation American Teaches Second Language Composition." *ESL Composition Tales: Reflections on Teaching.* Ed. Linda Lonon Blanton and Barbara Kroll. Ann Arbor, MI: U of Michigan P, 2002. 63-82.

As part of a collection of stories told by leaders in the field of ESL composition, this representative chapter chronicles, in an entertaining narrative format, Silva's personal and professional development into a world-renowned L2 writing researcher and scholar while simultaneously showcasing the evolution of the field. In this vivid and honest account, Silva speaks out about his own battles with textbooks and writing assignments and relates his conclusions: get to know the students and meet them where they are. Replete with practical, useful advice for writing instructors of all levels and experiences, Silva's story inspires and educates as he reminds teachers to be reflective and flexible, adjusting their pedagogies to each new group of students.

▶ ---. "On the Ethical Treatment of ESL Writers." *TESOL Quarterly* 31 (1997): 359-63. Rpt. in *Second-Language Writing in the Composition Classroom: A Critical Sourcebook.* Ed. Paul Kei Matsuda, Michelle Cox, Jay Jordan, and Christina Ortmeier-Hooper. Boston: Bedford/St. Martin's, 2006. 154-58.

In this essay Silva presents four fundamental principles for working with ESL writers: understand their differences, provide appropriate instructional contexts, offer programs that focus on writing and allow for student choices, and assess equitably students' writing. The article's thesis stresses the importance of treating ESL writers with respect, an inarguable tenet; yet, despite its relative simplicity, teachers, regardless of experience, need to consider seriously how they approach their ESL students. Practical and readily comprehensible, Silva's text provides sage advice and recommendations for accommodating the needs of this vastly growing student population.

▶ ---. "On the Philosophical Bases of Inquiry in Second Language Writing: Metaphysics, Inquiry Paradigms, and the Intellectual Zeitgeist." *Research on Second Language Writing: Perspectives on the Construction of Knowledge.* Mahwah, NJ: Erlbaum, 2005. 3-15.

In this first chapter of the edited compilation of essays on L2 writing research, Silva introduces readers to empirical research through a narrative history detailing his own initiation into and experiences with research methodologies. The text's primary objective is to present the terminology inherent to the inquiry process in L2 writing, which Silva successfully accomplishes in an engaging manner by providing clear explanations to complex concepts. Especially useful and insightful for novice researchers, Silva's chapter demystifies the myth that research be clear-cut and utilize only one mode of inquiry, instead promoting a mixed methodology.

▶ ---. "Second Language Composition Instruction: Developments, Issues, and Directions in ESL." *Second Language Writing: Research Insights for the Classroom.* Ed. Barbara Kroll. New York: Cambridge UP, 1990. 11-23.

Silva's book chapter highlights the evolution of approaches to L2 composition beginning in 1945, including controlled composition, current-traditional rhetoric, the process approach, and English for academic purposes, and offers suggestions for creating a more stable methodology for ESL writing instruction. This article critiques the manner in which approaches are conceptualized and become popular and proposes a model for viewing the relationship between research, theory, and practice that factors in all relevant aspects, namely the writer, reader, text, context, and their interactions. Despite the article's datedness, the historical sketches, analyses, and suggestions are still relevant and useful for today's L2 composition instructor.

▶ ---. "Toward an Understanding of the Distinct Nature of L2 Writing: The ESL Research and its Implications." *TESOL Quarterly* 27 (1993): 657-77. Rpt. in *Landmark Essays on ESL Writing*. Ed. Tony Silva and Paul Kei Matsuda. Mahwah, NJ: Erlbaum, 2001. 191-208.

In this article Silva examines 72 research reports comparing ESL and native-English speaking writers and their writings and analyzes the obvious differences in composing processes and textual features. The implications of his findings indicate the need for the development of more appropriate theories to explain the L2 writing phenomena. Thoroughly researched and articulately analyzed, Silva's report is an important addition to the field; however, more recent research in other second languages besides ESL may demand the article's revision.

▶ Silva, Tony, and Ilona Leki. "Family Matters: The Influence of Applied Linguistics and Composition Studies on Second Language Writing Studies—Past, Present, and Future." *Modern Language Journal* 88.1 (2004): 1-13.

In this article Silva and Leki investigate the history of L2 writing by examining its parent disciplines, namely composition studies and applied linguistics, as well as its grandparent disciplines, rhetoric and linguistics, to develop an understanding of how L2 writing studies have been and will continue to be influenced by them. A must-read for newcomers to L2 writing and other related interdisciplinary fields, this account provides helpful overviews of the histories of rhetoric, linguistics, composition studies, and applied linguistics and illustrates how each has played a role in the development of L2 writing. After appraising the differences and similarities between applied linguistics and composition studies, Silva and Leki conclude by recommending that L2 writing work to reconcile its differences with its parent fields by incorporating aspects from both that best serve its needs.

► Silva, Tony, Ilona Leki, and Joan Carson. "Broadening the Perspective of Mainstream Composition Studies: Some Thoughts from the Disciplinary Margins." *Written Communication* 14 (1997): 398-428.

In this article Silva, Leki, and Carson critique composition studies for being too narrowly focused, ethnocentric, monocultural, and monolinguistic. They first present their argument for the adoption of a broader perspective through an examination of L2 studies and then address specific aspects of the field that might be profitable to composition studies. Despite the intention of influencing positive change in the field, the writers' approach is somewhat harsh and their use of second language acquisition and second language writing instruction concepts too dense for individuals with limited knowledge or background in L2 studies.

► Silva, Tony, and Paul Kei Matsuda, eds. *On Second Language Writing*. Mahwah, NJ: Erlbaum, 2001.

This book is a compilation of essays written by scholars in the field of L2 writing who presented their research at the 1998 Symposium on Second Language Writing. The diversity of formats and writing styles on a wide range of topics, including theory, research, pedagogy, ideology and politics, gender, assessment, and the relationships between L2 writing and other related fields, provides a comprehensive overview of the field at the beginning of the 21st century; however, the collection's focus on college-level adult ESL writers limits the field of L2 writing by omitting other second language writers. Still, for the novice ESL researcher, *On Second Language Writing* is easily accessible and a good starting point for further research in the field.

Chapter 40:
Geneva Smitherman

(b. 1940)

Determined to be involved in the debate over language rights, Geneva Smitherman, affectionately known as "Dr. G," has become a prominent linguist, prolific author, and educational activist who is unwavering in her efforts to bring different languages, such as Ebonics, into the academic consciousness and support them as valid languages of study and use. A collaborator with other leaders in composition, such as Victor Villenueva and Lisa Delpit, Smitherman has published 11 books and countless articles on academic discourse and African American language. She received her BA (1960) from Wayne State University and began teaching English and Latin in the Detroit public school system. During this time, Smitherman also completed her MA (1962) and received her PhD (1969) from the University of Michigan. Although all of her degrees are in English Literature, Smitherman is best known for her work in linguistics. Upon completion of her PhD, Smitherman became an instructor of English at Wayne State where she stayed until 1971, when she went to be a lecturer in Afro-American studies at Harvard until 1973. She returned to Wayne State in 1973 as associate professor of Afro-American studies, and in 1975, she became professor of speech communication. She also held the titles of assistant director (1973-74) and director (1974-77) of the Center for Black Studies, and in 1977, she became a Senior Research associate before becoming Acting director of the Linguistics Program at Wayne State (1982-83). She is presently University Distinguished Professor at Michigan State University and director of their American Language and Literacy Program.

Not long after obtaining her PhD, Smitherman began publishing articles on the legitimacy of the black idiom and its place in the cultural revolution. In 1977, she published her seminal work *Talkin and Testifyin: The Language of Black America*, and with it, examined the place and importance of African American English, or what she refers to as "Black Dialect," within the context of African American lifestyle and culture. In this book, she claims that the concerns over educational programs that wish to bring about a dialect change in the speech of blacks have been generated by two important acts: the upheaval of the sixties brought about most notably by the 1954 Supreme Court desegregation decision, and the attempt of white America to deal with the new black pride. Smitherman went on to define Black Dialect as "an Africanized form of English reflecting Black America's linguistic-cultural African heritage and the conditions of servitude, oppression and life in America" (*Talkin* 2). Boldly publishing a work at the end of nearly two decades of cultural unrest, communal love, and political turmoil that stakes its claim in an individualized, discreet, and race-specialized language is just the sort of impression that Smitherman continues to make with her work.

Smitherman's obvious contribution to the field of composition is within her publications on Black Dialect and African American language and cultural diversity, but she has also published works on linguistics, education, and identity. In 2000, Smitherman published a revised version of her book *Black Talk: Words and Phrases from the Hood to the Amen Corner*, which serves as a sort of dictionary for Black dialect.

In addition to her many publications, Smitherman serves as the Chair of the Language Policy Committee for the CCCC, is a former member of the Standing Committee on Research for the

NCTE (2001-02), and a former member of the CEE Executive Committee (1992-95). She also serves as director of My Brother's Keeper, co-founded with Clifford Watson in 1990, a student mentoring program between Michigan State and the Detroit public school system for African American males in the area.

Smitherman has received many awards and recognitions for her long career, including the David H. Russell Research Award (2001), the Michigan State Distinguished Faculty Award (2000), the CCCC Exemplar Award (1999), the James B. Hamilton Award from the Mid-America Association of Education Opportunity Program Personnel (1994), a W.E.B. DuBois Scholarship Award from Wayne State, and the Zora Neale Hurston Anthropology Award from the Center for Black Studies at Wayne State.

Without Smitherman's contributions to the field of linguistics, education, and Black Dialect and culture, composition studies would not be as culturally aware or linguistically accepting of language diversity.

Rachel Robinson

Sources for Biographical Narrative

▶ "Geneva Smitherman." *Literature Resource Center*. James E. Walker Library. Middle Tennessee State University. Murfreesboro, TN. 28 Aug. 2006.

▶ Smitherman, Geneva. "About Me." African Studies Center home page. Michigan State University <www.msu.edu/~smither4/g/about.html>.

▶ ---. *Talkin and Testifyin: The Language of Black America*. Detroit: Wayne State UP, 1977.

Geneva Smitherman recommends these readings for novice composition instructors:

1. Gilyard, Keith. *Voice of the Self: A Study of Language Competence.* Detroit: Wayne State UP, 1991.
2. Gilyard, Keith, ed. *Race, Rhetoric, and Composition.* Portsmouth, NH: Heinemann   Boynton/Cook, 1999.
3. Richardson, Elaine. *African American Literacies.* London: Routledge, 2002.
4. Villanueva, Victor, Geneva Smitherman, and Suresh Canagarajah, eds. *Language Diversity in the Classroom: From Intention to Practice.* Carbondale, IL: SIUP, 2003.

 Annotated Bibliography

▶ Smitherman, Geneva. "A 'New Way of Talkin': Language, Social Change, and Political Theory." *Sage Race Relations Abstracts* 14.1 (1989): 5-23.

Referencing both Amiri Baraka and Alice Walker's *The Color Purple,* Smitherman addresses the idea that language plays an unforgettable role in ideology, consciousness, behavior, and social relations and claims that because of this, contemporary political and social theory need to address language in regards to social change. Smitherman brings up many provocative points in this article asking how far language has really come, and she points to three linguistic phenomena: White English, or the language spoken by typical upper-class whites; non-standard English, or that language spoken by working-class whites; and Black English, the language spoken by African Americans. Although the article is full of interesting linguistic theory, it sometimes gets bogged down with terms and ideas that are more aspiring than their reality.

▶ ---. *Black Talk: Words and Phrases from the Hood to the Amen Corner.* Boston: Houghton Mifflin, 1994.

In the "Explanatory Notes" section of this work, Smitherman claims that Black Talk is only completely understood within the "Black context," and asserts that grammar and pronunciation can fully change the authentic Black sound of any of the words or phrases that she defines in the book. Furthermore, Smitherman argues that the African American Language (AAL) has a widely-known core of words and phrases, such as "Blazin," "Hush Yo Mouf!," and "Ice," that do not change and are commonly known throughout the Black community. For those people wanting a more in-depth look at the etymology of these words and phrases, this book is not for you; however, people interested in basic definitions and familiar usages will find this work greatly useful.

▶ ---. "'Students' Right to Their Own Language': A Retrospective." *English Journal* 84 (1995): 21-7.

This article addresses the "Students' Right to Their Own Language" resolution policy adopted by CCCC in the 1970s. The policy, which almost immediately came under scrutiny, essentially affirmed that students had the right to their own language—whichever language they found their personal identity and style in—and called out the ignorance of deeming any one language unacceptable. Smitherman praises this policy, and reports that CCCC has long been a breeding ground for social, political, and power struggles that reflect the larger society after researching CCCC trends through back issues of *CCC.*

▶ ---. "Ebonics, King, and Oakland: Some Folks Don't Believe Fat Meat is Greasy." *Journal of English Linguistics* 26 (1998): 97-107. Rpt. in. *Talkin That Talk: Language, Culture, and Education in African America.* Geneva Smitherman. London: Routledge, 2000. 150-62.

Beginning with the Oakland, California school system's call for the recognition of Ebonics and moving to the *King v. Ann Arbor* case in which parents of young African American children argued that their children were being cheated of an education because of the difference between their speaking language and their school language resulting in being labeled as learning disabled, Smitherman highlights the importance of the recognition of language diversity within the public school system. A far cry for NCTE's 1917 "Better Speech Week" creed, which frowned upon "um-hum," "ya," and "nope," to name a few of its offenses, the recognition of Ebonics, Smitherman argues, would usher in an understanding of the most basic use of the Mother Tongue. Clearly and passionately argued, this article details a thorough history of Ebonics awareness and points to tips for helping integrate these differing dialects into the classroom.

▶ ---. "English Teacher, Why You be Doing the Thangs You Don't Do?" *English Journal* 61 (1972): 59-65.

An in-your-face reprimand to the English teachers who denigrate African Americans for not using "standard" English, this article confronts the problem of teaching African American students as if they had no differing dialect. Smitherman outlines five points for teaching English in the inner-city: an examination of alternative lifestyles; an emphasis on reading; an emphasis on oral work; an intensive study of language and culture and both social and regional dialects; and, finally, an emphasis on content, organization, development, and style. While Smitherman gives these tips as advice for teaching Black students, she fails to mention that any student would gain a better understanding of language and literacy if they were taught with these points.

▶ ---. "'It Bees Dat Way Sometime': Sounds and Structure of Present-Day Black English." *Language: Readings in Language and Culture.* 6th ed. Ed. Virginia P. Clark, Paul A. Eschholz, and Alfred F. Rosa. New York: St. Martin's, 1998. 328-43.

Like many of her articles on linguistics and Black Dialect, Smitherman opens this article with an explanation of what Black Dialect consists of—language and style. She further goes on to talk about the differing uses of the *be*, and she points out how different words are paired in Black English as opposed to White English: *done* and *been*, contractions and *nobody*, and *don't* and *but*, for example. Smitherman ends the article with a glimpse into the differing patterns of speech by quoting Langston Hughes and looking closely, and poetically, at Black English in practice.

▶ ---. "Review of Noam Chomsky's *Language and Responsibility*." *Language in Society* 12 (1983): 349-55.

Smitherman begins this article by drawing on the importance of timing for Chomsky's work and referring to the changing world in which it debuted (the 1970s), as well as her personal history at the time. Basically appreciating Chomsky but calling his bluff, Smitherman points out that Chomsky's ideas and views expressed in the book are simply an example of figuring and configuring—saying one thing but meaning a different. While Smitherman points out Chomsky's shortcomings, ultimately she praises his efforts at confronting diversity and contradiction.

▶ ---. *Talkin and Testifyin: The Language of Black America.* Detroit: Wayne State UP, 1977.

In this seminal work, Smitherman outlines her basis for the relevance and cultural importance of Black Dialect. While showing its relevance alongside white English, Smitherman claims that the levels of grammatical structure are the greatest differences between Black and white English, pointing out that the most apparent differences in Black Dialectical structure is the usage of the word "be." This is an essential work for anyone interested in gaining a greater awareness of the language diversity of Black Dialect on both linguistic and cultural levels.

▶ ---. "White English in Blackface, or Who Do I Be?" *Black Scholar* 4 (May-June 1973): 3-15.

Smitherman argues that black idioms have two important sides: linguistic, or those dimensions pertaining to phonology and syntax, and stylistic, those elements that include gestures, cadence, rhythm, and resonance. Because of these two differences, phrases and words that mean the same thing are oftentimes different. Straightforward, full of information, and peppered with Black Dialect, this article is a good base for any linguistic study of Black English.

▶ Villanueva, Victor, Geneva Smitherman, and Suresh Canagarajah, eds. *Language Diversity in the Classroom: From Intention to Practice*. Carbondale, IL: SIUP, 2003.

This compilation of essays focuses on diversity in the classroom, including language and nationalism, language and racism, teaching challenges, and different Englishes. The essays push the reader to see different dialects as respectable and even argues that the US is getting better at recognizing these diverse languages. While presenting a surprisingly positive look at diversity and the US, this book is essential to understanding and examining the ways in which the classroom needs to mirror the country, at times.

Chapter 41:
Nancy Sommers

(b. 1951)

Nancy Sommers received her BA (1971) from Northwestern University and her PhD (1978) from Boston University. Before settling into the field of composition, Sommers worked as a teacher in a Chicago junior high school and worked on a kibbutz in Israel (1972).

In 1976, Sommers became the director of Writing Programs at the Boston University School of Management, and in 1978 she became an assistant professor as well as the director of Composition at the University of Oklahoma. In 1985, she found herself at Rutgers, serving as a Henry Rutgers Research Scholar and the director of the New Jersey Center for the Study of Writing. Sommers later joined the faculty at Harvard University (1987), where during her first two years, she became a Senior Lecturer and the associate director of the Harvard College Expository Writing Program. Since 1994, Sommers has been the Sosland Director of this program, and she also teaches freshman composition.

Nancy Sommers has won many awards for her scholarship. Some of her recent accomplishments include the Promising Researcher Award from NCTE, the CCCC's Richard Braddock

Award (1983 for "Responding to Student Writing," 1993 for "Between the Drafts") for the best essay on teaching writing, the Editor's Choice Essay in *CE,* and a Notable Essay by Best American Essays.

Sommers names David Bartholomae and Mike Rose as influences on her work. She herself has been a developer of theories related to the process movement, WAC, revision, and feminism in composition studies. She now finds herself interested in the role of grammar in composition pedagogy, the scholarship of research, and the idea of feedback. In addition, Sommers recently completed a groundbreaking longitudinal study, in which she made a film of students speaking about their writing experiences. Her writing style could be classified as thought-provoking, personal, and accessible. Very fond of anecdotes, she uses her experiences as a mother, a daughter and a woman to personalize her pedagogy. This individualized method of expression is something that she encourages her students to do in their writing as well.

Michael S. Morris

 Sources for Biographical Narrative

▶ Sommers, Nancy. *Curriculum Vitae.* 30 Sept. 2004.

▶ —. "Re: Hello." Email to Michael Morris. 24 Sept. 2004.

▶ —. Telephone Interview. 27 Nov. 2004.

Nancy Sommers recommends these readings for novice composition instructors:

1. Shaughnessy, Mina. *Errors and Expectations: A Guide for the Teacher of Basic Writing.* New York: Oxford UP, 1977.
2. Bartholomae, David. "Inventing the University." *When a Writer Can't Write: Studies in Writer's Block and Other Composing-Process Problems.* Ed. Mike Rose. New York: Guilford, 1985. 134-66.
3. Joan Didion's essays.

Annotated Bibliography

▶ Sommers, Nancy. "Between the Drafts." *CCC* 43 (1992): 23-31.

In one of her most well known pieces, Sommers questions the nature of authority in scholarship, in writing, and in life. In this accessible article, Sommers examines the problems that occur when writers cling to the authority of others rather than trusting their own ideas. She urges the empowering practice of letting students find their own voices through the writing process. This essay is great for the new composition instructor because it shows that personality in writing can be a very effective rhetorical strategy.

▶ ---. "I Stand Here Writing." *CE* 55 (1993): 420-28.

In this essay Sommers explores the value of students' ideas and individuality while explaining some of the difficulties inherent in hiding behind the role of scholar, rather than using one's own voice. Sommers encourages students to see themselves as places of knowledge and ideas, which in turn will continue the process of giving and receiving information. Any composition instructor will appreciate the value placed on the individual in this essay as well as Sommers practical ideas for classroom application.

▶ ---. "The Language of Coats." *CE* 60 (1998): 421-25.

In this reflective article, Sommers analyzes her role as a teacher in light of her childhood. Writing more for instructors, Sommers reflects upon her composition work and illuminates the difficulty of knowing how well a composition teacher does with his or her students on a daily basis. This essay is good food for thought for the composition instructor and can aid in self reflection about classroom roles and student connections.

▶ ---. "The Need for Theory in Composition Research." *CCC* 30 (1979): 46-49.

In this theoretical article, Sommers makes the case for a well-defined theoretical approach to composition. She challenges the status quo by saying that there are only fragmented ideas being used in the composition community These fragments are linear in nature, and Sommers argues against this idea. Sommers offers instead the idea that writing is a much more recursive practice and should be studied as such. This article is especially useful for the composition instructor who is interested in composition theory and how it can be studied.

▶ ---. "Responding to Student Writing." *CCC* 33 (1982): 148-56.

Here Sommers examines what constitutes a good response to student writing. She looks at some of the mixed messages that instructors give their students and the effects these signals have on student writing. Sommers makes the case for individualized comments that lead to further reflection and revision rather than generic ones. She cautions instructors to avoid clichés such as "be specific" or "wordy," calling these statements impersonal and non-directive "rubber stamps." It is her contention that responses should encourage students to write more and to discover what they want to say (not what teachers want to hear). This article is invaluable for composition instructors who want to be more effective when grading papers.

▶ ---. "Revision Strategies of Student Writers and Experienced Adult Writers." *CCC* 31 (1980): 378-88.

In this piece, Sommers examines the revision strategies of both student writers and experienced writers. The experienced writers in this case were journalists and colleagues. Sommers discovered that students were more concerned with syntax than with content. Conversely, the experienced writers gave much insight into how they shape and re-shape their papers. Ultimately, Sommers concludes that if students can see the bigger picture in their writing, they will become more empowered. This essay is extremely useful for showing composition instructors the big picture and the importance of content.

▶ ---. *Shaped by Writing: The Undergraduate Writing Experience.*
Harvard University. VHS. Prod. Telequest, 2004.

A companion to the longitudinal study done at Harvard
University, this video shows students being interviewed about
their experiences as collegiate writers. The film focuses on the
personal aspects of each student's learning, giving insight into
what the writing process means from a student perspective,
and how writing affects the overall learning process. This is a
fun and interesting video that any composition instructor
would find interesting as well as inspiring.

▶ Sommers, Nancy, et al. *Fields of Reading.* 7th ed. New York:
St Martin's, 2004.

This anthology for freshman composition contains model essays
by various contemporary authors arranged both rhetorically
and thematically and encompassing a variety of topics from the
humanities, science, and technology. Topics covered include
audience, subject, and purpose. This text is very useful for the
composition instructor who has a variety of students from
many different backgrounds and majors.

▶ Sommers, Nancy, and Laura Saltz. "The Novice as Expert:
Writing the Freshman Year." *CCC* 56 (2004): 124-49.

In this longitudinal study, Sommers followed 400 students
through their four years at Harvard. The objective of this study
was to find out what writing meant to the students on a
personal level and beyond the writing assignment. Sommers
helps her students become comfortable with the term "novice
writers," which in turn gives them a base from which to learn.
This study is an excellent resource for composition instructors
who want to understand their craft from the eyes of the
student.

▶ Sommers, Nancy, and Linda Simon. *The HarperCollins
Guide to Writing.* New York: HarperCollins, 1993.

The authors organize this textbook into three sections: creating an
essay, purposes for writing, and the research essay. This text is
accessible and includes a handbook for reference, but most useful
are the numerous models taken from actual student papers.

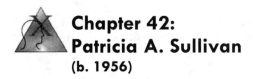

Chapter 42:
Patricia A. Sullivan
(b. 1956)

Patricia Sullivan earned both her BA (1977) and her MA (1981)
from the University of Utah. She received her PhD (1988) from
The Ohio State University. Sullivan spent several years UNH
before moving to the University of Colorado. While currently a
professor of English and director of the Program for Writing
and Rhetoric at Colorado, her areas of emphasis include
composition theory and practice, American literature, and
creative writing (nonfiction).

Sullivan has received numerous awards for her writing and
teaching abilities. These awards include the Excellence in
Teaching Award from the College of Liberal Arts at UNH
(2001), Faculty Scholarship from the HERS (Higher Education
Resource Services) Management Institute for Women in Higher
Education at Wellesley College (2001-02), Outstanding Faculty
Award from the President's Commission on the Status of
Women at UNH (1997), finalist for the CCCC Book Award
(*Methods and Methodology in Composition Research*, 1993), and
the James L. Kinneavy Award for most outstanding article in
JAC (1991).

Having co-written and co-edited books on pedagogy and
methodology, Sullivan has also written a variety of articles
dealing with issues ranging from writing in the graduate
classroom to images of women on the Internet. Sullivan's work
reflects an awareness of how the professor's and the student's
perspectives influence the activities of the writing classroom.
Whether discussing her personal story and how it shapes her
views, or how gender influences the writing process of her
students, Sullivan repeatedly urges her reader to recognize the
range of concerns brought into the classroom. Moving from the
first year composition classroom to the graduate literature
course, Sullivan encourages all levels of the academy to realize
the complexities of writing and the lack of a "finish line" for
writers. The majority of Sullivan's research focuses on how
research is conducted in the field of composition and rhetoric.

She has also made substantial contributions to feminist rhetoric and research as well as the discussions surrounding FYC and basic writers.

Sullivan not only writes and edits for publication, but also she has been known to write with her students. During one semester during her time at UNH, she wrote along with her students for each assignment. It is this work ethic and enthusiasm for writing and reading literature that gives her an interesting dynamic with her students. Rochelle Lieber, the department chair at UNH, was quoted as saying, "Students say that she is open and funny, that she makes herself available, and that she is excellent at giving constructive criticism on their writing" (Vento).

Laurel Taylor

Sources for Biographical Narrative

▶ "Patricia Sullivan." English Dept. faculty page. University of Colorado. 18 Nov. 2004 <http://www.colorado.edu/English/faculty/facpages/ sullivan.shtml>.

▶ Vento, Jennifer. UNH News Bureau. 2001. 18 Nov. 2004 <http://www.unh.edu/facultyexcellence/excellence2001/ sullivan.html>.

Annotated Bibliography

▶ Hawisher, Gail E., and Patricia A. Sullivan. "Fleeting Images: Women Visually Writing the Web." *Passions, Pedagogies, and 21st Century Technologies.* Ed. Gail E. Hawisher and Cynthia L. Selfe. Logan: Utah State UP, 1999. 268-91.

Hawisher and Sullivan discuss the ways that women portray themselves on their personal Web sites as well as the ways companies and universities portray their employees. While women on personal sites wrestle with balancing professional and unique images, women on business and university Web sites are often portrayed in stereotypical ways: sexy lingerie models or academic talking heads. This article offers practical considerations for women navigating the spheres of the Internet.

▶ Lunsford, Andrea, and Patricia A. Sullivan. "Who Are Basic Writers?" *Research in Basic Writing: A Bibliographic Sourcebook*. Ed. Michael G. Moran and Martin J. Jacobi. New York: Greenwood, 1990. 17-30.

Lunsford and Sullivan discuss the multitude of statistics collected concerning basic writers. While summing up the data, the authors conclude that basic writers are such a diverse group that they cannot be categorized. While this article sometimes presents recurring themes, it challenges instructors at all levels to view developmental students as individuals.

▶ Sullivan, Patricia A. "Charting a Course in First-Year English." *Nuts & Bolts: A Practical Guide to Teaching College Composition*. Ed. Thomas Newkirk. Portsmouth, NH: Boynton/Cook, 1993. 17-42.

With a practical feel and a conversational tone, Sullivan presents the week-by-week plan for her FYC course. Sullivan not only presents the strategies and tools she uses by presenting specific assignments, but also she includes personal narratives as well as bits of students' reactions to the class. This is a valuable resource for any instructor looking to explore new avenues in composition.

▶ ---. "Composing Culture: A Place for the Personal." *CE* 66 (2003): 41-54.

Sullivan tells stories of the things her students have written and the struggle for her students to find a sense of self in the writing process. She discusses the spectrum of writers ranging from those afraid of discussing their lives to those willing to discuss the intimate moments of their lives. She concludes by encouraging composition teachers to use the work of their students as a way of learning and experiencing the culture of their students.

► ---. "Ethnography and the Problem of the 'Other.'" *Ethics and Representation In Qualitative Studies of Literacy.* Ed. Gesa Kirsch and Peter Mortensen. Urbana, IL: NCTE, 1997. 97-114.

Incorporating the language and theories traditionally used to discuss sociology research, Sullivan discusses the ways in which the research done in the composition field must consider the theoretical other. Her encouragement to strive for more than research as an end in itself, but instead to use the voices of others as an influence in the research process is an important message to anyone currently conducting research in the ever-changing world of composition.

► ---. "Feminism and Methodology in Composition Studies." *Methods and Methodology in Composition Research.* Ed. Gesa E. Kirsch and Patricia A. Sullivan. Carbondale, IL: SIUP, 1992. 37-61.

Sullivan critiques two aspects of composition research: the way in which research is gathered and evaluated, and the assumptions that go behind researching the composing process. She argues that both aspects are tainted by gendered assumptions. Sullivan's push towards the consideration of both male and female perspectives in composition research is a useful read to those currently involved in composition research.

► ---. "Passing: A Family Dissemblance." *Coming to Class: Pedagogy and the Social Class of Teachers.* Ed. Alan Shepard, John McMillan, and Gary Tate. Portsmouth, NH: Boynton/Cook, 1998. 231-51.

Through her personal narrative, Sullivan discusses her struggles to succeed in college and how those struggles have influenced the way she views the students in her classes. She honestly explores the ways that her story of survival in her undergraduate experience has influenced the way she approaches students from different socioeconomic classes. Her awareness of relating better to students that share her past calls all composition teachers to rethink the way they interact with the range of students found in their classes.

▶ ---. "Revising the Myth of the Independent Scholar." *Writing With: New Directions in Collaborative Teaching, Learning, and Research*. Ed. Sally Barr Reagan, Thomas Fox, and David Bleich. Albany: SUNY P, 1994. 11-29.

In this article, Sullivan argues against the idea of the scholar as one that sits in an isolated environment to create knowledge. She argues for a feminist approach to scholarship in which collaboration is essential to defining the nature of knowledge. This is a helpful read to anyone considering a collaborative project in the classroom or in his or her own studies.

▶ ---. "Social Constructionism and Literacy Studies." *CE* 57 (1995): 950-59.

Sullivan uses a book review of three different texts to explore some of the problems and complications with social constructionism. This article provides a helpful summary of three key texts in the conversation, thereby, giving the reader a quick reminder of the conversation. Although the theory gets a bit confusing at times, the article is a great entry into the debate.

▶ ---. "Writing in the Graduate Curriculum: Literary Criticism as Composition." *JAC* 11 (1991): 283-99.

Dealing mainly with the need for brainstorming and revision time in the class, Sullivan challenges the traditional thought that graduate students already know how to write and, therefore, do not need time to discuss or develop their writing. Sullivan encourages professors to use the links between literature and writing to help graduate students improve both aspects of their scholarship. While this article is somewhat specialized because of its focus on graduate-level courses, it is still a challenge to all teachers to consider their assumptions about the separation of writing and reading in the classroom.

▶ Sullivan, Patricia A., and Donna J. Qualley. Introduction.
Pedagogy in the Age of Politics. Ed. Patricia A. Sullivan
and Donna J. Qualley. Urbana, IL: NCTE, 1994. 6-21.

The editors of this book spend the introduction establishing
that composition has always been surrounded by political
struggle and encouraging readers to wrestle with the issues of
politics in the classroom as they read the narratives of the
contributing writers. This introduction lays a thorough
groundwork for the range of articles included in the text. New
teachers can benefit from this text because of the challenge to
wrestle with politics in the classroom.

Chapter 43:
Gary Tate
(b. 1930)

Gary Tate has been a formidable force in composition studies since 1957. He has edited, with various co-editors such as Edward P. J. Corbett, E. Alworth, D. Hayden, Erika Lindemann, Alan Shepard, and John McMillan, 11 books. He served as founder and co-editor of *Freshman English News* and has written reviews, numerous articles, and book chapters. Tate received his BA (1952) in English from Baker University and both his MA (1956) and PhD (1958) in English from the University of New Mexico.

Tate began his teaching career at the University of Wyoming, Laramie, where he served as an instructor in English (1957-58) before moving to Ohio Wesleyan University, Delaware, as an assistant professor of English (1958-60). Tate was an associate professor of English at the University of Tulsa, Oklahoma (1960-70), and he was a professor of English at Northern Arizona University, Flagstaff (1970-71). In 1971, he became the Addie Levy Professor of Literature and later the Cecil and Ida Green Distinguished Emeritus Tutor at Texas Christian University, Fort Worth. He has recently retired and spends his summers in Maine teaching part-time at Senior College at the University of Maine's Hutchinson Center in Belfast. Additionally, he has served professionally with CCCC in numerous positions.

Tate has always been a strong supporter of using literature to help students learn to write. In his seminal article "A Place for Literature in the Composition Classroom," Tate lists the three reasons literature has been stripped from composition classrooms: "[T]he pedagogical sins of teachers in the past, the revival of rhetoric, and changing attitudes about the purposes and goals of freshman composition" (175). According to Tate, literature disappeared from the classroom in part because past teachers misused the one discipline they knew well. This disappearance left a vacuum that rhetoric quickly filled.

Tate abhors the "Rhetoric Police" who, in the 1960s, zealously removed literature from the classroom, and, in turn, became "the dreaded enforcement arm of the CCCC" (176). He points out that this replacement occurred without any professional deliberation. The actions of the CCCC effectively removed literature and contributed to the changing of attitudes toward the reasons for teaching freshman composition.

The idea that freshman composition should be the service course through which students might join the conversations that education enables is the stand that Tate's most famous opposition, Erika Lindemann, takes; however, Tate counters this by outlining the difficulties a professor would face if he or she had to teach each and every student according to the discipline or major he or she chooses.

Marcia M. Beene

Sources for Biographical Narrative

► "Gary Tate" *Contemporary Authors Online*. Literature Resource Center. Middle Tennessee State University, James E. Walker Library, Murfreesboro, TN. 2002. 1 July. 2006 <http://galenet.galegroup.com>.

► Lindemann, Erika, and Gary Tate. "Two Views on the Use of Literature in Composition." *CE* 55 (1993): 311-21.

► Tate, Gary. "A Place for Literature in Freshman Composition." *The Writing Teacher's Sourcebook*. Ed. Edward P.J. Corbett, Nancy Myers, and Gary Tate. New York: Oxford UP, 2000, 175-79.

Annotated Bibliography

► Corbett, Edward P. J., Nancy Myers, and Gary Tate, eds. *The Writing Teacher's Sourcebook*. 4th ed. New York: Oxford UP, 2000.

With contributions from composition leaders, such as Peter Elbow, James Berlin, Donald Murray, David Bartholomae, and Mina Shaughnessy, this source book is intended to provide a starting point for new teachers to familiarize themselves with composition pedagogy. The included essays, which were written as early as 1970 and as late as 1998, combine theoretical discussions with concrete examples from the authors' personal experiences and some discussion of practical application within the classroom. Topics covered include student-teacher relationships, writing center theory, expressivism, formalism, rhetorical pedagogy, mimetic theories of writing, group work, collaborative learning, computers and composition, cultural diversity, using literature in the composition classroom, writing for an audience, critical pedagogy, and responding to and evaluating student writing.

▶ Easterling, Heather, Gary Ettari, and John Webster. *Proceedings of the Sixth Annual Meeting of the Western States Composition Conference, October 24-26, 2002: Panel IIIc: Course as Conflict: Re-Thinking Literature-and-Composition Pedagogy.* Seattle: U of WA, 1989.6 July 2006 <http://Faculty.washington.edu/ bawarshi/program02.html>.

This panel examines the writing-with-literature course as a disciplinary and pedagogical intersection and the conflicts that arise from such. Titles of readings include Easterling's, "Towards a Pedagogy of Problems: The Acts of Composition and Literature"; Gary Ettari's, "Disparate Disciplines?: Student Responses to Reading in a Composition Classroom"; and John Webster's, "Teacher-Training and the Challenges of the Literature/Composition Classroom." Although this site provides only abstracts of the readings, it nevertheless provides interesting questions.

▶ Lindemann, Erika, and Gary Tate. "Two Views on the Use of Literature in Composition." *CE* 55 (1993): 311-21.

Lindemann and Tate recap their staged debate at the 1992 CCCC about the role of literature in the composition classroom. In "Freshman Composition: No Place for Literature," Lindemann argues against using imaginative literature, such as poetry, fiction, and drama, in the first-year composition course, arguing instead for a focus on academic discourse. In "A

Place for Literature in Freshman Composition," Tate implies that literature has already been eliminated in first-year classes only to satisfy a fad for rhetoric (by none other than the Rhetoric Police). This article is a fascinating read for both the composition teacher and the literature teacher.

▶ Miall, David S., and Don Kuiken. "Aspects of Literary Response: A New Questionnaire." *Research in the Teaching of English* 29 (1995): 37-58.

This article explains the *Literary Response Questionnaire* (*LRQ*), which was developed to measure a reader's orientation toward literary texts. The questionnaire designers, including Tate, identify seven relevant aspects of orientation: insight, empathy, imagery vividness, leisure escape, concern with author, story-driven reading, and rejection of literary values. This argument is clearly developed for supporters of reader-response theory but not very clear for those unfamiliar with statistics.

▶ Shepard, Alan, John McMillan, and Gary Tate, eds. *Coming to Class: Pedagogy and the Social Class of Teachers.* New York: Heinemann-Boynton/Cook, 1998.

This unusual collection of 21 essays focuses on the social/class histories of teachers and what they bring to the classroom based on their backgrounds. The essays included look at the way teachers' socio-economic histories influence their interactions with students and the influence their backgrounds have on their own pedagogical practices. Topics discussed include a scientific approach to class and the intersections of class and race. These essays cover a wide yet concentrated area that has, until now, not been researched.

▶ Steinberg, Erwin R., Michael Gamer, Erika Lindemann, Gary Tate, and Jane Peterson. "Symposium: Literature in the Composition Classroom." *CE* 57 (1995): 265-318.

Five scholars examine the earlier debate between Lindemann and Tate on whether or not literature should be taught in the first-year composition course. Steinberg's article, "Imaginative

Literature in Composition Classrooms?," is an outstanding companion piece to the Lindemann and Tate articles. Gamer, in "Fictionalizing the Disciplines: Literature and the Boundaries of Knowledge," discusses the needed use of imaginative texts in composition courses. In Lindemann's, "Three Views of English 101," the focus is shifted back to the first question in her original essay: "What is the purpose of the freshman writing course?" Tate, in his follow-up essay, "Notes on the Dying of a Conversation," concludes that in his earlier piece ("A Place for Composition") he may "have been wrong in picturing literature as driven from the composition classroom" (304). In the last article, "Through the Looking-Glass: A Response," Peterson indicates that a general agreement about the purpose of first-year composition is needed. Specifically, she advocates a Freshman Reading and Writing Course, which deals with all language experiences: reading, writing, speaking, and listening. Although a bit long, the symposium nevertheless reveals that the debate over the make-up of freshman composition will continue. This is a great article for seeing both sides of the literature versus composition debate.

▶ Tate, Gary, Amy Rupiper, and Kurt Schick, eds. *A Guide to Composition Pedagogies.* New York: Oxford UP, 2001.

An exceptional source for English graduate students as well as new teachers, this collection of essays written by well experienced teachers and scholars discusses many of the major pedagogies used in colleges and universities today, such as process, expressive, rhetorical, collaborative, cultural studies, critical, feminist, community-service, WAC, and writing center theories.

▶ Tate, Gary, ed. *Teaching Composition: Twelve Bibliographical Essays.* Fort Worth: Texas Christian UP, 1987.

A significantly revised and updated edition of the *Teaching Composition: Ten Bibliographic Essays* first published in 1976, this important book includes essays by many of the leaders of composition studies, such as Edward P.J. Corbett, Richard E.

Young, Mina P. Shaughnessy, Andrea A. Lunsford, James L. Kinneavy, Hugh Burns, and many others covering diverse topics from invention, non-narrative prose, style, testing, literary theory, and rhetoric and literature, to WAC, and computers and composition. This edition is a must-have for English graduate students who are still looking for their own teaching pedagogy.

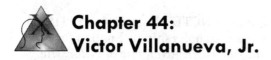

Chapter 44:
Victor Villanueva, Jr.

(b. 1948)

Victor Villanueva is one of the leading scholars in what many
writing teachers would call multiculturalism, although he
would not necessarily agree with that terminology, and has
published numerous articles on rhetoric and its connections
with racism, culture, and ideology. Villanueva was born to
Puerto Rican immigrants in Brooklyn, New York, in 1948.
After dropping out of high school, Villanueva entered military
service in 1968, serving for seven years, before entering
community college in 1975. Villanueva received his BA (1979)
and his MA (1982) from the University of Washington. He
earned his PhD (1986) with an emphasis in Rhetoric and
Composition Studies, also from the University of Washington.
During his post-graduate work, Villanueva was an instructor at
Big Bend Community College in Moses Lake, Washington, and
a pre-doctoral associate at the University of Washington.
Villanueva worked as an assistant professor at the University
of Missouri, Kansas City (1985) and then moved to Northern
Arizona University (1987). Villanueva is currently the Edward
R. Meyer Distinguished Professor of Liberal Arts and associate
dean at Washington State.

Villanueva was the recipient of NCTE's Russell Award (1995), for distinguished research and scholarship in English for his work *Bootstraps: From an American Academic of Color*, the Conference on English Education's Richard A. Meade Award (1994), for scholarship in English education, the Martin Luther King, Jr. Distinguished Service Award (1999) from Washington State, honoring "those who live Dr. King's vision," and was voted Rhetorician of the Year by the Young Rhetoricians Conference (1999), and chaired the CCCC (1998).

Villanueva's work has been influenced by several well-known literacy and composition theorists. The three most notable influences on his work are Paulo Freire, Frantz Fanon, and Antonio Gramsci, all of whom shaped Villanueva's assertion that racism is a product of colonialism and can be seen in the marginalization of the rhetoric of minorities in former colonized countries, including the Americas, the Caribbean, and other British and American colonies. Perhaps a greater influence on Villanueva's work is his own personal experience of being a minority in the academic community. Throughout his work, Villanueva uses personal experience as a catalyst for discussions of the rhetoric of racism.

Villanueva has impacted the field of rhetoric and composition studies through his unwavering and straightforward approach to literacy studies and the rhetoric of racism. His most well-known publication, *Bootstraps: From an American Academic of Color* (1993), examines the academic world and beyond through the lens of Villanueva's own experiences coming up through the ranks of academia. Other notable contributions include his article "On the Rhetoric and Precedents of Racism," published in *CCC* (1999) and the reader *Cross-Talk in Comp Theory* (2003), which provides writing teachers and composition students a collection of some of the most influential articles in composition theory from the past 35 years.

Villanueva's current and past research involves an examination of the connections between rhetoric, critical theory, and racism, and the way that the interplay between them affects literacy.

In addition to his research interests, Villanueva's teaching interests include composition theory, the teaching of writing to non-traditional students, and contemporary rhetorical theory.

Eric W. Atkins

 Sources for Biographical Narrative

▶ "The National Conference on Peer Tutoring in Writing and the International Writing Centers Association are proud to announce *Victor Villanueva* as the Keynote Speaker for our 2nd Joint Conference to be Held October 19-23, 2005 in Minneapolis at the Hyatt Regency." *IWCA Update.* The International Writing Center Association. Spring 2005. 2 July 2006 <http://writingcenters.org/ IWCA_Update_SP_05_V6_I1.pdf>.

▶ "Victor Villanueva." English Dept. home page. Washington State University, Pullman, WA. 30 June 2006 <http://libarts.wsu.edu/english/faculty/villanueva.html>

Victor Villanueva, Jr. recommends these readings for novice composition instructors:

1. Lindemann, Erika. *A Rhetoric for Writing Teachers.* 4th ed. New York: Oxford UP, 2001.
2. Grimm, Nancy. *Good Intentions: Writing Center Work for Postmodern Times.* Portsmouth, NH: Boynton/Cook, 1999.
3. Gilyard, Keith. *Race, Rhetoric, and Composition.* Portsmouth, NH: Boynton/Cook, 1999.

Annotated Bibliography

► Kells, Michelle Hall, Valerie Balester, and Victor Villanueva, eds. *Latino/a Discourses*. Portsmouth, NH: Boynton/Cook, 2004.

The authors in this collection highlight the ways in which Spanish discourse is ignored or marginalized in both the American academy and the American culture. The individual articles range from classic literacy studies to discourse analyses of Latino/a slang. This collection provides a wide overview of the ways in which Latino/a discourse has been pushed aside by the mainstream, English-speaking society. The text is useful for understanding discourse analysis at a high level and could help teachers better understand the minority voices in their classes.

► Villanueva, Victor. *Bootstraps: From an American Academic of Color*. Urbana, IL: NCTE, 1993.

This work, one part autobiography, one part theory, and one part critique of the current academic climate, offers a compelling and thought-provoking read for anyone interested in the rhetoric and composition field. The book may not be obviously practical (i.e., it may not provide lessons to take directly to the classroom), but the knowledge provided about the way rhetoric is used to diffuse minorities can be carried to the classroom with some adaptation. Because this book is at its heart a retelling of the struggles the author encountered as he rose through the ranks of academia, it is poignant and provides true insight into the world of the minority student and the minority teacher.

► ---, ed. *Cross-Talk in Comp Theory: A Reader*. 2nd ed. Urbana, IL: NCTE, 2003.

This text brings together over 40 of the most influential and well-known composition theory articles from the last 35 years. The collection provide a plethora of information on all aspects of composition theory, organized into the following categories: The Givens in Our Conversations: The Writing Process;

Talking in Terms of Discourse: What It Is, How It's Taught;
Scientific Talk: Developmental Schemes; Talking About
Writing in Society; Talking About Selves and Schools: On
Voices, Voices, and Other Voices; and Continuing the
Conversation. This collection is essential for anyone wishing to
gain a deeper understanding of composition theories.

▶ ---. "Hegemony: From an Organically Grown Intellectual."
    Pre/Text 13.1-2 (1992): 17-34.

This article explores the "concepts underlying hegemony:
ideology, its cultural multiplicity; civil society, the transmitter
of ideologies; intellectuals, their rules in either preserving or
countering hegemony; the war of positions, the discursive
practices that can change hegemony" (18). Advanced in its
theory, the article deals mainly with the ideas of Antonio
Gramsci, especially in connection with the ideas of hegemony
and ideology, counter hegemony, and the role of the American
intellectual in producing that counter hegemony.

▶ ---. "Memoria is a Friend of Ours: On the Discourse of Color."
    CE 67 (2004): 9-19.

This article provides a personalized, almost autobiographical
discussion of the discourse of racism. The author narrates small
glimpses of his past and uses them to examine the subtlety of
racist discourse. Encouraging the use of personal experience
and narrative in the classroom, Villanueva sheds light on the
importance of helping students, and teachers, understand
discourse in all its forms and the power that it holds. The
article has much the same feel of Villanueva's *Bootstraps* but
the article form condenses the message and in some ways
makes it more easily accessible.

▶ ---. "On the Rhetoric and Precedents of Racism." *CCC* 50
    (1999): 645-61.

This article, considered to be one of Villanueva's most
important works, argues that the root of racism in our
hemisphere lies in the colonization by Europeans. The article
draws from writers of many different backgrounds to illustrate

the point that scholarly voices from places other than Western
Europe are often ignored or given only token acknowledgment.
The article is, at heart, a call to action; the author demands
that academicians confront the marginalization of minority
voices by taking direct action, not circumventing it with short-
term fixes and cover-ups. All teachers of composition should
read this article as it points out the inadvertent racism found
in even the most forward-thinking members of the academic
community.

▶ ---. "On Syllabi." *Strategies for Teaching First Year
Composition.* Ed. Duane Roen, Veronica Pantoja,
Lauren Yena, Susan K. Miller, and Eric Waggoner.
Urbana, IL: NCTE, 2002. 98-102.

This article, which is in the form of a memorandum to all
teachers of English 101, is a romp through the following
considerations that both new and experienced teachers must
make when writing a syllabus: Common Goals, Common
Assumptions, The Books, The Syllabus, and Other
Considerations. The article is light and humorous but provides
a lot of valuable insight from an experienced teacher and will
help ease the nerves of new teachers trying to formulate their
first syllabi. While it is short and general, this article packs a
lot of information that will aid teachers in constructing syllabi
that are functional and organized.

▶ ---. "'Rhetoric Is Politics,' Said the Ancient. 'How Much So,' I
Wonder." *Writing Theory and Critical Theory.* Ed. John
Clifford and John Schilb. New York: MLA, 1994.
327-34.

This article again uses the personal narrative form to illustrate
the political currency of rhetoric in composition and language
itself. The author discusses several of his major influences,
including Antonio Gramsci and Paulo Freire, and reveals the
way he came to understand the effect these theorists would
have on his professional life and his world view. Ultimately, the
article asserts that rhetorical theory has not yet addressed fully
the rhetorics of the minority voices. While easily accessible

because of the personal narrative dispersed throughout, this article is deeply theoretical and may be difficult without further reading of Villanueva's influences.

► ---, ed. "Rhetorics From/Of Color." *CE* 67 (2004): 9-120.

This work is a special edition of *CE* edited by Villanueva and contains articles dealing with the rhetorics of several minority groups. The collection includes articles about Latino/a, American Indian, Native Hawaiian, and Black English rhetorics. The articles, while being independent of each other, all speak to the relative marginalization of the discourse of minorities. The most interesting aspect of the collection is that it deals with several minority rhetorics, such as American Indian and Native Hawaiian, which are not often discussed in detail. The articles are useful in understanding the oppressive nature of rhetoric.

► Villanueva, Victor, Geneva Smitherman, and Suresh Canagarajah, eds. *Language Diversity in the Classroom: From Intention to Practice*. Carbondale, IL: SIUP, 2003.

According to the editors, this collection "is about language and racism, about language and nationalism, about discussing and teaching the connections between language and racism and nationalism" (1). Each essay forces the English language teacher to look seriously at the way language itself is discussed in the classroom. This collection urges teachers to ask tough questions, but it does so in a way meant to encourage discourse about the ever-changing English language.

Chapter 45:
Edward White

(b. 1933)

Edward White has become an icon in composition studies through his research, teaching, and publishing in the field of student writing assessment. He has published eleven books and over 70 articles and book chapters, some published multiple times, resulting in a bibliography of almost 100 books, book chapters, articles, and reviews. Because of his extensive contributions of reviews and a regular newspaper column under the pseudonym "Eugen Eisen," White has also contributed to journalism. White received his BA (1955), in English from New York University his MA (1956), in English from Harvard University and stayed at Harvard to complete his PhD (1960).

White began his teaching career at Harvard, then moved to Wellesley College, where he taught Literature. He helped found the English Department at California State University at San Bernardino (CSUSB) in the mid-1960s, becoming the first chair of that department. While at CSUSB, he coordinated the Writing Improvement Program for California State University, the Credit by Evaluation Program, the English Equivalency Examination Program, and the federally-funded project,

"Research in Effective Teaching of Writing." After teaching several courses in Composition Studies, White retired as Emeritus Professor of English in 1997. He then joined the English Department of the University of Arizona at Tucson where he teaches writing assessment, research, and WPA in the PhD program.

White is a contributing member of many organizations. He has served as director of Program Evaluation and Executive Council Member of the WPA. He served on the Executive Committee and on the Braddock Award Committee for the CCCC, and was named to the Board of Directors for the California Association of Teachers of English. He was also a Sponsored Speaker for the NCTE as well as the Official Delegate to the Pacific Coast Regional Conference of Two-Year Colleges and a member of the Committee on Public Doublespeak. He was given a Lifetime Membership to the English Council of California State University, and he is a Lifetime Member of the MLA.

White was awarded the San Bernardino Chamber of Commerce Award for Excellence in Teaching (1993) and was named CSUSB Outstanding Professor (1994). Also, White was awarded an Honorable Mention in the MLA's Mina P. Shaughnessy Prize (1994) for outstanding research given for *Teaching and Assessing Writing*, considered required reading for students of composition studies.

Most recently, White collaborated on a new cultural studies in composition text, *The Promise of America*. He describes his current publication and research interests as "academic freedom, computer scoring of essays, a new and better way to score student portfolios, teaching in times of trauma, the misuse of writing assessment for political purposes, and the portfolio assessment project that the UA department of Electrical and Computer Engineering has been using for the last five years." White continues to teach graduate courses while consulting for *Research in the Teaching of English, CE, CCC, WPA, Advanced Composition*, and for institutions and universities on writing programs, assessment, and WAC.

Stacia Watkins

Sources for Biographical Narrative

► Eble, Kenneth E., and Edward M.White. "The Author." *Teaching and Assessing Writing: Second Edition, Revised and Expanded*. San Francisco: Jossey-Bass, 1994. xxi-xxii.

► "Edward M. White." English Dept. home page. California State University, San Bernardino. 2004. 26 Oct. 2004 <http://english.csusb.edu/>.

► "Mina P. Shaughnessy Prize." *Modern Language Association Web site*. 2004. 26 Oct. 2004 <http://www.mla.org/resources/awards/awards_winners /pastwinners_ annual/pastwinners_mps>.

► "Professor Edward M. White." English Dept. home page. University of Arizona. 2004. 26 Oct. 2004 <http://www.u.arizona.edu/~emwhite/index.html>.

► White, Edward M. "Class and Comfort: The Slums and the Greens." *Coming to Class: Pedagogy and the Social Class of Teachers*. Ed. Alan Shepard, Gary Tate, and John McMillan. Portsmouth, NH: Boynton-Cook, 1998. 278-90.

► ---. *Curriculum Vitae*. Email to Stacia Watkins. 18 Sept. 2004.

► ---. *Curriculum Vitae*. Email to Tanya McLaughlin. 20 June 2006.

► ---. *Developing Successful College Writing Programs*. San Francisco: Jossey-Bass, 1989.

► ---. *The Pop Culture Tradition*. New York: Norton, 1972.

► ---. "Re: Project." Email to Stacia Watkins. 18 Sept. 2004.

► ---. "Re: Recommendations for New TAs." Email to Tanya McLaughlin. 20 June 2006.

► ---. "Re: WPA Article." Email to Stacia Watkins. 1 Oct. 2004.

> **Edward White recommends these readings for novice composition instructors:**

1. North, Stephen. *The Making of Knowledge in Composition: Portrait of an Emerging Field*. Upper Montclair, NJ: Boynton/Cook, 1987.
2. Dobrin, Sidney. *Constructing Knowledges: The Politics of Theory-Building and Pedagogy in Composition*. Albany: SUNY Press, 1997.
3. Straub, Richard, and Ronald F. Lunsford. *12 Readers Reading: Responding to Student Writing*. Cresskill, NH: Hampton, 1995.

 ## Annotated Bibliography

▶ Bloom, Lynn Z, Donald A. Daiker, and Edward M.White, eds. *Composition in the 21st Century: Crisis and Change*. Carbondale, IL: SIUP, 1996.

Essays from Bartholomae, Elbow, Flower, Lunsford, Heath, and North are just a few selections exemplifying the significance of this collection of essays from the national Conference on Composition Studies in 1993. The Conference itself was a request for more development in the field of Composition Studies, and the text provides the answer to the request. Dealing with every issue from the teaching writing to new techniques and theories in teaching and assessing writing, the collection adequately maps a plan for the future of rhetoric and composition study.

▶ ---, eds. *Composition Studies in the 21st Century: Rereading the Past, Rewriting the Future*. Carbondale: SIUP, 2003.

In this collection of essays from the national WPA Conference on Composition Studies held in Miami, Ohio in October 2001, the recurring theme is attributed to the attacks of September 11 of that same year; the essays project the future of Composition Studies based on the field's past. The collection features the text of Peter Elbow's Keynote Address at the Conference in which he re-emphasizes the term *invention* as a necessary consideration for writers in the 21st century. Concerned with the change that occurred in the country after the terrorist attacks, the editors and authors explain a reinvigorated need for technology, research, and debate on politics in writing.

▶ White, Edward M. *Assigning, Responding, Evaluating: A Writing Teacher's Guide*. New York: St. Martin's, 1992.

White's seminal work acknowledges the common misconception that assessment has little to do with the learning process; however, the text defines assessment in two parts, as a tool for administration to examine student success and as a tool for teachers to understand their own students' progress in order to help them more fully develop. White discusses the development of appropriate writing assignments so that assessment is more effective. The text, a tool for beginning teachers or experienced educators who are interested in furthering their understanding of assessment, is primarily concerned with the process of essay testing, but also addresses portfolios and exit examinations.

▶ ---. "Class and Comfort: The Slums and the Greens." *Coming to Class: Pedagogy and the Social Class of Teachers*. Ed. Alan Shepard, Gary Tate, and John McMillan. Portsmouth, NH: Boynton-Cook, 1998. 278-90.

In this essay, White discusses his personal experiences with social class as it relates to teaching. Even though he began his career at a Wellesley, a private school for women, the author jumped at the chance to move to a fledgling English department at a school for the lower middle class, CSUSB, and he argues that his purpose was not to be a British Lit man, but to conduct research in composition that would impact a multitude of teachers and students. White also gives several examples of the parallels between teaching to the elite and primarily studying literature in this accessible narrative, which puts a face on the role that politics plays for a professional educator.

▶ ---. "Language and Reality in Writing Assessment." *CCC* 41
　　(1990): 187-200.

This article, written after White attended The Assessment
Forum of the American Association for Higher Education
Conference, is based on the author's recognition of the study of
assessment in various fields other than English and the
realization that these fields contain ideas much different from
those in his background. Because of his need to explain his
understanding of assessment, the article is a helpful tool for
anyone who is trying to understand an educator's point of view.
White argues that allowing for divisions in terminology and
language of writing and writing assessment is a destructive
practice, and he urges all with an interest in composition
studies to unite, debate, and solve problems that arise in the
field while discussing the value-added practice of evaluating
curriculum and negates it by advocating a value-free
assessment.

▶ ---. "On Being a Writer, Being a Teacher of Writing." *Living
　　Rhetoric and Composition: Stories of the Discipline*. Ed.
　　Duane H. Roen, Stuart C. Brown, and Theresa Enos.
　　Mahwah, NJ: Erlbaum, 1998. 171-92.

Through his understanding that he is a writer first and a
teacher second, the author addresses the issue of teaching
writing through a narrative form, and his progression through
a lifetime of writing to his retirement where, again, writing has
become an important part of his life. He begins with a personal
story of his first piano and how its destruction led to his first
experience of getting paid for writing, which leads into many
more narratives of White's writing experiences through
journalism, exposition, creative writing, and, finally, through
teaching. His growth as a teacher is shown through the many
examples of his strategies and, at the end, through his progress
with writing program administration.

▶ ---. "The Opening of the Modern Era of Writing Assessment:
　　A Narrative." *CE* 63 (2001): 306-20.

This article allows for the introduction of assessment into the
field of English Studies where definitions of internal
assessment (within the classroom relationship of students and

teachers) and external assessment (outside the classroom when English teachers are viewed as either grammar-oriented or flowery) are often considered unnecessary. In a history of the development of the field, White outlines a course from 1971 (the development of California State University's Writing Program) through the development of many programs, books, conferences, and journals in the field to the future of assessment studies. This article provides a detailed background for beginners in the field of composition and rhetoric.

▶ ---. *The Pop Culture Tradition.* New York: Norton, 1972.

In this collection of essays, narratives, and poems, White uses popular culture to develop the interests of his composition students. These selections, with authors from Shakespeare to Ellison, exemplify content, creativity, and development through their diversity of subject-matter and of the background of the authors, making it not only a guide, but also a tribute, to White's students who, as he writes, have the ability of "full perception." Though he admits that it is not often that his students have had the opportunity to read about the Beatles or *Playboy* in an English writing classroom, White's collection takes on the role of reaching the students on their level, and even though several popular culture texts have been published since the release of this text, it is a seminal work in the advancement of the field into the writing classroom.

▶ ---. *Teaching and Assessing Writing: Understanding, Evaluating and Improving Student Performance.* San Francisco: Jossey-Bass, 1985.

This text stresses the importance of the study of writing assessment for all teachers who use writing in their classes, not just English faculty members, and it discusses advances in writing assessment as well as new theories about assigning a grade to student papers. As they promote the text for teachers to use to argue for their assessing preferences and personal assessment experience, the author proves to be knowledgeable in all areas of assessment discussed. The text is divided into two parts, assessment in the classroom and assessment outside of the classroom, for easy research.

▶ White, Edward M., William Lutz, and Sandra Kamusikiri, eds. *Assessment of Writing: Politics, Policies, Practices.* Research and Scholarship in Composition. New York: MLA, 1996.

In this discussion of formal and informal assessment, the collection of essays addresses the politics of a teacher's many roles, the theories of different styles of writing assessment, and the way that assessment is actually interpreted by teachers in their own classrooms. Through an easy to access breakdown of the major areas of research within writing assessment, the text argues for an incorporation of assessment into all parts of the teaching process primarily through the definition of writing, and it acknowledges issues of reliability and validity, inclusion and gender, legalities, models of assessment, and the path of assessment for the future. Assessment affects the lives of students and teachers, and this text carefully considers this in its debates.

**Chapter 46:
Kathleen Blake Yancey**

(b. 1950)

A leading advocate for portfolios and reflection in the classroom, Kathleen Blake Yancey has also written extensively about assessment, voice, collaboration, WAC, and WPA. Yancey earned her BA (1972) and MA (1977) in English at Virginia Polytechnic Institute and State University before going on to Purdue University to complete her PhD (1983) in English.

Yancey's career appointments have included terms at Purdue (1977-90), where she served as director, English 109: English Fundamentals (1984-87) and director, Office of Writing Review (1987-90), and she was also at the University of North Carolina at Charlotte (1996-99). Yancey became the first R. Roy Pearce Professor of Professional Communication (1999-05) at Clemson University. As such, she directed the Pearce Center for Professional Communication (2000-05), a facility devoted to communication instruction at all levels and in all disciplines. Currently, she is the Kellogg W. Hunt professor of English (2005-present) and director of the Graduate Program in Rhetoric and Composition (2005-present) at Florida State University.

Committed to promoting and sharing research in composition, Yancey is an active member of several professional organizations. She has served as Chair (2004) of CCCC as well as leading numerous CCCC committees including Archives (2004-present), Nominating (2005-06), and Assessment (1993-95). Additionally, her involvement with NCTE includes terms as Vice-President (2005-06), member of the Task force on the SAT and ACT (2005), and Chair of both the College Section (1998-01) and the College Forum (1998-00). Yancey also belongs to the MLA and the WPA, of which she was President (2000-02). Her editorial responsibilities include board memberships on *CE*, *Kairos*, *Journal of Writing Assessment*, and *Computers and Composition*, for which she was guest editor for a special issue on electronic portfolios (July 1996).

Yancey's research has been validated by various grants and awards. She shared a NSF grant (2002-04) for investigating ways of teaching embedded computing, and she helped secure a $1 million gift at Clemson to establish The Class of 1941 Studio for Student Communication. At UNC-Charlotte, she completed numerous projects related to program assessment, portfolios, and curriculum development that were all funded by the university. Yancey's honors include membership in Phi Kappa Phi, appearing in *Who's Who in American Education* (1989-91), and being named Outstanding Young Woman in America (1984).

As her publications illustrate, Yancey is truly an advocate for students and teachers. In her prolific writing about portfolios, reflection, and voice, she seeks to improve students' writing and critical thinking, to give them shared responsibility for their own learning, to develop global citizens who make connections between their work and the world, and to maximize the ever-changing technology that characterizes their world. Similarly, Yancey urges teachers to continually reflect on their own practices, to learn from their students, and to make curricular changes as necessary. She is a leading innovator in the area of electronic portfolios and is enthusiastic about the new kind of student and learning that they could create. In a broader sense, Yancey is committed to the future of composition, its place in academia, and its successful evolution to meet the needs of students and writing programs.

Yancey recently edited *The Fifth Canon: Delivering College Composition* (Boynton/Cook, 2006), a collection of essays discussing diverse sites for teaching college-level composition, including universities, community colleges, and high schools. Currently, Yancey is working on a book about composition instruction in the 21st century and another book about electronic portfolios.

Karen Wright

Sources for Biographical Narrative

▶ "Clemson University Names First Pearce Professor." *CLEMSONews*. Clemson University Department of News Services. 12 May 2000. 26 June 2006 <http://clemsonews.clemson.edu/WWW_releases/2000/May2000/News_Briefs.html>.

▶ "Kathleen Blake Yancey." English Dept. home page. Florida State University. 26 June 2006 <http://english.fsu.edu/faculty/kyancey.htm>.

▶ Yancey, Kathleen Blake. *Curriculum Vitae*. 6 July 2006.

▶ ---. Email interview. 6 July 2006.

Kathleen Blake Yancey recommends these readings for novice composition instructors:

1. Bazerman, Charles, and David Russell, eds. *Introduction to Writing Selves, Writing Societies: Research from Activity Perspectives.* Fort Collins, CO: WAC Clearinghouse, 2003. 14 Aug. 2005 <http://wac.colostate.edu/books/selves_societies>.

2. Brandt, Deborah. "Accumulating Literacy: Writing and Learning to Write in the Twentieth Century." *CE* 57 (1995): 649-68.

3. Faigley, Lester. "Competing Theories of Process: A Critique and Proposal." *CE* 48 (1986): 527-42.

4. Fulkerson, Richard. "Summary and Critique: Composition at the Turn of the Twenty-first Century." *CCC* 56 (2005): 654-87.

5. Hairston, Maxine. "The Winds of Change: Thomas Kuhn and the Revolution in the Teaching of Writing." *CCC* 33 (1982): 75-88.

6. Johnson-Eilola, Johndan. "Writing About Writing." *Kairos* 7.3 <http://english.HU.edu/Kairos/7.3/features/johnsoneilola.htm>.

7. McLeod, Susan H. "Re-Visions: Rethinking Hairston's 'Breaking Our Bonds.'" *CCC* 57 (2006): 523-34.

8. Shipka, Jody. "A Multimodal Task-Based Framework for Composing." *CCC* 57 (2005): 277-306.

Annotated Bibliography

▶ Yancey, Kathleen Blake. "Getting Beyond Exhaustion: Reflection, Self-Assessment, and Learning." *Clearing House* 72 (1998): 13-17.

Yancey posits that self-assessment should be required of students and valued by instructors, thereby teaching students to critique their own writing and then revise according to those critiques. Yancey presents her own self-assessment schema, comprised of self-knowledge, content knowledge, task knowledge, and judgment, with which the student begins a dialogue about the text. She also offers advice on asking for, responding to, and grading self-assessment, which would benefit any instructor planning to use the portfolio assessment model.

▶ ---. "Introduction: Definition, Intersection, and Difference—Mapping the Landscape of Voice." *Voices on Voice: Perspectives, Definitions, Inquiry.* Ed. Kathleen Blake Yancey. Urbana, IL: NCTE, 1994. vii-xxiv.

In this introduction, Yancey presents a historical overview of voice as it relates to composition, including the influences of expressionism, multiple voices, reader, Bakhtin, poets, oppression, and discourse communities. Basic ideas, such as the existence of voice, the intersection of voice and discourse, and the relationship between voice and authority, position this discussion logically within composition studies, and Yancey previews this collection's reflective and pedagogical considerations of voice. This text will help instructors clarify their own feelings about voice, direct them to relevant resources, and guide them in helping their students develop voices of their own.

▶ ---. "Looking Back as We Look Forward: Historicizing Writing Assessment." *CCC* 50 (1999): 483-503.

Yancey describes three waves in the development of writing assessment since CCCC was founded in 1950: 1) multiple-choice placement tests that emphasized grammar, usage, and vocabulary; 2) holistic grading of student essays for placement and post-testing that more closely resembled classroom practice; and 3) portfolios, whose multiple genres and texts as well as creation in a classroom environment, offer increased validity to this style of assessment. In time, assessment resources were developed, composition specialists such as Edward White, Peter Elbow, and Pat Belanoff emerged and writing assessment became its own field, recursively transforming writing instruction. All composition instructors should be familiar with this history of assessment and anticipate Yancey's predicted fourth wave: program assessment.

▶ ---. "Made Not Only in Words: Composition in a New Key." *CCC* 56 (2004) 297-328.

From her 2004 CCCC's Chair's address, Yancey urges instructors to build on the technology that we already use, such as word processors, WebCT/Blackboard, projectors, and the Internet, to teach our students how to become part of a global writing public, selecting appropriate media and delivery for their messages and thinking critically about content and appropriate sites for that content. She calls for sweeping fundamental changes in the field of composition, including revising the curriculum, revamping our WAC initiatives, and establishing a major in composition and rhetoric in order to secure our place in academia. Yancey inspires even the most technologically reluctant instructors to embrace and forge the future of academia and, more specifically, the field of composition.

▶ ---. "Chapter One: On Reflection." *Reflection in the Writing Classroom*. By Kathleen Blake Yancey. Logan: Utah State UP, 1998. 1-22.

In the first chapter of the book, Yancey charts her development as a proponent of reflection in the writing classroom, building on the prior research of Janet Emig, Linda Flower and John Hayes, John Dewey, Lev Vygotsky, Michael Polanyi, and Donald Schon. She asserts that reflection helps students know their own texts as they concurrently learn about writing, and the book offers guidelines on what, how, and when to ask students for reflection. This selection would benefit any instructor regardless of the assessment model used because it stresses communicating with students about their writing, thus creating a context for it, instead of merely grading essays in isolation.

▶ ---. "Portfolios in the Writing Classroom: A Final Reflection."
   Portfolios in the Writing Classroom: An Introduction.
   Ed. Kathleen Blake Yancey. Urbana, IL: NCTE, 1992.
   102-16.

Yancey sums up this collection of essays by providing an
overview of portfolios, their characteristics, pitfalls, and
principles of practice. Benefits of using portfolios include the
extensive student/teacher dialogue about writing throughout
the term and the students' metacognitive work about their
development as writers. New instructors who are weighing
their assessment options would be well advised to consider the
argument for portfolios presented here.

▶ ---. "Postmodernism, Palimpsest, and Portfolios: Theoretical
   Issues in the Representation of Student Work." *CCC* 55
   (2004): 738-61.

Building on linear print portfolios, digital portfolios have the
potential to create a different kind of student, one who can
represent himself or herself through a multi-media gallery of
verbal texts, images, audio, and links both internal and
external. While this new technology holds promise for
developing deeply reflective and intellectual students, Yancey
asks important questions about the impact of digital portfolios
on composition, such as who will teach design, how the
teaching of writing will be affected, how programs will evolve,
and what teachers will need to learn to keep up. While this
article may foretell an academic future that is coming whether
or not we are ready, for now only the technologically savviest of
instructors will benefit from its considerations.

▶ ---. "Teacher Portfolios: Lessons in Resistance, Readiness,
   and Reflection." *Situating Portfolios: Four Perspectives.*
   Ed. Kathleen Blake Yancey and Irwin Weiser. Logan:
   Utah State UP, 1997. 244-61.

Yancey summarizes the teaching portfolios of three students in
her Teaching Methods class, explaining what the students
learned during the class and what she learned from the
students' portfolios. Her reflection yields several key concepts:

delivered curriculum vs. experienced curriculum, the productive intersection of the two, and the development of a teacher identity. Her reflection also suggests that resistance leads to, and may be necessary for, change to occur. New instructors will readily identify with the student narratives and, consequently, think seriously about the importance and path of their own professional development.

▶ ---. *Teaching Literature as Reflective Practice*. Urbana, IL: NCTE, 2004.

In creating critical readers of literature, Yancey moves her students through the delivered curriculum, the experienced curriculum, and portfolios. Through reflection, students clarify their own and others' understanding of texts, interpret texts in ways that are meaningful to them, and make connections between texts and the world. Yancey's reflective assignments could be applied to any required reading or text, not just literature, and would be appropriate for any writing instructor.

▶ Yancey, Kathleen Blake, and Michael Spooner. "A Single Good Mind: Collaboration, Cooperation, and the Writing Self." *CCC* 49 (1998): 45-62.

Referring to myriad scholars on collaboration, such as Ede and Lunsford, the authors piece together their online discussion about the effectiveness and processes of co-authorship. Yancey and Spooner represent their dialogue through different fonts and overlapping text blocks to convey the rhythm of their collaboration in the hope that this multivocality will mirror their interaction and create in the reader an appreciation of difference. Instructors and solitary writers will benefit from this introduction to collaboration and notable theorists in this area.

Chapter 47:
Vivian Zamel

(b. 1946)

Vivian Zamel received her MA (1969) in English Literature
from Boston University and her PhD (1977) from Columbia
University and is currently professor of English, director of the
ESL Program, and director of the Center for the Improvement
of Teaching at The University of Massachusetts, Boston. Zamel
has been working with college-level ESL students, researching
their experiences in composition, since the late 1970s and has
researched, presented, and written extensively on ESL theory
and pedagogy, focusing in particular on the writing of
multilingual learners.

Her early work explored multiple facets of how ESL students
compose in composition courses; this research was the
foundation for the work she would go on to do in other ESL
classes. Some of the students she worked with in these early
years would go on to become ESL teachers themselves,
enabling Zamel to study how these students functioned in the
university, how they acquired academic literacy, and,
ultimately, how they used what they learned to instruct other
ESL students. Zamel expanded upon her research in the 1980s
and began focusing on WAC, studying how instructors modify
their teaching methods to accommodate students with

linguistic diversity. Her recent work has focused on engaging ESL students across the disciplines, while promoting learning and growth.

Drawn together by their mutual interest in researching literacy and composition, Zamel and Ruth Spack, a Bentley College professor, have been working together since the early 1980s, co-editing several books together and sharing their research. Their books together include *Crossing the Curriculum: Multilingual Learners in College Classrooms, Enriching ESOL Pedagogy: Readings and Activities for Engagement, Reflection, and Inquiry,* and *Negotiating Academic Literacies: Teaching and Learning with Diverse Student Learners.* Both Zamel and Spack were recognized for their outstanding contribution to multicultural education with the Freedom to Learn Award (2203), sponsored by the Massachusetts Association of Teachers of Speakers of Other Languages. Zamel also received the UMass Pedagogy Professorship Award (1996-98) and was honored with the UMass Chancellor's Distinguished Service Award (2004). With Eleanor Kutz and Suzie Q. Groden, she co-authored the book *The Discovery of Competence: Teaching and Learning Across Languages and Cultures* (1998) and has presented at more than 100 conferences, including TESOL, CCCC, and The Conference on the Teaching of Composition. She is currently working with Ruth Spack on a book entitled *Language Lessons: Short Stories about Learners of English.* Her current teaching areas are English as a second language, composition theory & practice, and methodology of teaching ESL.

Will Ingram

Sources for Biographical Narrative

▶ "Brief Biodata for Vivian Zamel." Sent by mail from Vivian Zamel.

▶ "English Department Faculty." Dept. home page. University of Massachusetts, Boston. 19 Nov. 2004 <http://www2.www.umb.edu/directory/person_detail.php?id=1254>.

▶ "Faculty and Staff." English Dept. home page. University of Massachusetts, Boston. 20 Oct. 2004 <http://www.english.umb.edu/faculty.html>.

▶ Fassel, Melissa. "Professor is Honored for Contributions to Multicultural Education." *The University Reporter*. University of Massachusetts, Boston. Dec. 2003. 25 Oct. 2004 <http://www.umb.edu/news/2003news/reporter/november/zamel.html>.

▶ Zamel, Vivian. *Curriculum Vitae*.

▶ ---. "Re: Book Chapter." Email to Will Ingram. 12 July 2006.

Vivian Zamel recommends these readings for novice composition instructors:

1. Rose, Mike. *Lives on the Boundary: The Struggles and Achievements of America's Underprepared*. New York: Free Press, 1989.
2. Zamel, Vivian, and Ruth Spack, ed. *Negotiating Academic Literacies: Teaching and Learning Across Languages and Cultures*. Mahwah, NJ: Erlbaum, 1998.

Annotated Bibliography

▶ Zamel, Vivian. "Engaging Students in Writing-To-Learn: Promoting Language and Literacy Across the Curriculum." *Journal of Basic Writing* 19.2 (2000): 3-21.

In this article, Vivian Zamel discusses some of the speaking and writing based communication challenges faced by ESL students in a university setting. She recommends using writing-to-learn assignments such as assigning one-minute-papers at the end of class (prompting students to write about something they learned in class and also something that was confusing to them), assigning reading response journals to encourage students to reflect informally on what they have read, and also assigning short un-graded writings that allow students to gather their thoughts and rehearse what they want to say in class. These suggestions are not solely intended for the English classroom and can be used to help solidify students' understanding of course content in any discipline.

▶ ---. "From the Margins to the Center." *Enriching ESOL Pedagogy: Readings and Activities for Engagement, Reflection, and Inquiry.* Ed. Vivian Zamel and Ruth Spack. Mahwah: NJ: Erlbaum, 2002. 331-39.

This article recounts Zamel's personal experience teaching an ESL freshman composition course about the myths and realities surrounding the idea of the American dream. She encouraged her students to find research dealing with the experiences of immigrants in the United States, having them read and respond to poetry and select autobiographies that dealt with the topic. This article is concise, easy to understand, and would be helpful for any ESL instructor interested in approaching the topic of immigrant marginalization in the United States.

▶ ---. "Questioning Academic Discourse." *Negotiating Academic Literacies: Teaching and Learning Across Languages and Cultures.* Ed. Vivian Zamel and Ruth Spack. Mahwah, NJ: Erlbaum, 1998. 187-97.

Zamel addresses the problems students have (ESL students in particular) with negotiating academic discourse. She argues that academic discourse should not be viewed as one "thing," and because there are multiple ways to communicate within disciplines, the discourse of the university should not be presented as a rigidly structured way of writing that can and should be mastered once a student enters college. This article would be helpful to ESL and Non-ESL instructors and anyone interested in postcolonial issues in college composition; Zamel's arguments are communicated very clearly.

▶ ---. "Re-evaluating Sentence Combining Practice." *TESOL Quarterly* 14.1 (1980): 81-90.

In this article, Zamel explains that, because sentence-combining practice includes no grammar instruction and many ESL students lack the linguistic repertoire required for manipulating sentences in this way, these exercises do not often provide the opportunity for ESL students to create meaningful sentences. She argues that ESL students should be introduced to key grammar concepts gradually, using these concepts to build sentences and then to analyze the sentences they have created. Her article is clear, accessible, and includes helpful example exercises to use with ESL students.

▶ ---. "Responding to Student Writing." *TESOL Quarterly* 19.1 (1985): 79-97.

Zamel addresses the need for teachers of composition to develop and implement new types of responses to student writing, urging instructors to respond to their writing as a work in progress. She explains that many ESL students believe that accuracy and correctness are the most important factors in their writing, suggesting that, by raising questions about writers' intentions and meaning and seeking to clarify ambiguity, teachers can help students realize that content and meaning supercede "grammatical correctness" in importance. Zamel's arguments are clear and are supported by excellent examples of how instructors have misinterpreted their students' writing; this article offers helpful advice to both ESL and non-ESL composition instructors.

▶ ---. "Strangers in Academia: The Experience of Faculty and ESL Students Across the Curriculum." *CCC* 46 (1995): 506-21.

This article responds to the tendency of university instructors to foreground ESL students' communication deficiencies, citing these communication problems as evidence that more remediation courses are necessary to ensure success for these students. Zamel urges instructors to employ new teaching strategies focused on engaging not just ESL students, but all students in their texts, encouraging them to read, writing, and respond in meaningful ways. Zamel suggests that instructors should make stronger efforts to identify and appreciate evidence of their students' intelligence (and not to make value judgments of their work), to understand the challenges ESL students face in the university, to question the legitimacy of approaches that stress assimilation, and to understand and reflect upon the relationship between the work of ESL students and that of their instructors.

▶ ---. "Teaching Those Missing Links in Writing." *ELT Journal* 37 (1983): 22-29.

In this article, Zamel addresses the problems English language students have with using "conjuncts" (coordinating conjunctions, subordinating conjunctions, and conjunctive adverbs or transitions). She addresses some of the major problems instructors have with teaching these conjuncts and, through the use of multiple example exercises, outlines new methods of teaching these elements. This article is easy to understand and provides helpful exercises that can benefit both high school and college level students.

▶ ---. "Through Students' Eyes: The Experience of Three ESL Writers." *Journal of Basic Writing* 9.2 (1990): 83-98.

Zamel describes the results of a study she conducted that focused on the experiences of three ESL students in pre-composition and composition classes. The students in her study felt that their expectations for their composition courses differed dramatically from their instructor's expectations and that this difference led to their instructors labeling their work "inadequate." Zamel urges instructors to pay attention to students' reactions to their assignments and to consider their students' agendas in relation to their own agendas; her article in easy to follow and offers helpful advice to college composition instructors.

▶ ---. "Toward a Model of Transculturation." *TESOL Quarterly* 31 (1997): 341-52.

Zamel addresses the implicit problems with theories of composition that view ESL writers as unable to meet the requirements of university composition courses because they are seen as being trapped by their own cultural world views. She uses multiple testimonies from her students' experience in composition to argue against the conception that ESL students are resistant to writing that requires critical thinking, argumentation, or the adoption of skeptical viewpoints. Ultimately, Zamel suggests moving away from reductive theories about assimilation in writing and toward a model of transculturation which celebrates the inventive power of linguistics and reflects the ways in which different cultures and languages develop and also how language is infused and enriched by innovation.

▶ ---. "Writing One's Way into Reading." *TESOL Quarterly* 26 (1992): 463-85.

Zamel outlines strategies for engaging students in their reading through the use of writing exercises. She explains how writing allows students to learn about themselves by enabling them to establish their opinions and thoughts on paper and how reading is, itself, a form of composition. This article is very instructive and accessible, offering many helpful ideas for instructors across the disciplines.

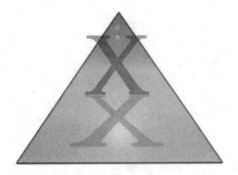

Section II:
Influences from
Other Disciplines

Chapter 48:
Education and Educational Psychology

Lisa Delpit
(b. 1952)

▶ Delpit, Lisa. "Educators as 'Seed People' Growing a New
   Future." *Educational Researcher* 32.7 (2003): 14-21.

Delpit calls for a move away from relying on test scores as the
measure of students' abilities and to replace them with getting
to know the students better and validating differing cultural
backgrounds evidenced through composition and oral language
use. She offers practical steps, a variety of real-life scenarios,
and examples of what excellence should be. The article
encourages rethinking of teaching practices.

▶ ---. *Other People's Children: Cultural Conflict in the*
   Classroom. New York: New Press, 1995.

Poignantly addressing the plight faced in American schools by
children of color, Delpit denounces stereotyping as a tragic
weakness in the educational system. Through a set of essays that
chronicle her own growth, which includes her seminal article "The
Silenced Dialogue: Power and Pedagogy in Educating Other
People's Children," she calls on educators to battle these
stereotypes to better educate this segment of the student
population. Delpit is candid in questioning innovations like process
writing and whole language instruction and in offering some
answers for future teachers.

John Dewey
(1859-1952)

▶ Dewey, John. *Experience and Education.* New York:
   Macmillan, 1938.

In this, his most important and last major work on education,
Dewey revisits his philosophy of education, reformulating the

link between learning and experience. He points to some abuses in the progressive system and calls for a return to the basic ideas he had initially proposed.

▶ ---. "The Reflex Arc Concept in Psychology." *Psychological Review* 3 (1896): 357-70.

Dewey's seminal article presents his revolutionary ideas about active engagement with the environment as key to learning, as opposed to the traditional practice of passive learning. Although written for an audience of psychologists, his ideas are still influential in today's theories of education.

Paulo Freire
(1921-1997)

▶ Freire, Paulo. *Pedagogy of the Oppressed*. Trans. Myra Bergman Ramos. New York: Herder and Herder, 1971.

Freire takes a stab at the traditional models of teaching, such as the banking method and introduces philosophies first brought up by Rousseau and John Dewey to a modern audience. His idea of a purely democratic classroom where students and teachers share a peer-like communication style is the crux of his notion that education will liberate the oppressed. While some of these concepts are dense, Freire's passion for this subject makes the reading enjoyable as well as educational.

▶ ---. *The Politics of Education: Culture, Power, and Liberation*. Trans. Donaldo Macedo. South Hadley, MA: Bergin and Garvey, 1985.

Freire focuses the essays in the work on liberation on a tri-fold: with adult literacy, within culture, and with the church's role within this pedagogy. The detailed essays offer specific explanations for each of these topics while still exploring Freire's personal cry for liberation. Those readers not familiar with Freire may find this work dense, but readers familiar with Freire will appreciate his continued passion.

Howard Gardner
(b. 1943)

▶ Gardner, Howard. "Audiences for the Theory of Multiple Intelligences." *Teachers College Record* 106 (2004): 212-20.

Gardner offers candid remarks about his misperceived audiences and the reception to his book *Frames of Mind*. Acknowledging his audience of educators as a surprise, he goes to recognize their long-time investment in the individual learner and in how best to meet his/her needs. Gardner calls for continued exploration in the field.

▶ ---. *Development of Education and the Mind: The Selected Works of Howard Gardner*. London: Routledge, 2006.

This book is a useful resource for those interested in educational psychology, since it gathers over 20 pieces of Gardner's work. Selected by the author himself, the pieces offer a glimpse into the development of his ideas, including his key contribution on multiple intelligences.

▶ ---. *Frames of Mind: The Theory of Multiple Intelligences*. New York: Basic Books, 1983.

In this ground-breaking book, Gardner argues against the concept of a single intelligence and further questions that it can be credibly measured by standard testing methods. He presents a then-revolutionary definition of intelligence, including eight criteria and identifies the various types, most of them not addressed by the educational system. Written in accessible language, although integrating a fair amount of psychological terminology, the book presents ideas that should be a basic part of every educator's concept of student potential.

bell hooks (Gloria Watkins)
(b. 1952)

▶ hooks, bell. *Teaching to Transgress: Education as the Practice of Freedom*. New York: Routledge, 1994.

hooks uses this work as a rallying cry for teachers to step up to the plate and realize that "[t]o educate as the practice of freedom is a way of teaching that anyone can learn," and learn from (13). Peppered with personal accounts of her own teaching and education, hooks yearns to introduce a pedagogy that incorporates the life experiences of each student so that none of them lose their voice in what hooks repeatedly refers to as the "white supremacist capitalist patriarchy." hooks offers real encouragement for the benefits of her theories; however, readers not familiar with hook's may be turned off by her political writing.

Mary Louise Pratt
(b. 1948)

▶ Pratt, Mary Louise. "Arts of the Contact Zone." *Profession* 91 (1991): 33-40.

Considered her seminal piece, this essay introduces the concept of the contact zone to education theory and practice. Pratt uses the term to define any space where groups of diverse status— cultural, ethnic, economic, and others—engage one another, usually gaining insight into each other's positions. The concept of contact zone has had significant impact in the culturally diverse composition classroom.

▶ ---."Building a New Public Idea about Language." *ADFL Bulletin* 34.3 (2003): 5-9.

Pratt points to the importance of bilingualism and multilingualism not only to achieve a more educated citizenry, but also to allow students to know the world better and function more smoothly in the contact zone. Four misconceptions about multilingualism are dispelled, and four new perspectives are proposed in their stead. The article is very readable and engaging in its timely message.

▶ ---. *Imperial Eyes: Travel Writing and Transculturation.*
   London: Routledge, 1992.

Applying her concept of contact zones through a discussion of
travel writing, Pratt's book presents her conclusion that
European imperialism found a disseminative medium through
that genre of composition. Her concerns focus on how language
is used to benefit only some segments of the population and
strives to decolonize knowledge. Although the text is at times
full of critical theory terminology, the travel accounts and what
they reveal about the observers are engaging and present an
interesting perspective on the issue of empowerment, critical in
the composition classroom.

Walter Ong
(1912-2003)

▶ Ong, Walter J. *Interfaces of the Word.* Ithaca, NY: Cornell
   UP, 1977.

In this work, Ong introduces the idea that writing is technology
and warns that the move from an orally-based culture to a
written-based culture is alienating some of the worlds' peoples.
He argues that oral speech is consistently arguing with the
written word. Though the work is exhaustive and slightly
dated, Ong's work can be appreciated for what it introduced
before its time.

▶ ---. *Orality and Literacy: The Technologizing of the Word.*
   London: Methuen, 1982.

This work opens with the impetus that educators and theorists
need to re-evaluate the human identity in relation to what they
consider native to the human experience: thought and
expression in literature, philosophy and science, and oral
discourse. Ong goes on to explain that literacy has evolved and
that its basis in orality is still imperative to its study. Ong does
a great service to the study of literacy with this work by
incorporating not just a study of Western literacies and oral
traditions.

Lev S(emenovich) Vygotsky
(1896-1934)

▶ Daniels, Harry. *Vygotsky and Pedagogy*. London:
    Routledge, 2001.

Daniels uses Vygotsky's theories to explore current educational
pedagogy and Vygotsky's theory of learning as a social process.
Daniels also examines Valsiner's re-evaluation of the Zone of
Proximal Development (ZPD), which includes the Zone of Free
Movement (ZFM) and the Zone of Promoted Action (ZPA).
Daniels work offers a fresh look at Vygotsky's theories within
education, but the reader shouldn't expect to find practical
pedagogical instruction.

▶ Vygotsky, Lev. *Thought and Language*. 1934. Trans. Alex
    Kozulin. Cambridge, MA: MIT Press, 1986. 1 Nov.
    2004 <http://www.netlibrary.com/Reader/>.

Knowledge of psychology greatly helps with Vygotsky's dense,
seminal work in which he explains his theories of inner speech
and the Zone of Proximal Development (ZPD) in regards to pre-
adolescent children. Vygotsky reacts to some of the
foundational psychologists' work, including Jean Piaget. While
this work is arduous, it is an imperative read for anyone
wanting more knowledge of the fields of thought and language.

▶ Zebroski, James Thomas. *Thinking Through Theory:
    Vygotskian Perspectives on the Teaching of Writing*.
    Portsmouth, NH: Boynton/Cook, 1994.

Zebroski champions the Zone of Proximal Development in this
work through his own use of it when teaching composition.
While Zebroski's theories and practices don't always match up,
he does offer practical examples of his theories for the
classroom. Zebroski shows that Vygotskian theory can be used
in a composition classroom.

Maria A. Clayton and Rachel Robinson
with Emileé LeClear, April Sivley, and Ruth Sundberg

Chapter 49:
Language and Linguistics

Dennis Baron
(b.1944)

▶ Baron, Dennis. "Forget Everything You Learned About
   Writing." *The WAC Casebook: Scenes for Faculty
   Reflection and Program Development.* Ed. Chris Anson.
   New York: Oxford UP, 2003. 261-65.

This short essay broaches the difficult topic of how teachers,
from high school through graduate school, present writing to
their students. Instead of giving answers, Baron inspires the
reader to think about ways to solve problems in writing
curricula. This is a valuable resource for teachers seeking to
bridge the gaps between different levels of education and
between different disciplines.

▶ ---. *Guide to Home Language Repair.* Urbana, IL: NCTE,
   1994.

In this entertaining and informative book, Baron dismisses
many of the myths about the decline of the English language.
He presents an easy-to-read discussion of the vitality of our
language and the joy of exploring the subject for its own sake.
Baron also covers controversial issues, such as language
policing and political correctness, in an easy, non-offensive
manner.

▶ ---. "Watching Our Grammar: The English Language for
   English Teachers." *On Literacy and Its Teaching: Issues
   in English Education.* Ed. Gail Hawisher and Anna
   Soter. Albany: SUNY P, 1990. 208-23.

In this article, Baron discusses the necessity of including
linguistic study in the college curricula of prospective English
teachers. Baron suggests courses that provide a general
overview of linguistic topics that every English teacher, often
expected to be a language expert by the general public, should

know. This highly readable and engaging essay is essential for any teacher seeking to enrich his or her knowledge of the English language, and it is especially useful for new teachers joining in the debate over whether grammar should be taught explicitly or implicitly in the writing classroom.

Noam Chomsky
(b.1928)

▶ Smith, Neil. *Chomsky: Ideas and Ideals*. New York: Cambridge UP, 1999.

Smith provides an excellent overview of Chomsky's linguistic theories, summarizing and clarifying them with readily understandable explanations. The book is a vital tool for the Chomsky student and is also useful for teachers exploring how Transformational Grammar and other Chomskyan ideas and theories have influenced the teaching of grammar in introductory language and writing classes.

Brock Haussamen

▶ Haussamen, Brock. *Grammar Alive: A Guide for Teachers*. Urbana, IL: NCTE, 2004.

In this book, Haussamen presents creative ways to teach grammar to students without using the typical methods of rote rule learning, worksheets, and constant correction. This readable book begins with the three grammar goals set forth by the NCTE and is filled with examples of nontraditional exercises being used in the classroom. The final chapter provides an overview of linguistic grammar, describing linguistic terms and ideas in language meant for English teachers rather than linguists.

▶ ---. *Revising The Rules: Traditional Grammar and Modern Linguistics*. Dubuque, IA: Kendall/Hunt, 1993, 1997, 2000.

Written for the student or teacher with at least a basic knowledge of grammar and grammar terminology, this book explores the main categories of traditional grammar, such as verb tense, subject-verb agreement, pronoun agreement, and adverbs, in a new way. The first chapter examines the history of traditional grammar, and each subsequent chapter discusses the history and linguistic viewpoint of each grammar rule. This is an interesting and useful source for expanding grammar knowledge but is not intended as an introductory text.

Shirley Brice Heath
(b.1939)

▶ Heath, Shirley Brice. "A Lot of Talk about Nothing." *The Heinemann Reader: Literacy in Process*. Ed. Brenda Miller Power and Ruth Hubbard. Portsmouth, NH: Heinemann, 1991. 79-88.

Heath presents an examination of a talk-centered classroom—one that attempts to strengthen the skills that students may, or may not, have acquired from their home environments. Very clearly written, the article is fairly readable and demonstrates forcibly how innovative classroom environments can expand student capabilities, and it effectively explores the differences between traditional classrooms and those centered on discussion and oral discourses. For those not familiar with *Ways with Words,* this essay provides an informative synoposis.

▶ ---. "The Literature Essay: Using Ethnography to Explode Myths." *Language, Literacy, and Culture: Issues of Society and Schooling*. Ed. Judith A. Langer. Norwood, NJ: Ablex, 1987. 89-109.

This interesting and self-reflective article explores the myths surrounding essays used in writing classrooms. Heath succeeds in exploding myths and proposing counter-statements to supplant or counterbalance those myths and is very lucid and effective. Heath provides a fun read but also proposes some interesting ways in which essays can be developed to differently construct the act of writing. Depending on the amount of freedom and control the TA is given over classroom activities, the application of some of Heath's ideas within TA classrooms are quite innovative.

▶ ---. *Ways With Words: Language, Life, and Work in Communities and Classrooms.* New York: Cambridge UP, 1983.

Heath's seminal work examines the ways in which children in three different communities acquire language and how this impacts their performance in school. Since the work constitutes an anthropological field study, it is difficult to follow in some particulars. However, Heath's conclusions seem strong and are well worth the time. Like several of the other articles presented in this bibliography, this book presents facts and observations that are not directly transferable to the classroom, but it encourages an awareness that is directly applicable. Because not every student has the same background in language use, major differences across students' writing occur.

▶ ---. "What No Bedtime Story Means: Narrative Skills at Home and School." *Language Socialization Across Culture.* Ed. Bambi B. Schieffelin and Elinor Ochs. New York: Cambridge UP, 1986. 97-127.

This article, one of Heath's favorites (Heath, email), builds off Heath's work in the Carolinas detailed in *Ways with Words.* With the help of clearly defined case studies, Heath argues effectively for the use of labeling, description, narrative, and question/answer behaviors with children—critical strategies that, according to the author, determine a child's success in school. Extremely readable and effective, the article's observations provide a sound pedagogical argument for the use of narrative and description papers as bridges to more academic writing.

Robert B. Kaplan
(b.1929)

▶ Grabe, William, and Robert B. Kaplan. *Theory and Practice of Writing: An Applied Linguistic Perspective.* New York: Longman, 1996.

The seventh chapter of this volume, which focuses on contrastive rhetoric, should be of particular interest to ESL teachers, as well as other composition teachers. Grabe and Kaplan provide a useful introduction and discussion for those teachers interested in the fundamental differences in written discourse found within several foreign language groups compared to writers of English.

▶ Kaplan, Robert B. "Cultural Thought Patterns in Inter-cultural Communication." *Readings on English as a Second Language.* Ed. Kenneth Croft. Boston: Little, Brown, 1980. 399-418.

This is the quintessential "doodles" article, which brought Kaplan to the forefront of the linguistics community. Originally published in *Language Learning* in 1966, the article introduces the concept of contrastive rhetoric to the academy. Upon publication, this article influenced ESL scholarship and pedagogy for many years afterward, although there are some scholars who question the framework.

▶ Kaplan, Robert, and William Grabe. "A Modern History of Written Discourse Analysis." *Journal of Second Language Writing* 11 (2002): 191-223.

Kaplan and Grabe examine the history of discourse analysis over the last 50 years as seen through the eyes of applied linguists. They distinguish the many types of linguists and the disciplines involved in written discourse analysis. This history is a must read for any student or teacher of composition for its focus on and acceptance of varieties of written English.

William Labov
(b.1927)

▶ Labov, William. *Principles of Linguistic Change. Volume II: Social Factors.* Oxford: Blackwell, 2000.

Labov provides an overview of some of his studies concerning language change influenced by social factors. The author details language changes related to class, ethnicity, gender, and other sociolinguistic variables. While written with the linguist in mind, this book is a valuable resource for teachers and students interested in language change and how this change affects the systems students bring to our writing classes.

▶ ---. "Recognizing Black English in the Classroom." *Black English: Educational Equity and the Law.* Ed. John W. Chamber, Jr. Ann Arbor: Karoma, 1983. 29-55.

In this article designed for reading instructors, Labov describes the various features of Black English in accessible, non-technical terms. Detailing aspects of this dialect, such as verb tenses, inflections, and final consonant deletion, he provides a useful introduction to the differences between Standard English and Black English. The final section includes five methods for reading teachers to assist Black English students as they learn to read without treating the students' home dialect as inferior.

Steven Pinker
(b.1954)

▶ Pinker, Steven. *How the Mind Works.* New York: Norton, 1997.

Pinker synthesizes theories from a broad variety of disciplines, such as neuroscience, cognitive science, evolutionary biology, and psychology, into a discussion of how our minds work. As Pinker states in the Preface, this book is intended to be a discussion of the problem of how our mind works rather than an absolute authority. More readable than many sources on this subject, Pinker makes this topic accessible to people from almost any background, and composition instructors could find it useful, especially when dealing with the intercultural rhetoric of the classroom.

▶ ---. *The Language Instinct: How the Mind Creates Language.* New York: HarperPerennial, 1994.

This accessible and engaging book is designed for anyone interested in how language works. Discussing how we learn language in understandable terms, Pinker brings together research from multiple disciplines in an entertaining and essential book for language lovers. Pinker broaches difficult topics, such as language critics, and dispels language myths in an open, candid manner.

▶ ---. *Words and Rules: The Ingredients of Language.* 1st ed. New York: Basic Books, 1999.

Continuing work from *The Language Instinct*, Pinker uses the structure of regular and irregular verbs to explore and explain the underlying structure of language wired into the human brain. Written in witty, engaging language, he presents complicated theories from cognitive science at a level understandable by the average reader. This is a good source for teachers who wish to delve deeper into the subjects of language cognition and language acquisition.

Ferdinand de Saussure
(1857-1913)

▶ Culler, Jonathan D. *Ferdinand de Saussure.* Ed. Frank Kermode. New York: Penguin, 1976.

Detailing the work of Saussure, considered to be the father of modern linguistics, Culler explains Saussure's theories in easily-understood, concise terms. Of particular importance is the detailed discussion of Saussure's most well-known theory about *langue* and *parole*, which differentiates the underlying structure of language, the *langue*, from the unique expressions, the *parole*, that individuals are able to construct from this structure. This is an essential source for understanding the beginning of modern linguistics and would be helpful for new writing teachers as they grapple with how students use language.

Constance Weaver

▶ Weaver, Constance, ed. *Lessons to Share on Teaching
Grammar in Context.* Portsmouth, NH: Boynton/Cook,
1998.

This sequel to Weaver's earlier *Teaching Grammar in Context*
contains 18 articles by educators from elementary school
through college. Subjects include language acquisition,
Ebonics, teaching grammar for ESL, methods of teaching
stylistic effect, positive methods of writing revision, teaching
grammar through writing, and more. Like its predecessor, this
book is essential for teachers at all levels who wish to improve
language and writing education in their classrooms.

▶ Weaver, Constance. *Teaching Grammar in Context.*
Portsmouth, NH: Boynton/Cook Publishers, 1996.

Arguing against the use of structural and transformational
grammar, Weaver instead suggests the use of the
constructiveness model of grammar, which uses mini-lessons
designed to allow students to construct isolated facts into
concepts. A broad variety of mini-lessons covering subjects
such as parts of speech, sentence construction, style, dialect
appropriateness, and mechanics are provided for teachers
wishing to use this theory to improve their students' writing.
This book is a valuable source for improving the variety and
effectiveness of grammar lessons or for learning how to
incorporate grammar instruction into the writing process.

▶ ---. *Understanding Whole Language: From Principles to
Practice.* Portsmouth, NH: Heinemann, 1990.

In this book, Weaver explains the philosophy of whole language
learning, developed from a variety of disciplines such as
linguistics, psychology, anthropology, and education, which
emphasizes teaching literacy through the use of natural
learning processes and of relevant, student-driven activities.
Designed for teachers, this book is filled with examples of this
philosophy as well as activities that can be used in any
classroom. This book is essential for any teacher looking for an
alternative to traditional teaching methods.

Rebecca Wheeler
(b.1952)

▶ Wheeler, Rebecca S. "Believing Is Seeing: Errors and
Expectations in 2002." *Journal of College Writing* 5
(2002): 5-21.

This easy-to-read article examines the difficulties that teachers
face when teaching students who speak a nonstandard dialect
and offers advice on how to teach the formal standard English
required by employers and universities. Using theories from
applied linguistics, Wheeler discusses the difference between
dialects, which are regional or social varieties of a language,
and "bad" English, a judgment based on the public's attitudes
toward a dialect. To bridge this gap, Wheeler suggests code-
switching, the act of choosing the appropriate dialect or
language variety based on the situation.

▶ Wheeler, Rebecca, and Rachel Swords. *Code-switching:
Teaching Standard English in Urban Classrooms.*
Urbana, IL: NCTE, 2006.

Wheeler, an academic linguist, and Swords, a classroom
teacher, have written a truly innovative guide to how teachers
can assist their students who speak vernacular varieties of
English code-switch to a variety of English that allows for a
more successful school experience. The book is organized into
two main sections: the first introduces the theory and research
behind code-switching, which is the act of restructuring the
patterns of one dialect of a language into the patterns of
another dialect; the second focuses on classroom practice. In
the theory section, the authors present common vernacular
patterns that will help teachers and their students identify
these patterns in student writing. The 14 chapters in the
classroom section are organized around sample lessons that
teachers can use to give their students practice in code-
switching. A valuable resource for K-16 literacy educators, this
book is an important addition to any library focused on the
connection between language use and writing.

▶ Wheeler, Rebecca, ed. *Language Alive in the Classroom.*
Westport: Praeger, 1999.

This book combines knowledge from the linguistics and
education fields to provide teachers with a careful analysis of
what works, and what doesn't, in English and composition
curriculums. A wide variety of experts contribute essays on
subjects such as dialect, writing, grammar, and literature, an
inclusive approach providing information valuable to both the
beginner and the expert alike. Highly readable and engaging,
this book contains valuable examples on ways to improve all
aspects of English teaching.

Walt Wolfram
(b.1941)

▶ Wolfram, Walt, Carolyn Adger, and Donna Christian.
Dialects in Schools and Communities. Mahwah, NJ:
Erlbaum, 1999.

The authors begin with an analysis of language varieties in the
US and a general discussion of linguistic, dialectal, and
cultural studies. In the second half of the book, the authors
discuss dialect and language instruction in oral and written
languages and in reading education, concluding with a chapter
on dialect awareness exercises designed to increase all
students' proficiencies in language analysis. This is an
important source for teachers dealing with dialect variety in
the classroom or for teachers who have an interest in dialect
diversity and discrimination.

▶ Wolfram, Walt, and Donna Christian. *Dialects and
Education: Issues and Answers.* Englewood Cliffs, NJ:
Prentice Hall, 1989.

As the title suggests, this book is written in an easy-to-read
question and answer format, with questions grouped under
main headings. Wolfram and Christian answer tough
questions often posed by educators concerning dialect,
particularly considering dialect equality, differences between
dialects, and the inclusion of dialect in Language Arts

programs. This is an essential book for understanding and dispelling dialect myths and for including the dialects of all students into the English, Language Arts, and writing curricula.

▶ Wolfram, Walt, and Natalie Schilling-Estes. *American English: Dialects and Variation.* 1st ed. Malden: Blackwell, 1998.

Wolfram and Schilling-Estes explore the subject of dialect outside of an educational setting. The authors explain the history, types, and styles of American dialects in language accessible to the average reader. For people fascinated with the phenomenon of dialect itself, this is a concise source detailing all aspects of American dialects and an excellent introduction to varieties of English found in the writing classroom.

Bethany Adams and Allison D. Smith
With Elke Bartel, Jeremy Brown, Vickie Knierim,
Abby Lockett, Ronald W. Scott, and Jennifer Wilson

 **Chapter 50:
Literary Theory**

Roland Barthes
(1915-1980)

▶ Barthes, Roland. "The Death of the Author." *Image-Music-Text*. Trans. and ed. Stephen Heath. New York: Hill, 1977. 142-48.

One of the most infamous essays of French poststucturalism, "The Death of the Author" challenges the prevalent notion that to understand literature, one must remain faithful to the author's intentions. Barthes argues that readers are not passive spectators; they actively construct meaning through language, a medium tinged with cultural values and assumptions. Barthes writes in beautiful, easily accessible prose; therefore, due to its extraordinary amount of influence, this article should prove useful for newcomers to literary theory.

Jacques Derrida
(b.1930)

▶ Derrida, Jacques. *Of Grammatology*. Trans. Gayatri Chakravorty Spivak. Baltimore: John Hopkins UP, 1976

In this, one of Derrida's most famous texts, the author examines the relationship between writing and speech and how they develop as language. Whereas many have argued that writing is a natural expression of speech and have thus investigated the development of language based on this assumption, Derrida disagrees with this argument and claims that neither is more important than the other and that language is actually a result of the interplay between the two. He first examines the origins of writing and then proceeds to deconstruct theories by such greats as Ferdinand de Saussure, Claude Lévi-Strass, and Rousseau as evidence that prior views on the relationship between speech and writing in the development of language are lacking.

▶ ---. "Meaning and Representation." *Critical Theory Since Plato*. 3rd ed. Ed. Hazard Adams and Leroy Searle. Boston: Thomson Wadsworth, 2005. 1215-20.

In this article, Derrida examines the correlations between meaning and representation and the act of language. He explores the meanings or such terms as *sign, signifier, representation*, and *re-presentation* as they relate to language in general and in particular to Husserl's idea that solitary discourse could "not take place because it would make no sense, and it would make no sense because there would be *no finality* to it" (1215). Derrida concludes that such solitary discourse is useless because it is false. Derrida's ideas as presented in this text, support the social constructionist pedagogies of the composition classroom and should inform instructor's practices.

Stanley Fish
(b. 1938)

▶ Fish, Stanley. *Is There a Text in This Class?* Cambridge, MA: Harvard UP, 1980.

In this seminal work, Stanley Fish' elaborates on interpretive communities. The first half collects his traditional reader-response criticism; of particular interest is "Interpreting the *Variorum*," where he analyzes one of Milton's poems and discusses how his reading strategies *created* the text. In the second half, Fish explores the implications for both the classroom and literary studies, often using his characteristic blend of personal narrative, humor, and dense argumentation.

▶ Fish, Stanley. "Anti-Foundationalism, Theory Hope, and the
   Teaching of Composition." *Doing What Comes
   Naturally: Change, Rhetoric, and the Practice of Theory
   in Literary and Legal Studies*. London: Duke UP, 1989.
   342-55.

Fish addresses composition specialists—in particular, figures
such as Kenneth Bruffee and Patricia Bizzell, who had
developed Fish's theories into a justification for peer tutoring
and collaborative learning. Following a characteristic line of
argumentation, he argues that social constructionism has no
implications; it leads to no revolutions, because that would
assume scholars, using a postmodern model, could impartially
examine their context. Even though his argument is
historically false, this article should fill scholars with caution,
especially those who exaggerate the importance of theory.

Gerald Graff
(b.1937)

▶ Graff, Gerald. *Beyond the Culture Wars: How Teaching the
   Conflicts Can Revitalize American Education*. New
   York: Norton, 1992.

Beyond the Culture Wars is directed toward the literature
classroom, but it offers a captivating glimpse into the politics of
English studies. Graff believes the academic system encourages
the development of a fragmented curriculum; as a result,
students often feel unable to make sense of each course's
divergent assumptions. Instead of viewing academic debate as
a liability, Graff recommends using these conflicts to spark
student interest.

▶ ---. "Hidden Intellectualism." *Pedagogy* 1 (2001): 21-36.

Graff argues that popular culture and the university share
many features. To help students make the same connection,
Graff advises problematizing the distinction—by forcing
students to defend why they are *not* intellectuals, professors
can both teach academic discourse and stimulate class
discussion. Written in an accessible style, which combines

personal narrative and theoretical argumentation, this article is a valuable resource for those interested in the problem of student motivation.

D(avid) G(ershom) Myers
(b.1942)

▶ Myers, D. G. *The Elephants Teach: Creative Writing Since 1880*. 1995. Chicago: U of Chicago P, 2006.

In this book, Myers outlines the complicated history of creative writing since the inception of the term at Harvard in the mid-19th century. Myers weaves important names and dates into the political narrative which shows how the many schisms have occurred within English departments. He notes how English studies have shifted from a study of the English language as a whole--complete with creative writing to study literature from the inside--to solely being associated with literature studies. The author unapologetically admits his prejudices against what the English department has become with its many factions, but the historical value of the text is not lost. For anyone in composition studies to understand the historical implications of departmental politics and the evolution of English studies in general, Myers offers a wealth of information and wisdom to learn from our past mistakes.

Richard Rorty
(b. 1931)

▶ Rorty, Richard. *Contingency, Irony, and Solidarity*. New York: Cambridge UP, 1989.

A compelling and well-written defense of social constructionism, Rorty's book argues that language does not produce accurate representations of the world; rather, vocabularies are best conceived as tools, which societies use to achieve certain objectives. Instead of searching for a culturally neutral, ahistorical truth, he advocates the creation an "ironist" utopia, where people embrace the contingency of their beliefs.

Rorty is a controversial figure, and while many have celebrated his move away from analytic philosophy's technical jargon, others have criticized him of radical skepticism and ethnocentrism.

Louise Rosenblatt
(1904-2005)

▶ Rosenblatt, Louise. *The Reader, the Text, the Poem: The Transactional Theory of The Literary Work.* Carbondale: SIUP, 1978.

Rosenblatt's transactional theory of reading asserts that what a reader brings to a text, or to the reading of a text, is just as important, if not more so, than what the author's text says. She sees the reading of a text as an event that takes place in a particular time and place at a particular moment in the reader's history; consequently, the printed marks on a page could possibly become different linguistic symbols by virtue of their transactions with specific readers.

Robert E. Scholes
(b.1929)

▶ Scholes, Robert. *The Rise and Fall of English.* New Haven: Yale UP, 1998.

In this accessible book, Scholes traces the origin of English studies. According to his historical narrative, by the end of the 19th century, literature had moved to the center of the discipline—canonical works had become a secular gospel, and teachers preached the virtues of reading these sacred texts. Today, many universities continue to live by the old faith, but for English departments to move forward, they must abandon this doctrine; he proposes a set of bold curricular reforms, which shift the discipline's focus to composition instruction and textual analysis.

▶ Scholes, Robert. *Textual Power: Literary Theory and the Teaching of English*. New Haven: Yale UP, 1985.

Textual Power explores the pedagogical implications of contemporary theory. Scholes advocates a revision of the English curriculum—instead of focusing exclusively on the traditional canon, instructors should aim to provide students with textual literacy. Along the way, he critiques several prominent theorists, including Derrida, Stanley Fish, and Frederic Jameson; therefore, before reading *Textual Power*, one should feel comfortable with the basic tenets of poststructuralism.

Kennie Rose and Trixie G. Smith
with Dianna Baldwin and Alan Coulter

Chapter 51:
Rhetoric—Classical to (Post)Modern

Aristotle
(384-322 BCE)

▶ Aristotle. *Rhetoric*. Trans. W. Rhys Roberts. *Poetics*. Trans.
  Ingram Bywater. Intro. Friedrich Solmsen. New York:
  Modern Library-Random House, 1954.

Noted classicist W. Rhys Roberts's translation seems to be the
edition of choice for many scholars. The user-friendly format
(e.g., the Table of Contents contains head notes for each
chapter within the three books) allows for effective navigation
of this intimidating text. According to Aristotle, rhetoric is an
intellectual skill that provides the student an avenue to search
for the best available reasons for believing something and
arranging those reasons into a logical order. *Rhetoric*'s
contribution to writing cannot be overstated for it serves as the
preeminent text on the art of persuasion. Its influence can be
traced throughout history, beginning with the writings of
Roman rhetoricians Cicero and Quintilian.

St. Augustine
(354-430 CE)

▶ St. Augustine. *De Doctrina Christiana*. Trans. D. W.
  Robertson. New York: Liberal Arts P, 1958.

St. Augustine dispenses with the Sophist's use of rhetoric as a
cosmetic tool. His text is often viewed as a transition between
the classical and the medieval/renaissance periods in rhetoric.
Organized in four books, the main discussion of rhetoric comes
in the final book; however, the Book I discussion establishing
principle categories of things and signs is helpful. Overall, this
work is especially useful when viewed as a synthesis of
Christianity and rhetoric.

Francis Bacon
(1561-1626)

▶ Bacon, Francis. *The Advancement of Learning*. Ed. G. W. Kitchin. London: Dent, 1965.

Although not dedicated to the topic of rhetoric, this is the best source of Bacon's discussion of the subject. Bacon is similar to Aristotle in that he attempts to logically organize human knowledge, categorizing it into history (memory), poetry (imagination), and philosophy (reason), with rhetoric being essential to all three areas. This is an essential work although it may be easier to read with a critical guide such as Karl R. Wallace's "Bacon's Conception of Rhetoric" (In *Historical Studies of Rhetoric and Rhetoricians*. Ed. Raymond F. Howes. Ithaca, NY: Cornell UP, 1961. 114-38).

Mikhail Bakhtin
(1895-1975)

▶ Bakhtin, Mikhail. *The Bakhtin Reader: Selected Writings of Bakhtin, Medvedev, and Voloshinov*. Ed. Pam Morris. New York: Edward Arnold, 1994.

This collection gives useful excerpts of Bakhtin's most important works, along with excerpts from two of the students who continued his work. The reader addresses many of Bakhtin's important ideas such as his attack on formalists and structuralists—in linguistics and literary criticism—in favor of social approaches that discuss heteroglossia and polyvocalism, as well as his ideas about the novel being better than both poetry and the epic because it is not frozen in time and includes multiple voices—dialogism.

▶ ----. *Speech Genres and Other Late Essays*. Trans by Vern McKee. Ed. Caryl Emerson and Michael Holquist. Austin: U of Texas P, 1986.

In the essay "The Problem of Speech Genres," Bakhtin anticipates genre theory when he claims that the utterances of speech are relatively stable types that occur in all realms of language and in all discourse communities. Bakhtin's dialogic approach recognizes both the speaker's intention to move the audience to action and the audience's active role in interpreting utterances in order to reply, react, or act—this audience role affects how the speaker constructs the initial utterance as well as later utterances or replies; genre sets up audience expectations.

Hugh Blair
(1718-1800)

▶ Blair, Hugh. *Lectures of Rhetoric and Belles Lettres*. New York: Garland, 1970.

Blair, Minister to St. Giles, Scotland, promotes literature, moral philosophy, writing, and rhetoric to a newly democratized educational system in 18th century England and Scotland in this much reproduced collection of lectures. He believes that the pursuit of clear and proper, or tasteful, communication is the pursuit of reason itself; consequently, he gives much attention to issues of taste, style, oration, and other elements of beautiful language and poetics. Blair also discusses the goals of education and pushes for more emphasis on oratory.

Wayne Booth
(1921-2005)

▶ Booth, Wayne C. " The Idea of a *University* – as Seen by a Rhetorician." *Professing the New Rhetorics: A Sourcebook*. Ed. Theresa Enos and Stuart C. Brown. Englewood Cliffs, NJ: Prentice Hall, 1994. 228-52.

Booth maintains that this was the most difficult essay he ever had to write because he was faced with discussing why rhetoric is important across the disciplines "to a pack of critically trained specialists in the 'harder' sciences" (228). He points out that most scholars understand little when it comes to lectures from fields of study other than their own and sometimes even within their own. Booth questions how the inhabitants of the university can claim to know their colleagues' works well enough to write recommendation letters and interdivisional memos if they do not understand the rhetoric being employed by them. He then describes three kinds of rhetoric: 1—"hard proof", 2—"general rhetoric", and 3—"the rhetoric of inquiry." Booth explains Donald T. Campbell's concept of knowledge as fish scales where each scale overlaps another thus adding knowledge to that scale and then Booth expands it to imagine that these scales have tentacles and can reach across the entire fish to an entirely new knowledge. He concludes that an image such as this would increase an individual's understanding of all three rhetorics and truly make the academic world a *University* where each discipline had some knowledge of another.

Kenneth Burke
(1897-1993)

▶ Burke, Kenneth. *Counter Statement*. 1931. Berkeley: U of California P, 1968.

Burke views literature not as an end in itself, but as a piece of self-revelation about the author. Burke's critical theory, anticipating elements of reader-response criticism, American formalism, and deconstruction, contends that literary forms are best understood by their effects on readers and that the study of rhetoric is precisely needed to comprehend the effects not only of literature but of all forms of discourse.

▶ ---. *A Grammar of Motives*. New York: Prentice Hall, 1945.

Dealing with the intrinsic nature of a work and focusing on dramatism and the pentad, Burke presents the dramatic system that unifies rhetoric and poetics within a single analytical framework. The system is a tool to study and compare statements about human motives by examining how writers, and consequently readers, treat the dramatic elements of human relations: act, scene, agent, agency, and purpose. Burke asserts that this pentad is intended to analyze descriptions of behaviors and not actual behavior.

▶ ---. *A Rhetoric of Motives.* Berkeley: U of California P, 1950.

Viewing rhetoric as a tool for literary criticism, Burke argues
that literature always attempts to persuade and that this
phenomena can facilitate the application of rhetorical terms to
purely poetical structures. The work reflects Burke's
Aristotelian interest in both drama and writing as cathartic
act, and Burke's appropriation of Karl Marx and Sigmund
Freud help to distinguish his formalism from that of the new
critics.

Judith Butler
(b. 1956)

▶ Butler, Judith. *Exciting Speech: A Politics of the
    Performative.* New York: Routledge, 1997.

In this text, Butler examines the power of speech: the power to
incite, excite, and injure. Her analysis of speech delves deeply
into such issues as hate speech, the military's "don't ask, don't
tell" policy concerning homosexuals, and pornography. She
explores the question of whether or not language could "injure
us if we were not, in some sense, linguistic beings, beings who
require language in order to be" (1-2). Butler's text explores a
realm of linguistics often ignored by linguists and
compositionists.

▶ ---. *Undoing Gender.* New York: Routledge, 2004.

This book is a collection of Butler's essays exploring the topics
of gender and sexuality and reexamines her previous views on
gender performativity. She combines feminist and queer
theory to analyze not only the undoing of gender, but also "the
experience of *becoming undone* in both good and bad ways" (1).
Butler's text is thought provoking and often triggers more
questions than it answers, but the topics it considers are
important when considering the make-up of many composition
classrooms.

George Campbell
(1719-1796)

▶ Campbell, George. *The Philosophy of Rhetoric*. Delmar, NY:
    Scholars' Facsimiles and Reprints, 1992.

This major work from Scottish intellectual Campbell seeks to
explain rhetoric in scientific terms. He traces the path of
rhetorical persuasion through the faculties as defined by Locke:
first understanding, then imagination, then the passions, and
then the will. At the same time, Locke separated argument into
two types, scientific and moral, associating rhetoric with
morality.

Cicero
(106-45 BCE)

▶ Cicero. *On Invention. The Best Kind of Orator. Topics*. Trans.
    H.M. Hubbell. *Loeb Classical Library*. Cambridge, MA:
    Harvard UP, 1949.

As a politician, Cicero experienced the rise and fall of Julius
Caesar. This collection of rhetorical treatises, written during
this tumultuous time in Roman history, demonstrates the
author's adroit ability to comprehend the importance of
composing sound rhetoric, pinpoint the best attributes of an
orator, and argue choice topics. These three writings (out of
only 58 that survive) are what remain of the 106 believed to
have been written by Cicero.

Michel Foucault
(1926-1984)

▶ Foucault, Michel. *The Archeology of Knowledge and The
    Discourse on Language*. Trans. A.M. Sheridan Smith.
    New York: Parthenon, 1972.

Foucault develops his theory of language as inextricably linked
to the exercise of power and his theory of knowledge as created
not by observation, but by discourse—a repudiation of

empiricism. Consequently, Foucault stresses the importance of digging down to the essential and original meanings of terms so that they can be used judiciously. While an important work, readers new to Foucault may want to start with secondary sources rather than his primary works.

▶ Hoy, David Couzens, ed. *Foucault: A Critical Reader*. Oxford: Basil Blackwell, 1986.

This collection of essays by various critical theorists attempts to explain and/or criticize the various theories of Foucault's *oeuvre*. The interpretative essays by critics such as Rorty and Dreyfus are helpful to students new to Foucault's work and make a nice companion to Foucault's original writings. The critical essays by theorists such as Habermas and Taylor are just as useful for reading Foucault and understanding his contributions to theories of language and power and the role of the author in both reading and writing.

Isocrates
(436-338 BCE)

▶ Isocrates. *Against the Sophists*. Trans. George Norlin. *Loeb Classical Library*. Cambridge, MA: Harvard UP, 1929.

Isocrates believes that moral knowledge is achieved by studying the art of oratory as a means to understand the moral choice of men and improve upon them. This fragment of his rant against the "wretched Sophists," offers great insight to what he believes is wrong with the sophists, which is not to be orators for a noble reason but in order to persuade for gain only.

Julia Kristeva
(b. 1941)

▶ Kristeva, Julia. *Powers of Horror*. Trans. Leon S. Roudiez. New York: Columbia, 1982.

Kristeva's first experiment with a more accessible style, *The Powers of Horror* features vivid and often poetic language. According to her seminal concept of abjection, for people to differentiate between themselves and their environment, they must violently expel certain aspects of their identities. Unfortunately, the book assumes knowledge of her previous work; therefore, for those new to Kristeva's ideas, *The Powers of Horror* could prove difficult.

▶ ---. *Revolution in Poetic Language*. Trans. Margaret Waller. New York: Columbia, 1984.

Infamous for its dense prose, *Revolution in Poetic Language* is a formidable challenge, but for those willing to brave the text, it offers a compelling description of the speaking and writing process. She introduces her seminal concepts of the semiotic, symbolic, and the *chora*, arguing that creating meaning is not just a mechanical process, but an act that includes one's unconscious drives.

John Locke
(1632-1704)

▶ Locke, John. *An Essay Concerning Human Understanding.* Ed. Peter H. Nidditch. Oxford: Oxford UP, 1975.

Although usually assigned a tangential place in discussions of rhetoric, this work was second only to the Bible as the most printed and widely read work of the 18th century. Locke examines fundamental questions of philosophy, including the philosophy of language explored in Book III, in which Locke follows a Platonic view of rhetoric as potentially corrupting. This text is most useful to read as a means of understanding human thought process as the initial step in communication.

James J. Murphy
(b. 1923)

▶ Murphy, James. J., and Richard A Katula, eds. *A Synoptic History of Classical Rhetoric.* 2nd ed. Davis, CA: Hermagoras, 1995.

A history of Greek and Roman rhetoric, this collection gathers essays by many notable scholars, including Donovan J. Ochs,

Forbes I. Hill, and Prentice A. Meador. It also contains
selections from Plato, Isocrates, Cicero, Pericles, and Lysias,
complete with introductions and commentary; in addition, the
appendices provides a bibliography of resources, a list of key
dates, and a subject outline. For those searching for an
overview of classical rhetoric, *A Synoptic History* provides a
thorough and highly readable introduction.

▶ Murphy, James J., ed. *A Short History of Writing
      Instruction: From Ancient Greece to Twentieth
      Century America.* Davis, CA: Hermagoras, 1990.

This collection discusses a variety of subjects, including
Quintilian's description of the Roman curriculum and teaching
practices in Renaissance Europe. Of particular interest is
James A Berlin's "Writing Instruction in School and College
English, 1890-1985," an article that covers both historical
trends and theoretical developments. *A Short History* concludes
with a detailed glossary and a short bibliography, making this
volume a wonderful resource for composition scholars.

Chaim Perelman
(1912-1984)

▶ Perelman, Chaim, and Lucie Olbrechts-Tyteca. *The New
      Rhetoric: A Treatise on Argumentation.* Trans. John
      Wilkinson and Purcell Weaver. Notre Dame, IN: U of
      Notre Dame P, 1969.

Originally a philosopher interested in law and legal arguments,
Perelman, with research partner Olbrechts-Tyteca examined
the arguments used by lawyers, politicians, and others. They
discovered connections to classical rhetoric, especially
Aristotle's idea of logos, and sought to revive the study and use
of classical rhetoric in Belgium. In this text, they focus on
argumentation, audience awareness, and usage which they say
is bound by communal and biological ties.

Plato
(ca 427-47 BCE)

▶ Plato. *Gorgias. Plato: Lysis, Symposium, Gorgias.* Vol. 3. Trans. W. R. M. Lamb. Cambridge, MA: Harvard UP, 1999.

One of Plato's earliest dialogues, the purpose of which is to investigate rhetoric as an art. Easy to follow as Plato, through the character of Socrates, dialogically defines rhetoric and identifies how it should be used as well as its potential for ill effects on morality, ultimately designating rhetoric as "cookery in the soul." As an argument, the *Gorgias* is based on flawed logic; however, it is useful to read as the root from which all other derogations of rhetoric spring.

▶ ---. *Phaedrus. Plato: Enthyphro, Apology, Crito, Phaedo, Phaedrus.* Vol. 1. Trans. Harold North Fowler. Cambridge, MA: Harvard UP, 1999.

Plato employs a complex use of Socratic dialogue centering on seduction to demonstrate the way in which the rhetoric can be used to corrupt and what a noble rhetoric would involve. A corrupted speech about love is first presented; then, the character of Socrates gives a more righteous speech on the same subject, which he then revises to improve. This work provides a richer discussion of rhetoric than the *Gorgias* or *The Republic* and offers a faint, albeit skeptical, acceptance of rhetoric as an art.

Quintilian
(ca 35-95 CE)

▶ Quintilian. *Institutio Oratio.* Trans. H. E. Butler. 4 vols. Cambridge, MA: Harvard UP, 1989.

Originally written in 12 books, the work not only provides a survey and commentary on traditional rhetorical material, but Quintilian also establishes his view of rhetoric as the capstone of a citizen's entire education. Book I begins with a child's earliest rhetorical training; the text progresses through to Book XII in which practical and ethical questions regarding the adult orator are considered. Although at times dismissed as disingenuous, this work has often been viewed by noted critics in the field as the authoritative statement on classical rhetoric.

I.A. Richards
(1893-1979)

▶ Richards, I. A. *Interpretation in Teaching*. New York: Humanities P, 1973.

In this text written specifically for teachers in 1938, Richards argues against the artificial separation of rhetoric, grammar, and logic, especially when teaching students to write, as all three must be studied in context and in conjunction with each other; separating them only leads to confusion and frustration. Likewise, he calls for more reflection on our language— including writing—as language is the chief vehicle for thinking and for improving our thinking. This is an important early text for the study of both rhetoric and grammar and their relationship to thinking and writing.

▶ ---. "Speculative Instruments." *Professing the New Rhetorics: A Sourcebook*. Ed. Theresa Enos and Stuart C. Brown. Englewood Cliffs, NJ: Prentice Hall, 1994. 38-9.

Richards, in this brief essay, takes a metaphysical look at misunderstood words. He compares what he calls the wanderings of these words to that of the planets, stating that misconstrued words, like the wandering of the planets, wander systematically. A person needs only to understand the "laws of their motions . . ." (38) to begin to understand their courses. He argues that the same misunderstandings recur constantly and that the study of one of these misinterpretations would shed light on the same recurrence in other fields of study. He wraps up the essay by noting that we do not "benefit as we should from the limited variety of our stupidities" (39) because we have not developed the appropriate exercises.

Stephen Toulmin
(b. 1922)

▶ Toulmin, Stephen. *The Uses of Argument*. New York:
    Cambridge UP, 1958.

Toulmin claimed that mathematically-based analytical or
syllogistic arguments don't really work, so he turned to legal
reasoning to construct more practical or "substantive"
arguments. He delineates six parts to an argument: (1) Data or
grounds, (2) the claim based on the data, (3) the warrant, or
operating principles that exist between the data and the claim,
(4) the modal qualifier, (5) the rebuttal conditions—if true
these would keep the warrant from being applicable, and (6)
the backing or proof that the warrant is acceptable.

Patricia Baines, Marcia Beene, and Trixie G. Smith
with Dianna Baldwin, Satwik Dasgupta,
Kennie Rose, and Stan Williams

Section III:
Influences from Writing
Program Administration

**Chapter 52:
Writing Program Administration**

► Barnett, Robert W., and Jacob S. Blumner, eds. *The Allyn
   and Bacon Guide to Writing Center Theory and
   Practice*. Boston: Allyn and Bacon, 2001.

In this anthology, Barnett and Blumner have pulled together
45 key articles for understanding the history, ideology, and
practice of writing centers. Foundational texts, like North's
"The Idea of a Writing Center" foreground more recent
discussions of online writing centers, the importance of space
and place for writing center location, the role of writing centers
in WAC, varied tutoring practices, and working with diverse
populations. While all of the articles are reprints, their
collection in one place makes this an extremely useful text for
introducing students and new faculty to both theoretical and
practical considerations for operating an effective writing
center.

► Bishop, Wendy, and Deborah Coxwell Teague. *Finding Our
   Way: A Writing Teacher's Sourcebook*. Boston,
   Houghton Mifflin, 2005.

In an attempt to "bring seldom-discussed topics to the surface
in a collection written by relatively new writing teachers for
even newer writing teachers" (xii), Bishop and Teague produced
a book in which the personal experience and reflection of new
teachers is followed by responses from experienced leaders in
the field, such as Chris Anson, Kathleen Blake Yancey, and
Doug Hesse, reminding new teachers that experienced teachers
still grapple with similar issues. Contributors explore topics
ranging from pedagogical conflicts within writing programs to
issues of race, gender, and sexuality. Written in tremendously
personal tones, each contribution grapples with important
theoretical issues.

▶ Boquet, Elizabeth H. *Noise from the Writing Center*. Logan, UT: Utah State UP, 2002.

Advocating "noise" in writing centers as a means to finding meaning and direction within the unplanned, unexpected occurrences common to the learning process, Boquet examines tutor and student personalities, writing center history, metaphors for writing centers and the writing process, and the development of writing center practices in recent years. Boquet draws heavily on her experiences at the Fairfield University Writing Center in Connecticut and those of a colleague at Rhode Island College.

▶ Bousquet, Marc, Tony Scott, and Leo Parascondola, eds. *Tenured Bosses and Disposable Teachers: Writing Instruction in the Managed University*. Carbondale, IL: SIUP, 2004.

The introduction and 22 essays in this collection critique the capitalist managerial systems that are now in place in many university writing programs and how this style of management provides a breeding ground for unfair labor practices. The majority of the essays not only present a description of the managed labor pool of "disposable" teachers and the unfair economic hardships they encounter, the authors also provide suggestions to solve this crisis of today. Any graduate student considering the profession of literacy educator needs to read this introduction to the harsh realities sometimes inherent in adjunct teaching.

▶ Bramblett, Anne, and Alison Knoblauch, eds. *What to Expect When You're Expected to Teach: The Anxious Craft of Teaching Composition*. Portsmouth, NH: Boynton/Cook, 2002.

Wanting other graduate teaching assistants to know that everyone makes mistakes and everyone has insecurities, Bramblett and Knoblauch compiled first person stories in which new teachers share their difficult experiences, failures, and disappointments. Each contributor shares his or her difficulties and the lessons learned from them. Topics covered include silence, resistance, problem students, and plagiarism.

▶ Breslin-Myers, Linda. *Administrative Problem-Solving for Writing Programs and Writing Centers: Scenarios in Effective Program Management*. Urbana, IL: NCTE, 1999.

This volume collects an assortment of real and fictional "case studies"—stories of dilemmas faced by experienced WPAs: raising funds, training graduate assistants, developing a writing center, and handling political conflicts. Due to the limited scope of the collection, the contributors rarely generalize beyond their institutional context. However, the book remains a valuable source of first-hand experience, offering a glimpse into the relationship between FYC, writing assessment, and university politics.

▶ *CCC*. Urbana, IL: NCTE/CCCC.

The *CCC* journal is one of the cornerstones of the field of composition studies, and no composition student or WPA should be without a personal subscription. Each issue contains articles and reviews on composition theory and pedagogy; these sections are often supplemented by Review Essays, Poetry, Interchanges, and Re-Visions. For information on becoming a member of NCTE and CCCC, which includes a subscription to *CCC*, see their Web site at http://www.ncte.org.

▶ Corbett, Edward P. J., Nancy Myers, and Gary Tate, eds. *The Writing Teacher's Sourcebook*. 4th ed. New York: Oxford UP, 2000.

With contributions from composition leaders, such as Peter Elbow, James Berlin, Donald Murray, David Bartholomae, and Mina Shaughnessy, this source book is intended to provide a starting point for new teachers to familiarize themselves with composition pedagogy. The included essays, which were written as early as 1970 and as late as 1998, combine theoretical discussions with concrete examples from the authors' personal experiences and some discussion of practical application within the classroom. Topics covered include student-teacher relationships, writing center theory, expressivism, formalism, rhetorical pedagogy, mimetic theories of writing, group work, collaborative learning, computers and composition, cultural diversity, using literature in the composition classroom, writing for an audience, critical pedagogy, and responding to and evaluating student writing.

▶ Ebest, Sally Barr. *Changing the Way We Teach: Writing and Resistance in the Training of Teaching Assistants.* Carbondale, IL: SIUP, 2005.

Ebest shares 18 case studies conducted over a five-year period, which she uses to investigate how TAs respond to and resist composition pedagogy presented to them through courses and workshops. The book is divided into two main sections, one focused on context and theory and the other on descriptions and discussions of the case studies. She suggests that graduate students need to be provided opportunities for personalized teacher research, in order to build their own pedagogy and to strengthen their own voices, which, in turn, will strengthen our profession.

▶ George, Diana, ed. *Kitchen Cooks, Plate Twirlers, and Troubadours: Writing Program Administrators Tell Their Stories.* Cross Currents: New Perspectives in Rhetoric and Composition. Portsmouth, NH: Boynton/Cook Heinemann, 1999.

This collection uses personal stories as a foundation for the political and theoretical work of WPAs. In the Foreward, Patricia Bizzell asserts that these stories are necessary because effective administrators must draw on everything they know in order to have institutional vision and theoretical purpose while accomplishing the daily tasks of program operation, e.g., scheduling, hiring, training, budgets. The various authors write to illustrate, explain, and theorize this complicated job and provide a snapshot of the people who have made this job their life—even if just for a time. This is a useful text for its personal approach to WPA work as well as its call for ongoing mentoring across all levels.

▶ Gillespie, Paula, and Neal Lerner. *The Allyn and Bacon Guide to Peer Tutoring*. 2nd ed. Boston: Allyn & Bacon, 2003.

Lerner and Gillespie walk peer tutors through every aspect of tutoring sessions from introductions to goodbyes, intermingling theory, practical advice, and mock sessions. Topics include the purpose of peer tutoring, the writing process, the tutoring process, cultural influences on tutoring, the value of observing sessions, note-taking during sessions, reading in the center, working with ESL students, discourse analysis, online tutoring, writing center ethics, and dealing with difficult sessions. This must-have work offers new tutors a top notch how-to guide and an invaluable reading list.

▶ Golub, Jeffrey N., ed. *More Ways to Handle the Paper Load: On Paper and Online*. Urbana, IL: NCTE, 2005.

In 23 essays, experienced teachers share their personal experiences of feeling overwhelmed by the paper load and how they handled it. Their suggestions include designing your courses to reduce the paper load through increasing in-class and peer responses to student writing, allowing for credit/no credit assignments, learning to not mark everything, using comments rather than editing, and adjusting your grading system to something more manageable.

▶ Good, Tina Lavonne, and Leanne B. Warshauer, eds. *In Our Own Voice: Graduate Students Teach Writing*. Boston: Allyn & Bacon, 2000.

With 30 essays from graduate teaching assistants, Good and Warshauer attempt to balance theory and practical application in their exploration of composition pedagogy. Intended to "Serve as a tangible reminder to graduate student teachers of composition that they are not alone" (x), this work explores issues of authority within departments and in the classroom, the advantages and disadvantages of bringing social issues into the classroom, combining the personal with academic discourse, responding to and evaluating student writing, and addressing instruction in grammar and mechanics.

▶ Grimm, Nancy Maloney. *Good Intentions: Writing Center Work for Postmodern Times*. Portsmouth, NH: Boynton/Cook, 1999.

Grimm explores ways for writing centers to actively engage in the improvement of higher education for students outside the dominant culture. Grimm argues that writing center work must include a consideration of the cultural role of literacy and should be grounded in a new, revolutionized concept of academic fairness. Political and proactive, *Good Intentions* uses postmodern theory to challenge present conceptions of the role of writing centers.

▶ Haswell, Richard H., ed. *Beyond Outcomes: Assessment and Instruction Within a University Writing Program*. Perspectives on Writing: Theory, Research, and Practice. Vol. 5. Westport, CT: Ablex, 2001.

This extensive case study of the university-wide writing and assessment program at Washington State University provides a realistic view of a healthy working program, as well as the problems inherent in running such a wide-ranging network that involves faculty from across the curriculum. The authors, all associated with Washington State at one time or another, delve into issues of basic writing, first-year composition, WAC, writing in the disciplines, writing centers, portfolio assessment, and pulling students in as stakeholders in the assessment process. This frank look at the development and implementation of an extensive program is both interesting and instructive. The time line in the appendix is especially informative.

▶ Haswell, Richard, and Glenn Blalock. *CompPile*. <http://comppile.tamucc.edu/>.

Haswell, the bibliographer, and Blalock, the site master, provide this valuable online resource and research tool with 82,734 entries on post-secondary writing as of July 2006. *CompPile* includes journal articles, books, dissertations, edited collections, and many other 20th century works on composition and rhetoric. This Web site should be one of the first stops when doing research on composition.

► Haswell, Richard H., and Min-Zhan Lu. *COMP Tales*. New
    York: Addison Wesley Longman, 2000.

COMP Tales is a wonderful collection of stories told by new and
experienced instructors about their first, most challenging, or
most rewarding classroom experience. The individual stories
are organized as one larger story, in which many members of
the composition community share their sometimes unique and
often encouraging tales of teaching, administering, and
researching composition.

► Janangelo, Joseph, and Kristine Hansen, eds. *Resituating
    Writing: Constructing and Administering Writing
    Programs*. Cross Currents: New Perspectives in
    Rhetoric and Composition. Portsmouth, NH:
    Heinemann Boynton/Cook, 1995.

The editors, and other authors in this collection, such as
Edward White and Susan McLeod, share their stories of how
the work of WPAs is significant. Important topics covered
include the need to professionalize both part-time and full-time
writing faculty and how WPAs need to reposition their
scholarship within more expansive political and scholarly
frameworks, in order to take the center, rather than be on the
margins, of the academic community. The entire group of
essays covers a wide range of difficulties encountered in the
recruitment and retention of quality teachers, the creation of
writing centers and WAC programs, and the evaluation of
writing programs.

► Johnson, T. R. *Teaching Composition: Background Readings*
    2nd Ed. Boston: Bedford/St. Martin's, 2005.

This valuable reader offers teaching assistants a broad
theoretical background in composition theory and an extensive
annotated bibliography, covering all of the following aspects of
teaching in the composition classroom: composition pedagogies,
the writing process, incorporating technology into the
composition classroom, methods of responding to and
evaluating student writing, visual literacy, understanding and
teaching academic discourse, the social constructions that

385

accompany teachers and students into the classroom, ignoring and acknowledging audience, dealing with cultural diversity, and negotiating the politics of the university. Contributors include Paulo Friere, Mike Rose, James Berlin, David Bartholomae, Peter Elbow, Chris Anson, Ann Berthoff, Cynthia Selfe, Doug Hesse, Nancy Sommers, Muriel Harris, and Tony Silva.

► Lindemann, Erika. *A Rhetoric for Writing Teachers.* 4th ed. New York: Oxford UP, 2001.

In this book, first published in 1982, Lindemann attempts to share the advice of colleagues and personal experience "about students, about writing, and about teaching" without getting too technical, "keeping in mind an audience of prospective classroom teachers" (xi). Lindemann includes an introduction to the basics of composition theory and its major theorists, rhetorical theory and pedagogy, linguistics, and cognitive theory. In addition, she examines practical topics, such why we write, why writing is important to students, the writing process, developing writing assignments, designing courses, responding to and evaluating student writing, and incorporating technology into the composition classroom.

► Marshall, Margaret J. *Response to Reform: Composition and the Professionalism of Teaching.* Carbondale, IL: SIUP, 2004.

Marshall provides an overview of the history and language used to describe writing instructors and their undervalued work. In chapters on teacher training and retraining, she is particularly insightful when she stresses the need for us as teachers to engage public audiences outside of our particular disciplines and the academy at large. Marshall suggests that when we hide our work from the public, we end up devaluing it and our profession as well. For those teachers considering a career as a literacy instructor at the college level, this book is an excellent source on how teachers can present what they as valuable.

▶ McDonald, James C. *The Allyn and Bacon Sourcebook for College Writing Teachers*. 2nd ed. Boston: Allyn and Bacon, 2000.

Intended to be a "useful collection of writings on important theories and pedagogies in composition theory" (vii), this sourcebook contains contributions from composition leaders, such as Edward P. J. Corbett, Anne Ruggles Gere, Mike Rose, Kenneth Bruffee, Ann Berthoff, Muriel Harris, Chris Anson, and Peter Elbow. In addition to foundational theoretical discussions, each section includes a valuable list of suggested readings. Topics covered include the writing process, general pedagogical perspectives, historical trends in composition theory, incorporating literature and critical theory into the composition classroom, using group work, and addressing concerns of audience, form, style, and grammar.

▶ McGee, Sharon James, and Carolyn Handa, eds. *Discord & Direction: The Postmodern Writing Program Administrator*. Logan, UT: Utah State UP, 2005.

At the center of this volume's introduction and 12 essays is an acknowledgment of how postmodern culture and thought is reflected daily in the life of a writing program and how WPAs can use postmodernism as a guide through the daily necessity of leading a program within a larger university community that is constantly conflicted and changing. The editors and other authors, such as Deborah Holdstein and Brian Huot, detail problems that they have faced at their own universities and share innovative and productive ways to deal with these problems. This collection is a very useful tool for new WPAs working to fit into their departments and universities.

▶ Mullin, Joan A., and Ray Wallace, eds. *Intersections: Theory-Practice in the Writing Center*. Urbana, IL: NCTE, 1994.

This is one of the earliest writing center-focused texts that seek to move beyond the practice of writing centers to the theory that informs this practice. As editor Joan Mullin describes, the collection serves a three-fold purpose: to provide a theoretical background for developing new writing centers, to aid writing center professionals in self reflection and program review, and to provide a picture of writing center work for the larger composition and English studies communities. The essays, arranged in chronological order, give a broad picture of the development of writing center theory, showing how it has become more and more complex over time, and, yet, continues to call for dialogue and collaboration with students, tutors, and administrators within local contexts and across the field in general.

▶ Murphy, Christina, and Steve Sherwood, eds. *The St. Martin's Sourcebook for Writing Tutors*. 2nd ed. Boston: Bedford/St. Martin's, 2003.

A thorough introduction to writing center theory, this sourcebook covers the history of writing centers, collaborative learning, cultural studies, aggression in the center, minimalist tutoring, tutoring ESL students, tutoring nontraditional students, and online tutoring. In addition to writings from composition leaders such as Stephen North, Andrea Lunsford, Toby Fulwiler, and Muriel Harris, Murphy and Sherwood included a useful list of resources for further reading.

▶ Pytlik, Betty, and Sarah Liggett. *Preparing College Teachers of Writing*. New York: Oxford UP, 2002.

An introduction to the scholarship on TA preparation, this collection features essays of interest to both experienced and novice administrators. The book contains four sections: the first contains a historical overview of TA programs; the second proposes a variety of theoretical models; the third provides information on specific programs around the country; and the fourth offers advice on individual practices, such as peer mentoring, teaching journals, and portfolios. Throughout the book, the contributors remain focused on informing practice; therefore, for those interested in the field, *Preparing Teachers of College Writing* should prove an invaluable resource.

▶ Roen, Duane, ed. *Views from the Center: The CCCC Chairs' Addresses 1977-2005*. New York: Bedford/St. Martins, 2006.

With addresses from composition leaders such as David Bartholomae, Andrea Lunsford, Anne Ruggles Gere, Jacqueline Jones Royster, Lester Faigley, Cynthia Selfe, Victor Villanueva, Keith Gilyard, Wendy Bishop, Kathleen Blake Yancey, Doug Hesse, *Views from the Center* includes topics ranging from authority and politics in the composition classroom to computer literacy and writing to learn. The introduction includes a brief history of CCCC and the role of the CCCC Chair, a look at the biographies of former Chairs, and an examination of how these Chairs felt about giving their addresses. In addition, Roen includes a comprehensive table of the Chair addresses beginning in 1949 and ending in 2005; the table includes the year of each address, location of the conference, session type, speech title, published title, and *CCC* article (year, volume, number, and pages).

▶ Rose, Shirley K., and Irwin Weiser, eds. *The Writing Program Administrator as Researcher: Inquiry in Action and Reflection*. Portsmouth, NH: Boynton/Cook, 1999.

This collection of essays is devoted to understanding the research of WPAs. The first half provides an overview of research methodologies—discussing their application in specific projects and demonstrating the strengths and weaknesses of each approach. In the second half, the contributors examine the subject on a theoretical level, exploring issues such as historical research and political conflict. For those interested in the struggles faced by WPAs, this volume focuses on the rhetorical aims of empirical research, making this book valuable on both a scholarly and practical level.

▶ Rose, Shirley K., and Irwin Weiser, ed. *The Writing Program Administrator as Theorist: Making Knowledge Work*. Portsmouth, NH: Boynton/Cook Heinemann, 2002.

This text takes a two-pronged approach to the intersection of writing program administration and theory, or the act of theorizing—explained as "conceptualizing, organizing, explaining, analyzing, reflecting on, and interpreting experiences and specialized knowledge" (2) gained through the everyday work of program administration. In part one, WPAs describe their local programs and delineate the theories that circumscribe their operations. In part two, WPAs explore writing program administration as profession and broad community, exploring how local work can have global implications. This text is a must read for WPAs at all levels, but especially for those seeking ways to show the theory behind their practical work to colleagues and administrators, as well as graduate students in composition and rhetoric programs.

▶ Ryan, Leigh, and Lisa Zimmerelli, eds. *The Bedford Guide for Writing Tutors*. 4th ed. Boston: Bedford/St. Martin's, 2006.

This short but thorough tutor training manual covers topics including professionalism in the center, the writing process, tools for conducting sessions and helping students through the writing process, learning styles, using technology to tutor, WAC in the center, and coping with difficult session. Ryan and Zimmerelli include helpful exercises and a useful annotated bibliography. In addition, appendices cover outside tutoring and editing jobs, presenting at conferences, commonly asked questions, and a list of problematic comments commonly made by tutors to students.

▶ Stenberg, Shari J. *Professing & Pedagogy: Learning the Teaching of English*. Urbana, IL: NCTE, 2005.

Stenberg maintains that the current prevalent model of pedagogy that is introduced to graduate students is based on the idea of their becoming tenure-track professors at research universities, a myth she debunks early on. She encourages a move from the research-based teacher training taking place in composition pedagogy courses required of new TAs to true pedagogical and professional development. Her ideas for disciplinary revisions are appropriate and needed in the current climate of FYC, where many new TAs are viewed as disposable temporary labor, rather than valuable tenure-track hires.

▶ Tate, Gary, Amy Rupiper, and Kurt Schick, eds. *A Guide to Composition Pedagogies.* Oxford: Oxford UP, 2001.

Designed to introduce graduate students and new teachers to the theories and practices encompassed by the term composition pedagogy, this anthology includes discussions of process pedagogy, expressivism, rhetorical pedagogy, collaborative learning, cultural studies, critical pedagogy, feminism, community-service pedagogy, writing center theory, basic writing instruction, and computers and composition. The book includes 12 essays by various leaders in composition theory and pedagogy who combine theoretical discussions with brief histories and practical applications for the classroom.

▶ Villanueva, Victor, ed. *Cross-Talk in Composition Theory: A Reader.* 2nd ed. Urbana, IL: NCTE, 2003.

Villanueva's purpose in compiling this dense 883-page volume is "to introduce you to some of the concepts and methods available to writing teachers today and to have you regard some of the controversy" in composition theory (xiv). Contributors include Donald Murray, Janet Emig, Nancy Sommers, Walter Ong, Lisa Ede, Andrea Lunsford, James Kinneavy, Lester Faigley, James Berlin, Linda Flower, Mina Shaughnessy, Patricia Bizzell, Ann Berthoff, Mike Rose, Kenneth Bruffee, Min-Zhan Lu, David Bartholomae, Jacqueline Jones Royster, Paul Kei Matsuda, and Chris Anson. Updated to include technological developments, the second edition covers topics including but not limited to process versus product, post-process theory, the role of audience, the artificial nature of academic discourse, global versus local concerns, basic writing instruction, cognitive theory, collaborative learning, contact zone theory, ESL instruction, and cultural studies.

▶ Ward, Irene, and William J. Carpenter. *The Allyn and Bacon Sourcebook for Writing Program Administrators.* New York: Longman, 2002.

An introductory text for WPAS, this collection offers a wealth of information from experienced directors. It contains advice on handling the administrative role, overviews of the latest scholarly research, hints for dealing with assessment, and details on how to achieve tenure. In addition to reprints of well-known scholarly articles, *The Allyn and Bacon Sourcebook* also features extensive bibliographies and key professional documents, such as "The Portland Resolution"; for those new to the subject of program administration, this book provides an accessible introduction to the field.

▶ Wilhoit, Stephen W. *The Allyn & Bacon Teaching Assistant's Handbook: A Guide for Graduate Instructors of Writing and Literature.* New York: Longman, 2003.

A helpful mix of practical advice, exercises, checklists, and resource lists, this handbook reminds TAs that they are not alone in their struggles to negotiate the difficult dual roles graduate teaching assistants fulfill. Wilhoit includes subjects such as preparing for class, developing writing assignments, responding to and grading student writing, effectively presenting materials to students, working with technology, dealing with troublesome students, conducting student conferences, teaching literature, learning how to improve teaching, and preparing for the job market. Wilhoit repeatedly suggests looking to peer and faculty mentors for advice and support rather than suffering in silence.

▶ *WPA: Writing Program Administration.* Tempe, AZ: Arizona State U, Council of Writing Program Administrators.

The official journal of the Council of Writing Program Administrators, written for and by WPAs, each issue includes articles, reviews, and announcements; the Announcements section is always a valuable resource. For information on becoming a member of the Council of the Writing Program Administrators, which includes a subscription to the journal, see their Web site at http://www.wpacouncil.org/.

▶ Yancey, Kathleen Blake, and Brian Huot, eds. *Assessing Writing Across the Curriculum: Diverse Approaches and Practices.* Greenwich, CT: Ablex, 1997.

With 14 essays from composition leaders such as Toby Fulwiler, Cynthia Selfe, and Gail Hawisher, this collection contains a thorough examination of WAC. Topics include the roles of WAC faculty and students, dispelling myths about WAC programs, sharing experiences across the curriculum, contextualizing assessment of WAC programs, methods of assessing the effectiveness of WAC programs, and integrating WAC into general education courses.

▶ Yancey, Kathleen Blake, and Irwin Weiser, eds. *Situating Portfolios: Four Perspectives*. Logan, UT: Utah State UP, 1997.

The 24 essays in this work include contributions from various composition leaders, such as Bill Condon, Gail Hawisher, Cynthia Selfe, and Peter Elbow. The book is divided into four sections: "Theory and Power," which covers the theoretical backing for portfolios and a discussion of the recent popularity of such practices; "Pedagogy," which examines practical techniques for using portfolios in the classroom; "Teaching and Professional Development," which discusses the use of portfolios in assessing teachers and explores some ways for teachers to learn from portfolio systems; and "Technology," which offers some alternative formats for portfolios.

Tanya McLaughlin, Kennie Rose,
Allison D. Smith, and Trixie G. Smith

Topic Index

R

Racism 288, 307-308, 311-313

Reflection 4-6, 33, 64, 79-80, 106, 117, 158, 251-252, 254, 276, 291-292, 323-324, 326, 328-330, 332, 334, 347, 375, 379, 388-389

Remedial 29, 45, 47, 122, 177, 180, 231, 241-242, 244-247, 270

Research, student (ref. plagiarism) 4-8, 10-11, 14, 24-27, 32-35, 38-39, 43, 46, 50-53, 56, 63-64, 69-75, 83, 88-93, 97-100, 102, 108, 110-114, 117, 125-127, 135-136, 139-144, 148, 154, 166-189, 191, 197, 201-203, 207, 212-222, 229, 231-234, 236, 239, 242, 259, 271, 273-279, 285, 290, 293, 295-299, 308-309, 315-316, 319, 321-324, 328, 331-334, 353, 355, 373, 382, 384-385, 389-391

Revision 10, 20, 22, 24-25, 50, 73, 85, 92-93, 96, 98, 101, 189, 278, 290, 292, 299, 354, 364, 390

S

Second-language learners (L2) 168, 171-172, 211-218, 275-279

Silence 75, 115-116, 126, 128, 193, 195, 341, 380, 392

Social constructionism 33, 39, 299, 361-362

Social-epistemic rhetoric 18

Sociolinguistics 119

Standard American English 269

Student-centered 144, 230-231

Subject position 253

T

Teaching English as a Second Language (TESL) 168, 212, 214, 215, 273-274

Teaching English to Speakers of Other Languages (TESOL) 79, 167-172, 195, 212, 274-278, 332, 335-337

Technology 5, 7, 10, 40, 43, 51, 91, 94-95, 132, 140, 144-146, 154-155, 176, 179, 184, 209, 233, 237-239, 257-264, 293, 319, 324, 328-329, 345, 385-386, 390, 392-393

Transculturation 336-337, 345

Tutor, tutoring 35, 36-38, 41, 44, 46-48, 53, 54, 118, 131-132, 134-137, 142, 158, 175, 177-179, 203, 222, 228, 231-232, 235, 238-239, 247, 301, 309, 361, 379-380, 383, 388, 390

U

Under-prepared students 265-266, 268

V

Visual rhetoric 91-92, 95, 259

W

Writing Across the Curriculum (WAC) 3-5, 7, 12, 22, 49-50, 55,
        96, 101, 105-106, 108, 110-111, 114, 116, , 137, 140-141,
        143, 150, 162, 165, 175-176, 181, 216, 233, 237-238,
        247, 290, 305-306, 316, 323, 326, 328, 331, 347, 379,
        384-385, 390, 392-393
Writing apprehension 259
Writing center, lab, clinic 23, 28, 36-38, 41, 43-48, 53, 55, 67,
        70, 71, 73, 77, 91, 128, 131-137, 142, 158-159, 175-181,
        192, 203, 228-239, 249, 252, 303, 309, 379-381, 383-385,
        387, 388, 391
Writing center history, politics 45, 179-180, 380
Writing center theory 28, 41, 43-45, 67, 73, 91, 128, 132, 137,
        175, 180, 203, 239, 303, 379, 381, 388, 391
Writing in the Disciplines (WID) 92, 96, 384
Writing program administration, WPA 3-4, 6, 24, 28-29, 36, 49,
        52-54, 119, 136, 147-148, 150, 154, 159, 183-184, 212,
        234, 274-276, 316-318, 320, 323-324, 377, 379-393

People Index